ABOUT THE AUTHORS

WARRICK DUNN was a first-round draft pick of the Tampa Bay
Buccaneers in 1997. After five years at Tampa and six years
with the Atlanta Falcons, he returned to the Bucs for the 2008
season. In 2008, Dunn was overwhelmingly selected as the in-
augural recipient of the Home Depot NFL Neighborhood MVP
Award, which recognizes NFL players who are making a positive
impact in their local communities through charitable programs
and contributions. Dunn has also received the 2004 Walter
Payton Man of the Year Award, been named one of *Sporting
News*'s Top 75 Good Guys in Sports three times, and been recognized as one of *Sports Illustrated*'s Most Influential Minorities
in Sports. He founded the Warrick Dunn Foundation and its
Homes for the Holidays program, which has awarded 84 homes
to single parents and sheltered 224 children in its twelve years
of operation.

DON YAEGER is a four-time *New York Times* bestselling au-
thor, a former *Sports Illustrated* associate editor, and an award-
winning motivational speaker. He lives in Tallahassee, Florida,
with his wife and son.

RUNNING FOR MY LIFE

ALSO BY DON YAEGER

IT'S NOT ABOUT THE TRUTH: THE UNTOLD STORY OF THE DUKE LACROSSE CASE AND THE LIVES IT SHATTERED (WITH MIKE PRESSLER)

TURNING OF THE TIDE: HOW ONE GAME CHANGED THE SOUTH (WITH SAM CUNNINGHAM AND JOHN PAPADAKIS)

YA GOTTA BELIEVE: MY ROLLER-COASTER LIFE AS A SCREWBALL PITCHER AND PART-TIME FATHER, AND MY HOPE-FILLED FIGHT AGAINST BRAIN CANCER (WITH TUG MCGRAW)

UNDER THE TARNISHED DOME: HOW NOTRE DAME BETRAYED ITS IDEALS FOR FOOTBALL GLORY (WITH DOUGLAS S. LOONEY)

SOLE INFLUENCE: BASKETBALL, CORPORATE GREED, AND THE COR-RUPTION OF AMERICA'S YOUTH (WITH DAN WETZEL)

PROS AND CONS: THE CRIMINALS WHO PLAY IN THE NFL (WITH JEFF BENEDICT)

LIVING THE DREAM (WITH DOT RICHARDSON)

THIS GAME'S THE BEST: SO WHY DON'T THEY QUIT SCREWING WITH IT (WITH GEORGE KARL)

TIGER IN A LION'S DEN: ADVENTURES IN LSU BASKETBALL (WITH DALE BROWN)

A SHARK NEVER SLEEPS: WHEELING AND DEALING WITH THE NFL'S MOST RUTHLESS AGENT (WITH DREW ROSENHAUS)

SHARK ATTACK: JERRY TARKANIAN AND HIS BATTLE WITH THE NCAA AND UNLV (WITH JERRY TARKANIAN)

UNDUE PROCESS: THE NCAA'S INJUSTICE FOR ALL

TARNISHED HEISMAN: DID REGGIE BUSH TURN HIS FINAL COLLEGE SEASON INTO A SIX-FIGURE JOB?

RUNNING
FOR MY
LIFE

My Journey in the Game of
Football and Beyond

WARRICK DUNN
and Don Yaeger

HARPER

NEW YORK • LONDON • TORONTO • SYDNEY

HARPER

A hardcover edition of this book was published in 2008 by HarperCollins Publishers.

HarperCollins books may be purchased for educational, business, or sales promotional use. For information please write: Special Markets Department, HarperCollins Publishers, 10 East 53rd Street, New York, NY 10022.

FIRST HARPER PAPERBACK PUBLISHED 2009.

Designed by Lovedog Studio

The Library of Congress has catalogued the hardcover edition as follows:

Dunn, Warrick, 1975–
    Running for my life: my journey in the game of football and beyond / Warrick Dunn and Don Yaeger.—1st ed.
        p. cm.
    ISBN 978-0-06-143264-4
    1. Dunn, Warrick, 1975–   2. Football players—United States—Biography. 3. Children of murder victims—United States—Biography.   I. Yaeger, Don.   II. Title.

    GV939.D85A33 2008
    796.332092—dc22
    [B]   2008011032

ISBN 978-0-06-143265-1 (pbk.)

09 10 11 12 13 WBC/RRD 10 9 8 7 6 5 4 3 2 1

To my mom, who sacrificed her life to provide for my brothers and sisters; my grandmother, who stepped up and put her life on hold to raise us when my mom died; my brothers and sisters, who stuck together in tough times, supporting each other; my pops, Maelen "Choo Choo" Brooks, who helped me to become a man; and to the great people of Baton Rouge, Tallahassee, Tampa, and Atlanta, who helped shape my journey and allowed me to become who I am today. I love you all.

—WD

To my new son, Will: may you have your mother's polish and Warrick Dunn's grace. I cannot wait to watch you grow into an amazing young man.

—DWY

CONTENTS

FOREWORD

I first met Warrick Dunn in January 1997 at the National Scouting Combine. I was beginning my second year as head coach of the Tampa Bay Buccaneers and Warrick had just completed his senior year at Florida State University. Each team is allotted fifteen minutes to speak to the draft-eligible college football players. I came away from that meeting, as brief as it was, highly impressed. Without saying a lot, Warrick demonstrated to me that he was a special person. He was never boastful, but he told me in a matter-of-fact tone that he was what the Buccaneers needed. He was right. In the eleven years since then, I have come to the conclusion that he is more than just special—he is one of the most remarkable people that I've ever met.

I admire him not just because of what he has done on the football field. To play running back in the NFL at his size for eleven years is a feat in itself. To do it well enough to become only the twenty-second person in history to run for 10,000 yards is truly amazing. But football statistics don't even begin to tell the story of Warrick Dunn.

By taking lessons from his mother, from his coaches, and from his life experiences, Warrick has become what he never wanted to be—a role model. He didn't seek attention, hoping others would look at him and utter that phrase, but he has become a role model to thousands because he quietly used his gifts to change the lives of others. Most of us want to take the training of our parents and mentors and the dreams they have for us and let that shape our lives. We would love to have those people who have been so significant in our lives look at us with pride and see that we've carried on their legacy. Warrick's life has been a testimony to those who have guided him and believed in him.

The Buccaneers did draft Warrick in the first round in 1997, and I had the privilege of coaching him during his first five years in the NFL. Watching him mature into a young adult, I saw his determination on the field. More impressive, though, was his determination off the field. Warrick lost his mother when he was a senior in high school, and at eighteen inherited the position of head of the household. He was driven to be the leader of his family and to protect and provide for his younger siblings. I marveled at his ability, at twenty-one years old, to handle both his career and the care of five teenagers. He had a lot of talks with my wife, Lauren, about parenting, nurturing, discipline, and improving academic performance.

I thought that I understood Warrick's challenges. But having read this book, I realize that I never knew all the things that were going on in his world, all the pressures he had been facing.

Warrick didn't open up with me a lot—I think he did more so with Lauren—but he did share with me his goals. He wanted to be the best player at his position in the NFL but even more than that to be the best provider he could be for his family and to give back as much as he could to his community. He was very quiet and introverted at that time, but when he stated those goals, in his own humble way, you never doubted that he would accomplish them.

He has done that and much more. Along the way Warrick was also able to find help in dealing with some incidents that really scarred him as a young man. Things that I never knew about as his coach, things he didn't want other people to know because he didn't want them to be seen as excuses. He didn't want people to see those hurts as a sign of weakness, so he kept them inside. Because of that, I don't think many people in Tampa—including me—got to know the "real" Warrick Dunn.

In 2002 we parted ways. I went to Indianapolis to coach the Indianapolis Colts and Warrick went to Atlanta to play for the Falcons. We stayed in contact over the years and I could tell that he was enjoying Atlanta and that he was growing as a person. However, when I saw him in the Tampa airport in 2007, I felt I was seeing a different man. He was so relaxed and so much more outgoing that I wondered what had happened to him.

In this book he shares how counseling and also finding new meaning in his relationship with Christ have allowed him to move forward, to open up with people, and to really enjoy life again. Because of his willingness to open up and talk about those parts of his life—about how he rediscovered the ability to trust people and build relationships—I truly believe this book is going to help as many people as he has helped through his charitable ventures.

Reading this was an eye-opening experience for me. The deeper I got into this book, the more I was able to look back at our years together and understand Warrick's challenges. As those moments became clearer to me, my appreciation for the "real" Warrick Dunn grew immeasurably. I was proud of him before. Now *proud* seems too simple a word.

Warrick Dunn to me epitomizes what we should want in our National Football League players. He is a winner and a great role model for our young people. He's a leader and has been a beacon in the community, both in Tampa and Atlanta. His desire to play in the

NFL was not so he could make money and be a star, but so he could change the lives of other people. His dream was to translate the talent that God gave him on the football field into something truly meaningful for society. It's a dream he got from his mother and one that, because of his unbelievable desire and perseverance, he has made into a reality. I'm so happy that I got to know him and to experience a small part of his journey.

—Coach Tony Dungy

CHAPTER 1

FACE TO FACE

TO GET TO ANGOLA STATE PRISON FROM BATON ROUGE, Louisiana—a distance of fifty-six miles—you go north on Highway 61, then take a hard left on Highway 66. Or you can get there by committing the most serious of crimes.

For years I had wondered about Kevan Brumfield. He had confessed to killing my mother, Baton Rouge police corporal Betty Smothers, in the early morning of January 7, 1993, in an ambush at a local bank. Two years later a jury deliberated a little more than sixty minutes and decided that Brumfield should die for murdering Mom in the fatal attempted robbery.

In the months and years afterward, I wrestled with one question that was never answered: Why? What was on Brumfield's mind as he and another man, Henri Broadway, lay in wait in near-total-darkness as Mom's police cruiser pulled up to the bank's night deposit box? What did Brumfield think when he and Broadway charged out from behind bushes and fired shots into the car, killing my mother and wounding her passenger, Kimen Lee, night manager at a local Piggly Wiggly store, as she made a store deposit? Did Brumfield understand the severity of his actions as he and Broadway piled into the getaway car driven by a third man named West Paul?

It made absolutely no sense. Why?

Then an opportunity presented itself in October 2007 to go to Angola State Prison and actually get the chance to ask Brumfield the questions that have haunted me for years. Questions that kept me awake for so many nights. Questions that caused me to cry. Questions about a moment that changed my life like no other.

The meeting took months and countless telephone calls to arrange. There were casual and personal conversations with lawyers, prison officials, and football coaches. There were delays, changes of minds, emotional highs and lows. But it finally all came together on Tuesday, October 23, in a bye week of my NFL season with the Atlanta Falcons. My coaches realized how important this was and they decided to cut me loose for a day.

I flew from Atlanta into New Orleans, where my younger brother Derrick Green picked me up and drove me back to my hometown of Baton Rouge. I was accompanied to the prison by Maelen "Choo-Choo" Brooks, my youth football coach and mentor. I was also accompanied by Don Yaeger, this book's coauthor. Choo-Choo is probably as much like a father as anybody I'll ever have. He was one of the first people I saw after Mom's murder, and his guidance and support have been invaluable over the years. Still, Choo-Choo couldn't believe I wanted to do this. That was the reaction I got from almost everybody. Most people couldn't believe I wanted to make this visit. But I knew it was important for me to finally face my demons.

Before I went to Angola, I spent hours in conversation with my Atlanta counselor, Pauline Clance. She believed it was a good idea, a positive move, because she clearly understood that there were some things in my life that I would never get over until I sat across the table from him.

It was set.

I found myself in a small break room on Death Row at Angola State Prison, eye to eye with Kevan Brumfield.

THE DAYS AND NIGHTS leading up to the visit were somewhat unsettling. I tried not to let it dominate my mind, even pretending the meeting wasn't happening. I went to the movies. I slept a lot. I started gathering my thoughts and talking to my brothers and sisters, compiling questions they wanted me to ask. The weekend prior to the trip was difficult because we also lost to the New Orleans Saints on that Sunday. It was our third consecutive defeat and the sixth in our first seven games. Drained and tired, I actually just wanted to relax and enjoy the time off. It was really my first break since the start of the 2007 season.

As I prepared for the visit, however, people often said or asked, "Do you need anyone to go with you? Do you need anyone to be there for you? How do you feel? I'm proud of you that you have the courage to do this. Hopefully, you will find the answers you are looking for." It was crazy. I think they made it more of a big deal than I had. The truth is, I was nervous but really didn't want to let it show. How would the conversation go? What if he said something horrible or acted as if this were no big deal? How would I maintain control?

There were more questions than answers. Friends tried to caution me, prepare me. What I have always tried to tell people is that sometimes in life, you really don't know what you can do until you have to go through it. If my mom were still on this earth, I would probably tell people that I couldn't go on without her. But I have overcome that one. I knew that no matter how bad this meeting was, I could overcome that, too.

It was a calm, cloudy morning on Tuesday, October 23. We had an official escort named Chad who drove us to Angola State Prison from Baton Rouge in a prison SUV. While we navigated the long roads in near silence, the text message alert on my cell phone kept going off. It was my sister Summer Smothers and others all sending me notes wishing me luck, praying for me. An earlier text nearly brought tears to my eyes. It was from Hue Jackson, my offensive co-ordinator with the Falcons, who encouraged me to remain strong. He hoped that I would find the answers and peace my heart looked for.

As we got closer, there's no question that I became more physically tight. It had been a roller coaster of emotion. One day I was ready for the visit, another day I wasn't. Earlier dates had been scheduled but were snatched away. I also contemplated asking Summer and Derrick to join me, since they are only a few years younger than me and they remembered that horrific night vivdly. While Mom's murder also had greatly affected them, I just didn't think either one was in the right frame of mind to meet face to face with Brumfield. I still appreciated their support, along with that of my three other brothers and sisters, because everyone felt this meeting could offer some type of freedom for me.

I also know that Choo-Choo, who I wanted at my side, had concerns about my decision. He wondered what my reaction would be if Brumfield wasn't sorry or repentant, or if Brumfield simply gloated over the fact that he had taken something away from a successful, professional athlete. Choo-Choo wanted me to feel sorrow, not hatred, for Brumfield if that was the case. I also knew Brumfield might not say anything at all. If that happened, that was fine, but I wanted Brumfield to sit there and listen to whatever I had to say. I wanted him to understand the change he had made to our lives.

Another friend wondered how I would react if Brumfield asked for forgiveness. Would I forgive him? I decided in advance that I would do it for me, not for him. I would do it for myself because my life has been a struggle for so long, and I held on to so much anger and hatred. I had so much bottled up inside that it stopped me from being whole. To let someone know that he has that much control over me and my life, I can't continue to live like that. It took me a long time just to get to this point.

I had to play many years of college and professional football to reach the point where I went to counseling just to seek help so I could be sane and happy. Because I was hiding so much inside, I knew I needed help to get to the point where I wasn't depressed, wasn't sad all the time, so that I could laugh more, smile more. This visit was part of that journey. I was doing this for my soul, for my life. It was time for me to move forward. In God's eyes, you have to forgive. I won't ever forget it, but I have to forgive to get that burden off of me.

In the end, Brumfield and Broadway are going to get what's due in their lives, so I can't hold that hatred inside. I've tried to tell Derrick the same thing. It's crazy because we discussed on the drive from New Orleans that you can't hold onto something for so long, because it eats you up. It stops you from growing as a person—in my case and in my brother's, as men. We are still alive. We are still doing well. We are starting families. We are moving on and starting our own traditions. We're not holding onto the things that woulda, shoulda, coulda been. That's done and over with. This is your path and you have to live that life.

My heart started to race as we closed in on Angola. Usually, when I play football, my heart doesn't race until I get ready to pull up to the stadium. That's just from my love and excitement for the game. This was going to be a lot different because it was not about football. It was about life. Now I would have to face another fear in my life that I didn't know anything about or understand. I didn't know if I was going to talk straight or be nervous the whole time. I could tell I was nervous because my voice was cracking; it was just one of those things where I would have to try to stay calm.

We were en route to one of the most desolate spots in all of Louisiana. Highway 66 ends at a prison that's known as the most notorious in the South, a prison from which 91 percent of all inmates never leave. They either die on Death Row or because their sentences are longer than their lives. I was surprised when Richard Vannoy, the prison's deputy warden for security, met us at the gates and asked me to get in his truck with him. As I got out of the car, our driver, Chad, looked at me and said, "Man to man, I respect what you are doing." That really hit me. This was going to happen.

Vannoy joined the prison staff at age eighteen and has worked at Angola for thirty-three years. He explained how inmates on Death Row such as Brumfield and Broadway are locked in single-man cells. They are allowed out an hour each day to shower and an hour alone in the yard five times a week on a rotation basis that's kept a secret even from them for safety reasons. Inmates are moved in full restraints: leg irons and waist chains. The only time their hands are unbuckled from their waist chains is when they are alone in their exercise pen. They are never in the proximity of anyone when they are not fully restrained.

The 18,000-acre penitentiary is surrounded on three sides by the Mississippi River. Vannoy also told me that the prison is still run as a working farm—inmates grow and harvest their own vegetables and raise cattle. Vannoy drove me through what seemed like miles of dirt roads to get back to an area that was guarded with rolls and rolls of razor wire. The building's official name is Camp F. It was as dank and dark a place as you would ever see.

This was Death Row.

BRUMFIELD'S LAWYERS, THE HUSBAND-AND-WIFE team of Nick Trenticosta and Susan Herrero, were very quizzical about my visit. They've represented Death Row inmates for many years and really never had a request quite like mine, to sit down with one of their clients. I tried to explain to them that sometimes you just have to do it, that this was just a matter of opportunity for me to do something that I never before really thought I should even try.

The rules surrounding my visit had changed, however. I had hoped to meet with both Brumfield and Broadway. Brumfield agreed to the meeting, but Broadway did not after he initially said he would. Paul, meanwhile, had been released months earlier from another institution and had returned to Baton Rouge after serving 13½ years of his 25-year prison sentence.

As I walked into the prison staff's multipurpose break room, Room 116, Brumfield was already seated at a round brown table. He wore a white shirt, jeans, and Reebok tennis shoes. His hands were shackled to his waist. He was bald, with glasses; a scar was visible over his upper lip, and I noticed he had gold-capped teeth.

I have to admit that I was shocked when I first saw Brumfield. It didn't seem like this was real. It didn't seem like I recognized him at all. I didn't imagine him looking like he did. I thought he was going to be a smaller man, but he was a big guy, broad and wide-shouldered. At thirty-four years old, Brumfield was just two years older than I was. Still, I didn't think I would see a guy with a bald head and glasses. It had been so many years since I had seen him at his sentencing in a Baton Rouge courtroom in July 1995. I remembered him with hair and looking much different.

After a few moments of awkward silence, Brumfield spoke first. He explained how he had changed as a person, that he shouldn't have done some of the things that he did in the past and that he had grown into a better human being. He apologized for what happened to my family.

And then he said it.

"I didn't kill your mother. They got the wrong guy."

I had been previously warned by Warden Burl Cain to expect that response, and I certainly understood that with an appeal pending, this was the way Brumfield would handle himself. Brumfield has claimed he is mentally retarded, and his appeals have argued that the U.S. Constitution prohibits the execution of mentally retarded people. But judges have ruled that Brumfield's IQ shows that he's not retarded. I listened to Brumfield explain how, because of the life he had lived, he would have probably been dead by now if he hadn't been arrested for this crime that he now claims he didn't do . . . but to which he confessed.

Brumfield also told me that he had "messed over" people on the street like himself, but he had never "messed over" a family like mine, that he had never "messed over" hard-working people. Brumfield also pointed out that he had seven children, including a daughter who was in the courtroom when Brumfield was tried and convicted twelve years earlier, and was now in college. I asked him what his daughter thought of him being in prison, and he responded, "She's not proud." Brumfield also showed me the scars on his arms and recalled his shootouts on the streets with others like himself. He told me I needed to understand that when my mom was murdered, the police were looking for somebody. They had to have somebody. "I was that somebody," he said.

As I listened to Brumfield, I realized that most of the questions I had crafted in a spiral pocket notebook that I brought with me, questions that I had compiled from my family, were suddenly irrelevant. If he wasn't going to admit that he murdered my mom, as he did in his confession to police, I couldn't ask him questions about that night. It changed the dynamic of the conversation I had come to have.

After Brumfield professed his innocence, I told him that I didn't come to Angola to say "you, you, you" and get in his face. I had been through a lot and I wanted to tell him about it. I quickly flipped through the first three pages of my notebook, which had these hand-written questions in black pen:

Why did you rob the Piggly Wiggly that night?

How do you feel today about your situation?

Why did you guys shoot a police officer? Didn't you think she had kids, husband, family?

How could you guys do something so dreadful without even thinking who you may be hurting in the long run?

Why would you shoot a police officer and not think about the consequences?

Do you feel remorseful towards what you have done that night?

How would you feel if someone did to you what you did to my family?

Why did you guys agree to the meeting?

What made you guys feel comfortable enough to talk about the killing of our mother?

As you had the time to examine your life and the killing, was it worth the time and effort that you guys put in planning and carrying out this selfish act?

When you took the time to plot and accomplish this killing, what did you think would be the outcome of your deed?

It has been almost 15 years since the killing. If you could say anything to our family, what would it be and why?

Finally, after listening to Brumfield for a while longer, I decided I just wanted to tell him about what that night did to me and how that night changed my life. I wanted him to know that I used to play football with passion and emotion. I still play with the passion for the game, but I no longer play the game with emotion because the night Mom was murdered took all the emotion from me. When you loved somebody like I loved my mom, it is as great an emotional experience as you could have. I wanted to explain to Brumfield how it affected the lives of my brothers, Derrick, Bricson, and Travis, and sisters, Summer and Samantha. I wanted him to know that I remembered that growing up as a kid, I wanted to be a father, I wanted to be a husband, I wanted to be a dad. I wanted him to know that what he did that night to my mom ruined a lot of that for me. I flipped to the fourth page in my notebook. My hands trembled slightly as I began to read:

I have struggled with this loss. My family has struggled.

I don't think you realize the life changing experience it has caused.

You took my life away, changed my dreams and made them desires.

I am the oldest and it was my responsibility to look after my family. My life will never be the same. My best friend in the world was taken away from me by you guys.

Thank God that she raised and prepared me for that day.

Things have not been easy. I've been depressed for years, lying to myself that I am OK.

I've cheated people in my life because I wasn't giving them Warrick. I've had a tough relationship with my brother Derrick who I love, 'cause you took his opportunity to be my mom's little man.

It has been up and down with my family because I had to become Daddy, not just Big Brother. It wasn't easy deciding someone else's life when you can't decide your own.

I've had some serious issues over the years in my personal life: afraid of commitment, fully committing myself to anything other than my family; not wanting to have kids or get married; not enjoying life, laughing or smiling; not letting people love me.

Over the last few years, I've been trying to be at peace with things in my life because I have to move forward. I am yearning for something new, a new start. Family, kids—just to get my life started.

I guess I am searching for answers. You guys have short-changed my family.

As I looked at this man who I never met, I bared my soul to him. I told him how in the years after my mom's death I had been hesitant about being in a committed relationship, how I've been afraid to lose people. I've been in counseling for many years over this very concept of having a true committed relationship because I don't want to lose somebody I love twice in my life. I don't think I can do it. I don't think I could suffer that pain again.

Tears started to well in my eyes when I realized that I was laying it all on the line for a guy who had killed my mom. As I looked around the room, I realized everyone else in the room had tears in their eyes, too—Brumfield included. I took thirty seconds, paused, collected my thoughts, and finally looked at him and told him:

"If you didn't do it, I don't know why you are here today, but I know why I am here today. I am here because I need to forgive somebody. I am here because it has been fourteen years and it's time for me to move on. I was searching for answers. I've been going to counseling. I've started smiling. I've started laughing. I even had my first drink two years ago during a fun moment. It is time for me to forgive and move on."

Everyone went silent. I had said it. I was there to forgive.

Brumfield stuttered for a moment, then told me that as he watched me on television over the years, he wondered what path I would have taken, or the life I would have lived, if that night never had happened. He promised me that the Lord would take care of me. Brumfield added that he wasn't blessed with a support system and a mother like mine. He told me a story that in 1987, my mother, working security at a store, caught him stealing and made him put back whatever he took. Brumfield said my mom told him, "Boy, get your butt out of here." Brumfield said my mom could have made an example of him that day, but she elected not to. I thought to myself, that was Mom—always giving people second chances to do right.

Brumfield looked at me and asked, "Why now? Why meet?" I told him I was finally strong enough to do this, that years of counseling had made this possible. Brumfield told me not to hold onto my anger anymore, and he said that he prayed for me and my family. I answered that God has a path for all of us, and that I was happy that his life hadn't been taken away. I told Brumfield that it took me a long time to stop blaming God for that night.

I also had a letter and poem written by Summer that I pulled out and read to Brumfield.

> On behalf of the Betty Dunn Smothers family, I would like to say, I am appalled that we live in a society, where black-on-black crime is the highest-ranked type of homicide in the country. We were raised with the belief that we are free and equal, and that slavery, racism and prejudice no longer exist in our society. As we evolve into the different phases of our life, we have learned that these things are still heavily portrayed in our society. While living in this world, one believes our worst enemies are of the other cultural descent; however, the most dangerous people to us are our own people (African Americans).
>
> Now as my family and I try to cross another hurdle in our lives we are constantly brought back to January 7, 1993 as one of life's greatest tragedies, the loss of our mother, the great Betty Dunn Smothers. When our mother took her oath to protect and serve the citizens of Baton Rouge, Louisiana, she gave her life doing

what she promised the citizens and her fellow officers. In return, the city of Baton Rouge helped raise money for my siblings and me, and for that we are grateful. For them, showing their support and unconditional love, we thank you.

Now as the years keep growing and our joy becomes our pain, our life has this immense void where no one can even imagine because of the damage you and your friends cost our family. Can you imagine life at 14 without your mother, no father to step up and take responsibility for his seed? Not knowing where your next meal will come from, or where you are going to lay your head at night, or even who's going to sacrifice their life to raise six children because of someone's selfish acts. Do you know what this can to do a 14-year-old's physical, emotional and mental state of mind? Did you ever wonder, the effect you'd have on our lives for the rest of our life? Do you?

Poem

The Feeling of a Hurt Soul

As I tried not to hate,
I just keep my faith.
To have mercy on your soul,
For your action and your role.
I pray that justice will prevail,
As you sit in your cell.
You start to ponder,
Only to wonder.
How you took her life,
To leave her six children full of strife.
We were adolescent without a mother fighting for our wealth,
Now you sit and wait until your death.

With that said and done, I would like to leave you with a famous quote from Dr. Martin Luther King, Jr.—"the ultimate measure of a man is not where he stands in moments of comfort and conveniences, but where he stands at times of challenge and controversy."

Brumfield peered at me and said he was proud of me. "You stood up after all this. I ain't got no hate for you all," he said. I told him that my mom still beats in my heart. Brumfield responded that Mom was looking down on me at that very moment and smiling. Brumfield then encouraged me to get married, to have kids, to find the happiness I deserved. He told me I needed to be the Warrick Dunn who I said was robbed from others following that night. Brumfield also mentioned that I was a better man than him, because if his mom had been murdered, "there would have been street justice."

I was also surprised that Brumfield had followed my career and knew all of my stats and the fact that I was nearing 10,000 career rushing yards as we sat there that day. Brumfield actually had followed the athletic exploits of all of my brothers and sisters, with the exception of Samantha. He also knew of my Homes for the Holidays Program, which helps single parents become first-time home owners. Brumfield said one of the homes that I gave away in Baton Rouge was near his mother's house on Peach Street. He said his mother showed up and watched the presentation.

As the meeting began to draw to a close, Brumfield said he appreciated me showing up. I told him I appreciated it as well, and explained that I really had no idea what to expect. I told him that I didn't hold any ill feelings or hatred toward him. Brumfield answered, "I always felt you were an amazing person. Today proved it. Just live life, man. I'll continue praying for both of us."

After guards came and took Brumfield back to his cell, his lawyer Nick Trenticosta told me that only days earlier he had attended a friend's funeral. As he sat and listened to the exchange between my-self and his client, he thought of a saying that he had once heard: "Death is common but a life well lived is very rare." Nick looked at me and said, "Your mother's life was a life well lived. It was proven by what you did here today."

My meeting with Brumfield lasted sixty minutes—the same amount of time it took a jury to give him a death sentence over life in prison twelve years earlier.

AS I LEFT THE PRISON, I walked the same path that Brumfield and Broadway will walk when they are executed by lethal injection within the next two to four years. Inmates in Louisiana were previ-ously executed in the electric chair, but state laws changed in 1986 and they are now put to death by lethal injection. Angola's old elec-tric chair is actually on display at the prison's museum.

Deputy Warden Vannoy invited me to visit the chamber where Brumfield will be executed, first walking me into the holding cell where inmates are moved the day before their execution. There's a television and a telephone in the cell. An officer would be stationed out front. On the day of their execution, inmates can visit with their families, religious advisors, and attorneys. They are fed their last meal between two and three o'clock in the afternoon after their fam-ily leaves. Prior to the execution at sundown, inmates are dressed in a T-shirt and blue jeans. They are fully restrained and then walked to the death chamber.

Thirty to forty minutes before the execution, the witnesses are brought in and seated in a room adjacent to the death chamber. One side is for the victim's family and the other side is for the press, the inmate's attorney, and whoever else he wants. A locked door sepa-rates the groups. The warden will then ask the condemned person if he wants to make a last statement; he will stand behind a microphone to make it.

Once the inmate finishes his statement, he is strapped down on a table. The curtains are closed as medical technicians start an IV in each arm. The IV is run through a hole to a stand behind a one-way mirror. A bag is set up with the drugs and three syringes. Once the warden nods his head to begin, the drugs are administered. The first one is sodium pentothal, which puts the inmate to sleep. The second one is potassium bromide, and the third is potassium chloride. One stops his heart, the other stops his breath. A heart monitor is hooked up to the inmate. When the monitor flatlines, the warden is alerted. A physician is called in and will pronounce the inmate dead. Once the witnesses are cleared out, the body is placed on a gurney, bagged, wheeled out to an ambulance in back of the prison, and driven to either the morgue or the hospital, where it is picked up by his family.

As I walked out of the prison through the front door, I felt it. I felt the weight being lifted from my shoulders.

I looked back over my shoulder. Kevan Brumfield was still on Death Row.

I walked out a free man.

AS I SAT IN THE CAR, I tried to come to grips with the meeting. Brumfield, of course, denied that he murdered my mother. When his attorneys informed me that he wasn't going to answer any direct questions concerning his involvement or if he killed my mother, I knew I had to adjust my train of thought.

Obviously, with more time to reflect, I wish I had found ways to ask more direct questions. But I was a little overwhelmed. I had just sat face to face with a man who was convicted of killing my mother.

But I still had the opportunity to say my piece and to say some of the things my family wanted to share. I believe Summer's message, her poem, and the quote said it all.

I thought it was good for Brumfield to say I needed to release my anger and live my life. He had followed my career so closely and followed my family, too. That made me wonder: why would someone who didn't do it follow my family so closely? Did he really kill my mother and just didn't want to admit that he did it? Or was he really not there at the bank, his confession coerced by police, as he has claimed? His mention of street justice didn't affect me because I grew up on the streets. My uncles and cousins grew up on the streets, too. That's the first thing that everyone wants to think, retaliation. You want to retaliate through the streets. But we all had the sense to try to let the police do their jobs.

I know I had tears in my eyes and at times had to collect my thoughts during the meeting. When I was in the moment and it was happening so fast, I just needed to take a break and gather my thoughts and just realize what was happening. Honestly, I was surprised that I stayed calm and levelheaded, and that I was neither overly emotional nor emotionless. I was really just trying to concentrate on what I wanted to say. I think that I am at a point in my life where I've forgiven him, or whoever. I've forgiven them and it's in God's hands.

Yes, it might have been a better experience if he had confessed to me that he killed my mother. It would have provided some answers to a mystery. What Brumfield and his attorneys are obviously trying to do is question the judicial system and the Baton Rouge police force that my mom worked for. This is the same guy who, in his confession to police, said he viewed my mother's body at the funeral home before she was buried.

While Choo-Choo thought that Brumfield was a changed man based on the conversation, he also questioned whether those changes were genuine. Choo-Choo said it might be true sorrow, but he pointed out that it also might be the sorrow of a man who doesn't want to die and will say anything. All I know is that being strapped to a table in the death chamber at Angola State Prison is not the way you want to go out. It's not how you want to end your life, and it should be a lesson to people.

Even though Brumfield's lawyers asked me to stick around for a few minutes to listen to their plea, it didn't have any affect on me. They have to do what they have to do. Brumfield has already been tried in a court of law and he's had a million appeals, so it doesn't bother me one bit that he now may die for this crime. If they can prove something else, I will listen. But today he's guilty, and he's on Death Row for a reason. I am sure he's asking himself a lot of questions and praying to God for guidance and help.

I am praying for him, too.

TO GET TO ANGOLA State Prison from Baton Rouge, you drive right by St. Francisville. It's a small, quaint town on the bluffs of the Mississippi River. It's actually the last town you pass heading to Angola, or the first town you come to heading out of Angola. St. Francisville is also where my mother was born in 1957, and it's where my mother was buried in 1993, right next to her grandmother.

I was asked if I had ever given any thought over the years to driving from St. Francisville to Angola State Prison during one of my visits to her grave site. Honestly, I never had the desire in years past to meet the person who shot and killed my mother. I never even thought about it until recently. I tried to stay focused on football and the things that I had going on in my life. I tried to make sure I was on course at all times.

Well, that course finally led me to Angola.

A few quick turns off Highway 61, with the prison in our rearview mirror, and we found ourselves on a winding, narrow road to the St. Francisville cemetery. The small church and graveyard are surrounded by a chain-link fence. I jumped the fence and stood at Mom's grave site. Our family tries to meet here once a year on Good Friday before Easter. We talk to Mom. We laugh. We cry. We pray. I am sure Mom knew I had just met and talked with Brumfield. I am sure Mom heard every word, too.

But I wanted to stop and let her hear it again.

I love you, Mom.

CHAPTER 2

MURDER SHATTERS HOME

I T WASN'T UNCOMMON FOR MY MOTHER, AS A SINGLE mom with six children, to work fourteen- to sixteen-hour days. As a Baton Rouge police officer, Mom often took on off-hours security work at department stores, convenience stores, and football games to make ends meet on her $36,000-a-year salary.

Any time my mother worked late at night, I slept in her bed until she got home. That may sound kind of strange, but it was a comforting habit for me, even as her oldest child at eighteen years old. I always wanted to know when she returned home safe and sound. I would then get up and head to my room that I shared with my three younger brothers. My two younger sisters shared their own room across the hall.

The evening of January 6, 1993, wasn't any different for me. It was a Wednesday night, a school night, and everyone had gone to bed. Mom was working an extra-duty security job at a Piggly Wiggly grocery store on Florida Boulevard and Donmoor Avenue in East Baton Rouge. She had worked at this store many other times. Mom knew the neighborhood, knew the store's co-owners, Skipper Jones and Ted Harvey, knew the store's employees, and, best yet, the store was close to our home. I climbed into my mother's bed and fell asleep to the sound of rain hitting the roof.

The telephone rang around 12:30 in the morning of January 7. It startled me.

I got up and shuffled to the kitchen. The phone was on the counter near the refrigerator. I picked up the telephone and said hello. It was Baton Rouge police officer Theodore Jordan, who worked with my mother and was a family friend. I could sense something was wrong by his tone. Officer Jordan told me my mother had been shot, and she was at Our Lady of the Lake Regional Medical Center, about twenty minutes from our home in East Baton Rouge. My mind was spinning, not knowing what to think. I actually thought Officer Jordan was joking at first, but he said he was serious and then repeated himself.

That's when I knew.

I don't know how, but I knew.

Mom wasn't coming home.

I dressed quietly so as not to wake up my brothers and sisters. Officer Jordan picked me up in front of the house and we sped to the hospital. It was crazy. Nurses, doctors, and police officers were everywhere. That's when I was told my mother had died from her gunshot wounds; Mom was pronounced dead at 12:45 A.M. It was like the air had been squeezed from my body. I was the first family member to arrive, so I had to identify my mother's body. I didn't recognize Mom. She lay motionless on a table, still in her police uniform, her head bloodied, bandaged, and swollen. One bullet had struck her in the head behind her left ear. I immediately noticed that my mom was wearing the white pearl earrings I had given to her as a present. They were covered in blood. Mom's blood.

It felt as if my world had collapsed on top of me.

The scene at our house, as one might imagine, was emotional and chaotic. I didn't know it at the time, since I had already left for the hospital, but my sixteen-year-old brother Derrick said he woke up to the swirling reflection of blue lights inside and outside our home. A marked police car was parked at the side of the house where our mother normally parked her unit. Derrick got up and opened the door that led outside from our kitchen near the carport. He noticed it wasn't our mother's police cruiser because the blue emergency lights on top of the car were different, so he turned back inside, figuring somebody had been pulled over by the police.

A few minutes later, the nightmare started for our entire family.

That's when Derrick said the police officer in the car got out and knocked on the side door to let him know she was waiting on other officers. Although the officer wouldn't tell Derrick the reason she was waiting on other officers, Derrick found out soon enough when friends, family, and other officers started to arrive in waves. Our coaches from the local K-Y Track Club were the first to show—Choo-Choo, a man so close to me that I call him Pops to this day, Willie Williams, and Amos Harrison had hurried over. I am not sure how they had heard the news, but it spread quickly among the adults.

Derrick will be the first to tell you he's hotheaded. Initially, the people who arrived at the house didn't say much of anything about what had happened. They asked Derrick if his other brothers and sisters were in the house. He said yes, they were sleeping, but why did that matter? Coach Williams tried to grab and hug Derrick, calling Derrick by his nickname, "Pee Wee." But Derrick pushed him away, wanting to know what the heck was going on. Coach Williams finally answered, "Betty was shot." Derrick thought it was a "sickass joke" to play on the family. It was sick, but it wasn't a joke.

Around this time, Willie Wheeler, my mother's mom and my grandmother, showed up at the house. She had been out playing bingo. Derrick was inside, but he could hear Grandma outside screaming and wailing as more and more people, mainly police officers, started to arrive. Derrick looked for me in the house, but somebody told him I had already gone to the hospital. My other brothers and sisters—Bricson (11 years old), Travis (10 years old), Summer (14 years old), and Samantha (9 years old)—were asleep in the girls' room. Sometimes the girls would push their beds together and everyone piled into it at night—the boys at the foot of the bed, the girls at the head of the bed, all sprawled across it. As more and more people arrived at the house, Summer, Bricson, Travis, and Samantha got up and were told the horrible news.

There was shock, disbelief, and tears, but the realization that Mom was gone was hard to register at that age. Everyone tried their best to comfort our family and comfort one another. Officer Jordan left me at the hospital and went to my house to pick up Derrick and Grandma. When Derrick arrived at the hospital, he was furious. He didn't understand how this had happened, and at one point stormed out of the room with officers in pursuit. I sat in a corner with my head down, trying to figure out what I was going to do next. How would our family cope? What was I supposed to do?

My senior year at Catholic High School really couldn't have gone any better athletically. National Signing Day was four weeks away, and I was being recruited by some of the nation's top colleges and universities to play football. Mom and I had planned our recruiting visits—we were scheduled to drive to Tuscaloosa, Alabama, that Saturday—and I was so close to fulfilling a childhood dream. But college and football seemed unimportant as I stared at my mother's lifeless body on that table. Mom was my best friend, my soul mate, my guardian angel. We were so close that we knew each other's thoughts and finished each other's sentences. And Mom was gone, thirty-six years old, murdered in the line of duty.

Greg Brown, a family friend and K-Y's longtime president, showed up at the hospital. I told Greg right there, on the spot, that I planned to stay home and take care of my family, that college football was no longer an option. Greg told me my mother wouldn't be happy with that decision. He said that I needed to be strong, chase my dream, and make something of myself. Greg said the first child in a family has to set the tone. That's exactly what my mother used to tell me, too. Mom would call me her Little Man. She was the mother and I was the father figure in the house.

And now it was just me.

As we headed back to the house, I saw Coach Brooks standing in the front yard. He was my first youth football coach at age ten when I played for the Rams. Coach Brooks was a father to me. He taught me everything about life. He taught me to be humble. He taught me to be strong. And that's what he repeated as he put his arm around me and told me not to cry and to be strong for my family. He consoled and counseled me in the same breath. His message echoed in my mind.

Don't cry. I had to be strong.

Those hours were a blur. Nobody knew exactly at this point what had happened to my mother, but the police officers at our house shared bits and pieces. The motive of the shooting was likely robbery. They said my mother was shot along with a grocery store night manager. My mom, a fourteen-year veteran police officer who was dressed in her uniform and was in her marked police unit, was dead, and the night manager survived multiple gunshot wounds. It didn't make any sense.

People continued to show up at our house. Many of my high school teammates and friends started to arrive early Thursday morning. What do teenagers say to one another when one of them loses his mother? But I was glad they showed. A miserable, rainy night turned into a miserable, rainy Thursday morning. It seemed as if everyone we knew—and my mother knew—was crammed into our small house on Bradley Street. It was chaotic. The telephone rang nonstop.

People were crying, but I knew I had to be strong. It got really crazy. Grandma, sprawled out on the couch, was comforted by family and friends. My brothers and sisters were upset and dazed. It seemed as if I was being pulled in a hundred different directions.

Coaches, parents, teachers, and students from Catholic High were piled in the kitchen by midmorning. Head coach Dale Weiner, assistant coaches Joe LeBlanc and Sid Edwards, and athletic director Pete Boudreaux were some of those who arrived and offered their support. Coach Weiner was struck by my mind-set. He called it remarkable, saying he would have thought I was a forty-five-year-old man in charge. I was businesslike, absorbed in the details that needed to be done for our family. Coach Weiner didn't think I was in denial over my mother's murder, but he figured the busywork probably helped keep the deep pain away from me. The media also began to show up at our home with their cameras and notepads, and I tried to be as accommodating as possible. But it was hard. Finally, I had to step away and breathe, too.

The police continued to seek clues to my mom's death, and it was being played out in our local newspaper, the *Advocate*, and on television and radio shows. Police Chief Greg Phares said my mom's murder was "one of the boldest crimes I've ever been involved with in 21 years." The slaying was termed a "planned ambush." Assistant District Attorney Prem Burns promised to seek the death penalty for the person responsible for the murder and attempted murder. Also, Louisiana governor Edwin Edwards, calling the case "a double tragedy," personally offered a $5,000 reward for information leading to the arrest of the gunman or gunmen.

Mom's death was so hard to comprehend. The natural reaction was to think of your last moment with her, your last words. Those thoughts crossed my mind during the confusion. I had talked to Mom after she arrived for work at the Piggly Wiggly on Wednesday. I had an upset stomach, and Mom told me to ride to the store and meet her to buy medicine to settle my stomach. But I was like, Nah, I'll be fine. I'll just wait until you get home. I should have gone to see Mom. I regret that decision each day of my life. Summer and Mom also talked on the telephone before she left for work that night. Summer was upset because she was supposed to go to the mall that night with Mom to buy new shoes. Travis was in the kitchen when Mom headed out the door to the Piggly Wiggly, and she reminded him to finish frying the fish, which was our dinner that evening.

Two weeks earlier, Derrick and Mom had gotten into an argument. Words were exchanged, and Mom asked him what he would do if something happened to her. Derrick loved Mom and he loved us, but he was admittedly rebellious and hotheaded and could be mean-spirited. Derrick told Mom he would cry for about five minutes and then wouldn't shed a tear after that if something happened to her. He told Mom that it was her choice to be a police officer and that she needed to accept the job's responsibilities and risks. Derrick knew the words hurt Mom, but he said he didn't care. But truthfully, Derrick did care.

It seemed as if the entire city of Baton Rouge cared about Mom. Immediately following my mother's death, the Betty Smothers Memorial Fund was established at City Federal Credit Union for us. More than forty people showed up at the credit union on Friday, the day after the murder, and donated more than $1,260—and Friday wasn't even a payday for city-parish employees. The owner of our home, George Godso Jr., also said he wasn't going to charge us rent for three months, a sum equaling a donation of $1,150. Friends and family dropped off enough food to feed an army.

This was supposed to be a great weekend for Mom and me. We were scheduled to drive to Tuscaloosa, Alabama, on Saturday to visit the University of Alabama, which was one of a dozen schools recruiting me. But that was a distant thought. I wasn't worried about football. Instead, I had to plan my mom's funeral and burial, which were set for the following Monday and Tuesday. Football? I was more concerned about my family.

The investigation into my mom's murder also continued into the weekend. Police asked the public for help in solving the case, publishing telephone numbers for Crime Stoppers and the Homicide Division. More details continued to surface and were reported in the *Advocate*. The events seem to have unfolded like this:

The shooting occurred about 12:15 A.M. Thursday morning, when my mom and the thirty-year-old night manager, Kimen Lee, of a Florida Boulevard Piggly Wiggly drove to deposit the store's receipts. Mom pulled her marked police car into the exit lane of the drive-through area at the Citizens Bank & Trust on Jefferson Highway, a short drive from the store. The store manager was on the passenger side of the car. The car stopped at the night deposit box and the store manager rolled down her window to use her key to open the box. That's when at least one gunman opened fire on my mom and the night manager. The gunman or gunmen fired several shots into my mom's police car. Lee told police "she knew instantly what was happening." Mom was struck in the head and killed, and Lee was struck several times.

As the shots were being fired, Lee, severely wounded, managed to take control of the car and drive it through the teller lane. The car glanced off a metal box on the drive-through curb behind the bank before it continued onto Jefferson Highway. Lee drove northwest on Jefferson Highway to a nearby Circle K store for help. The store's bank deposit bag remained in the car, and the robbers got nothing. Police said there was no indication that the gunman tried to follow the police car after it left the bank. Lee was reported in stable condition and was expected to live.

After the shooting, police blocked streets in the area. They stopped motorists and asked for identification in an effort to locate a suspect. Corporal Kevin Cavel explained in a story that appeared in the *Advocate* that Mom was working "extra duty," or off-duty private work, as a police officer for Piggly Wiggly. Off-duty police officers were routinely hired by LSU, state agencies, federal agencies, and private individuals to provide security. They were allowed to wear their uniforms and drive their police cruisers. Even when off-duty, police officers have the power of arrest.

My family, of course, was left emotionally drained and with a broken heart. But I was determined to keep the family together and mend that heart. Grandma, who was fifty-six years old, also decided at that moment to move into our house. We weren't going to let the kids go anywhere else, and Grandma helped take charge of Mom's funeral plans. On Saturday, the police department released a composite drawing of a suspect in my mom's murder. The police also announced it was almost certain that the shooting was committed by two people.

According to information handed out by police, the suspect was described as a black male, possibly twenty-five to thirty-five years old, between five feet six inches and five feet ten inches tall and weighing between 170 and 185 pounds. The suspect's hair was curly, possibly Jheri-curled, and highlighted gray on the sides. He was also wearing a dark, possibly camouflage baseball cap, camouflage jacket, and plastic-rimmed glasses. Police said the suspect should be considered armed and dangerous. Police also asked the occupants of two vehicles seen near the shooting scene to contact them. One of the vehicles, a 1980–85 metallic blue Nissan 280Z with heavily tinted windows, was seen near the bank police said. Police said the second vehicle, which was not described, was almost struck when the night manager sped out of the bank parking lot onto Jefferson Highway.

The reward money for the capture and conviction of the suspects in the case grew to at least $8,000, and the police department said it was swamped with calls from people wanting to know what they could do to make a visible show of support for our family. The police asked people to drive with their headlights on during the Monday and Tuesday following the murder. All I know was that the support was unbelievable when you thought of the folks who had shown up at our home since early that Thursday morning and extended a helping hand.

CHAPTER 3

BECOMING DAD

WHY HER?

That's the question everyone asked one another following my mom's murder. I know Mom's fellow police officers were confused and angry that someone would blow away a police officer in full uniform in a marked car. Betty Smothers was a woman and a single mother, a combination that made her murder even more heinous, they said. I was just as confused and angry, too, but I couldn't let myself wallow in emotion. I had to step in and take care of my family. I honestly believed Mom prepared me for this day, but really, I had no idea where to start. As the police department's investigation continued into Mom's murder, we prepared for the two hardest days of our lives—Mom's funeral and burial.

It was time to say goodbye.

Nearly three thousand people attended my mother's funeral on Monday night, January 11, 1993, at the Centroplex Exhibition Hall in downtown Baton Rouge. The funeral was too large to hold at a local church. A four-hour visitation earlier in the day at the Winnfield Funeral Home also drew thousands of mourners. That entire day was a blur. I know the funeral was emotional for everyone. Hundreds of uniformed law enforcement officers from throughout Louisiana and other states attended the service. Many wore black strips over their badges. The police department also kept a close eye on us, too, since no arrests had been made in the case. When Summer needed to go to the bathroom before the funeral, two officers accompanied her.

During the service a number of speakers, including Police Chief Greg Phares, family friends Greg Brown and Gertrude Thomasson, and Catholic High coach and athletic director Pete Boudreaux, instructed us to follow our mother's footsteps. The crowd applauded when Brown directed his words toward me and said it was Mom's time, that we shouldn't quit and we needed to move on. He encouraged me to go to college and play football and said that my brothers and sisters would be looked after by our grandmother. Brown also told us that it was our mother's dream to own a home and to make sure we were educated. Coach Boudreaux said our mother had an "inner toughness" and often talked about her dreams to make our neighborhood, her police beat, and her children better. He told us we had athletic skills and academic skills and we could make those dreams come true. That foundation had been laid.

I sat there motionless. I didn't break down and cry because I knew I had to be strong for my brothers and sisters. But Mom's death affected everyone at the funeral.

Officer Murial Hall trained with my mother following his graduation from the police academy in 1990. Officer Hall was actually assigned to another officer at first, but Mom wasn't comfortable with the way Hall was being trained. That's when Mom asked her supervisor if she could train him instead. Mom and Officer Hall became good friends, and she always called him "Junior." We got to know Officer Hall pretty well, too. He stopped by the house to visit. Officer Hall was in the honor guard and was stationed next to Mom's casket at the funeral. As he saluted, tears rolled down his face.

Tuesday was the dismissal service and burial at the cemetery in St. Francisville, not far from where my mother lived as a child. We returned to the Centroplex Exhibition Hall for the dismissal. More than 2,400 people gathered for the service and heard the spiritual "May the Work I've Done Speak for Me." Mayor Tom Ed McHugh spoke and said my mom made the community a better place for all of us, and the community died a little bit inside "when we lost a person of this caliber." On behalf of the city, he promised my family, "We stand ready to help each and every one of you." The last words of Mom's obituary gave the perfect punctuation to the life she led: "VP of track club, secretary of Rams Football Team, Catholic High Mothers Club"—she had been involved and active about serving others. Of course, the most emotional moment came when all six of us, her children, leaned into Mom's coffin and kissed her goodbye.

The funeral procession left downtown for Magnolia Baptist Church in West Feliciana Parish. A caravan of mourners, including an estimated 300 police cars from all over Louisiana, made its way to the small, muddy hillside cemetery in St. Francisville. At the cemetery, many of the people who came to pay their last respects had to walk more than a mile to reach the grave site. By the time the people at the back of the procession walked up the hill, the people at the front were already returning. Cars clogged the narrow road that led to the church. Baton Rouge is like a lot of Southern cities with racial animosity, but my mom had brought everyone together for a little while.

We sat in chairs under a canopy near the grave site and the Reverends Robert Early and Sam Bell led the brief ceremony. My mom was buried beside her grandmother. During the burial ceremony, three Baton Rouge police officers folded the American flag that had covered Mom's casket. An honor guard from the Livingston Parish Sherriff's Office fired three rifle volleys and a trumpeter played "Taps." Police Chief Greg Phares then presented the flag to me, while honor guard commander Abe Ross gave me a commemorative pin. Very few people had ever seen me let go of my emotions, but it finally hit me.

I buried my head in my hands and cried.

The same day my mother was laid to rest, it was announced that four men had been arrested in connection with her murder. The *Advocate* reported that the big break had come two days earlier, on Sunday, when one of the suspects called detectives to tell them about his involvement. The first suspect was arrested at his apartment Sunday night and the other three were arrested at various locations Monday night and Tuesday evening.

The three men who were accused of taking part in Mom's murder were identified as Kevan T. Brumfield, twenty; Henri Carity Broadway, twenty-two; and West Paul, twenty, all from Baton Rouge. Each was booked on first-degree murder, attempted first-degree murder, and principal to attempted armed robbery. The fourth man, Eddie Paul, was brought to the police station as a material witness.

Police said Brumfield allegedly fired the shots that killed my mom, Broadway allegedly fired the shots that wounded Mom's passenger, and Paul was the alleged driver of a getaway car parked nearby. Paul's cousin, forty-nine-year-old Eddie Paul, was booked as a principal to first-degree murder, principal to attempted first-degree murder, and principal to attempted armed robbery. Assistant District Attorney Prem Burns said all four men confessed their involvement in the case.

According to an arrest warrant for Eddie Paul, investigators believed my mom's murder was planned in Eddie Paul's apartment. Prosecutors said there was evidence that two weapons were used in the shootings. The suspects were inside the detectives' office most of the day Tuesday, under intense security. The office was locked while a detective stood guard in the hallway. Even police weren't allowed inside unless they had business there. The *Advocate* reported that

Police Chief Greg Phares felt "tremendous relief" that the suspects in the case were arrested. Burns said the investigation was "the finest cooperative effort that I have ever seen" in eighteen years as a prosecutor. It also was reported that two of the suspects—Brumfield and West Paul—were suspects in a Christmas Day armed robbery in which Brumfield allegedly tried to shoot two Clinton residents. Brumfield also was free on bond awaiting sentencing on unrelated drug and theft charges when he was accused of shooting my mother.

But I wasn't aware of any of this as I stood staring at my mother's casket at the cemetery, asking myself, *Did this really happen? Are we really putting my mom into the ground?* Everyone talks about how you lose a part of you when somebody close dies. I didn't feel like I lost a part of me.

I felt like I lost *all* of me.

But, again, I knew I couldn't feel sorry for myself. Life continued, and I had a decision to make concerning college. Two weeks after my mom's murder, I made my official visit to Florida State in Tallahassee with family friend Greg Brown. I had a genuine connection with Coach Bowden when we met in his office, and I immediately knew I wanted to be a Seminole. Coach said he would try to take care of me, and I believed him. I also knew Mom wanted me to be a Seminole, too. There were many people who believed I needed to stay at home and attend Louisiana State, and I admit the thought crossed my mind, too. But as I sat in Coach Bowden's office and looked around, I knew.

FSU felt like the perfect fit.

When I signed with Florida State on National Signing Day, February, 3, 1993—less than a month after Mom's murder—I was part of an FSU recruiting class that was voted tops in the country by recruiting analysts. Max Emfinger, Tom Lemming, Allen Wallace, and all the others stamped our class as the nation's finest. Even University of Florida coach Steve Spurrier acknowledged as much when he went on television and said, "I think Florida State has the best recruiters in college football. The way those guys have the ability to convince players that they can come up there and beat out high school All-Americans who are already there is beyond me. They do it year after year. I am not taking about every other year. I am talking about every year."

Our class included players such as linebacker Peter Boulware of Columbia, South Carolina; offensive lineman Tra Thomas of Deland, Florida; linebacker Reinard Wilson of Lake City, Florida; running back Rock Preston of Miami, Florida; quarterback Thad Busby of Pace, Florida; kicker Scott Bentley of Aurora, Colorado; and receiver Andre Cooper of Jacksonville, Florida. It was a versatile class, too. Twenty of the twenty-four players who signed on National Signing Day played more than one sport. Coach Bowden was pleased and said, "It was like Santa Claus came to see me."

My Catholic High teammate, Kevin Franklin, meanwhile, decided to stay in town and sign with LSU. Including Kevin and me, our senior class had eight players sign Division I scholarships. But I couldn't get caught up in the euphoria of Signing Day the way everyone else seemed to. They were looking down the road. I was looking at the immediate. As I said, there were many people locally who believed I should have stayed home and signed with LSU, too. I was criticized by those who said I owed the community for the help and appreciation it showed following my mom's murder. Mom gave her life to our community; wasn't that enough?

Mom's murder, of course, shattered our home and changed our lives. Track season was especially tough for me. I was so used to seeing Mom, in her police uniform, hanging over the fence near the finish line, shouting words of encouragement. I swallowed hard that first time when I locked into the starting blocks, looked up, and saw the empty runway. Mom was really gone. But as I pushed off, I knew my family couldn't stop moving forward, either. The days and months following her death were extremely painful, though friends and relatives popped in and out and did their best to help out. Like a team, the community also rallied around us. The outpouring of sympathy and financial, educational, and other support was overwhelming. Each day we received letters from people we didn't even know, from all across the country, offering condolences and help.

The Betty Smothers Memorial Fund, which began January 8, the day after my mother was murdered, reached $235,000 by early March. The *Advocate* reported that Stella Cranfield, the manager of the Baton Rouge City-Parish Employees Credit Union, where the money was being collected, said organizers initially had hoped they could raise $50,000. It only took a few days before the goal was reached. A month later, in April, we were informed that our family would receive $60,000 in state benefits for officers killed in the line of duty. The state benefits are paid through the Louisiana Law Enforcement and Firefighters Survivors Benefits Board and funded by the state legislature. All the contributions were placed in a trust fund.

Not all the experiences were positive, however.

Everyone knew where we lived, since Mom's murder was splashed across the newspapers and reported on all the television and radio shows. But now people must have thought we had money, since the trust fund's amount was constantly publicized. We had telephone calls offering investment opportunities and real estate deals. Mom had actually made plans to look at new houses the day she was shot. Nearly a month to the day of Mom's murder, somebody stole my car, a white Mitsubishi Galant, from outside our home, thinking I might have had money in it. Police found the car in Baker, Louisiana, in a ditch. It was totaled.

We also knew we couldn't stay in our house on Bradley Street. The memories were just too painful, and honestly, I was afraid to live there. Mom's murder changed me. I always thought somebody was chasing me. I constantly looked over my shoulder, and I didn't trust anyone. If somebody asked me a question, I wanted to know why the question was being asked. I thought somebody was trying to figure out my whereabouts, where I was headed next. Subconsciously, because I knew my mom was ambushed, I thought somebody was going to set me up and murder me, too.

I was afraid to go home by myself. If the lights weren't on and nobody was home, I kept driving. I was at home one night hanging clothes in my closet when I noticed somebody outside my window. I could see the person's eyes staring at me. I turned on the lights and ran outside, and the person had ran behind the house and jumped the fence. You could see the footprints in the dirt. It was crazy. After Mom died, the television had to be on when I went to bed. I didn't care where I was, the television had to be on. It was my nightlight. I was eighteen years old, but scared of the dark.

There were days when I was late to track practice at Catholic High because I was out looking to buy a house. A couple of months later I finally found one in the Park Forest neighborhood, not far from where we lived. I paid $89,000 for it out of the insurance money we received following Mom's murder. Mom was gone. It used to be that she was the mom and I was the father figure of the house. Now it was just me, and I had to make these kinds of decisions and take action.

I was the dad.

And it was up to me to make sure that everybody grew up to be somebody.

CHAPTER 4

MOTHER'S TOUCH

F OR BEING SUCH A TINY LADY, MY MOM LEFT SOME pretty big shoes to fill.

Everyone seemed to know her and, what was more, everyone seemed to love her. As a teenager, she was well known throughout Baton Rouge for being a standout athlete. She was involved in a number of sports but was best known for being a track star and team captain at Scotlandville High School, which is part of the East Baton Rouge Parish Public Schools system. Mom was a state champion in hurdles. She actually trained with the Southern University track team and was breaking records on their track—while she was still in high school!

Mom was born on July 16, 1957, in St. Francisville, which is located on the bluffs of the Mississippi River and has been described by historians as two miles long and two yards wide. Mom grew up down the street from Doug Williams, a football star who became the first black quarterback to win a Super Bowl when he led the Washington Redskins over the Denver Broncos in 1988.

St. Francisville is a small, quiet town, about twenty-seven miles as the crow flies to Baton Rouge. Mom lived in St. Francisville until she moved to Scotlandville in the metro Baton Rouge area for high school. Mom had one older sister, Mary, who was born in 1955 and still lives in the Baton Rouge neighborhood, The Avenues, where our family grew up. Mom's mother, Willie D. Wheeler, obviously has been—and continues to be—a big part of our lives. Grandma says Mom's best trait was her upbeat personality. "She was a sweet person," Grandma said. "She liked everybody. She would do anything for anybody."

Mom met the man who would become my father while running track at Scotlandville. Apparently he was also an incredible athlete—just one of those guys who blows your mind with the way he can sprint. I guess with those genes coming at me from both sides, there was no way that I couldn't be both a runner and a leaper on the football field. Mom was just eighteen when she had me, and obviously, that put an end to her athletic career. You can't really clear hurdles when you've got a baby in tow. But she never seemed to mind it. Instead, she seemed to feel like she was just moving on to her next adventure, one where she proved herself every bit as spectacular as she had on the track.

Being a police officer was never Mom's lifelong dream. But with two children at the time, Mom needed a job. And once she made up her mind to enter the police academy in 1979, nobody could talk her out of it, not even her mother. "I didn't want her to go, but that's what she wanted to do," Grandma said. "I had to support her. She enjoyed working with people, but I knew it was dangerous. I tried to talk to her, but she said, 'Momma, I want to do it.' So I told her to go ahead."

Mom apparently never talked about the dangers of police work, but that's probably the norm for most police officers. Law enforcement is a demanding job, but one that Mom found worthwhile. Over her fourteen-year career, Mom worked in several jobs with the Baton Rouge police department. She earned the rank of corporal, which meant she obviously enjoyed shift work and the opportunity to work hand in hand with citizens. Two weeks before her murder, Mom was placed in the community policing division, the department's attempt to bring officers closer to the neighborhoods they patrol. Sergeant Mike Morris, the head of the community policing program, told the *Advocate* that he selected my mom for the unit "because of her police skills and her people skills." Morris was also Mom's training officer when she graduated from the academy, telling the newspaper, "I can't think of a time that I've known her that she didn't do something for someone."

There was really a unique relationship between us because I was born when she was still so young. As a result, our bond was different than between most parents and children because we kind of grew up together. We were best friends as much as we were mother and child. She wasn't afraid to be tough and be a parent when she needed to, but because we depended on each other in a different way, she didn't need to crack down and get tough too often because I never wanted to let her down. She didn't really ever have to punish me because just knowing she was disappointed in a choice I had made or in something I had done was enough to motivate me to never make that same mistake again.

We always seemed to know what the other one was thinking or feeling. When I was hurting, she could feel it, and I truly believe that. It was just like when I had my first car wreck. I had just gotten a car, and the first week I had it I had a wreck. I wasn't even in the city of Baton Rouge. I called her to tell her, but she already knew. She just said in a calm, cool voice, "I know you just had a wreck. I knew something had happened. It's okay." The police hadn't even gotten there yet, but somehow Mom just seemed to know. Our bond was just that strong.

Of course, despite our unique bond, that's not to say Mom and I never argued or disagreed. There was one time when she really got angry with me and pushed me backward with a quick right jab to my chest. It was so quick and powerful that her ring left a small imprint in the center of my chest!

She was such a wonderful mother to my entire family. For as much as she worked to make ends meet, she wasn't someone who brought her work home with her. When she was at home, she was completely ours. She made sure that we knew she would always have time for us—every track meet or football game or school show, she'd be there. She'd work double shifts in order to trade with people, and would make sure to do her "decompression" from work away from home. If she was in her "Mom capacity," she didn't let anything else interfere. Family time was family time—she could deal with work later.

Dale Weiner, my high school football coach, has always said how impressed he was with my mother's involvement and interest in my life. When I first got to Catholic, they never even talked about football or playing or what position I'd be in or anything like that. She was only worried about academics—how I was doing in class, what my attitude was like, if I was getting into trouble, and that sort of thing. She knew I could play football, so she wasn't concerned about that. She made sure she stayed on top of my schooling. That's what she was concerned with: Would I graduate high school? Would I be prepared for college? She just wanted to make sure that I was taking care of the things that mattered in the big picture.

And it wasn't just the people close to our family who recognized how special she was. Everyone who met her seemed to love her. You just couldn't help it because she was so humble and kind. Everyone called her "Miss Betty," too. She was a mom to everyone she met. After Mom died, it seemed as if everyone had a story to tell about a way she had quietly helped them out or encouraged them or just given them joy. I remember more than once she would stop people walking down the street, figure out where they were going, and give them a ride to make sure they got there safely. It didn't bother us kids, but we might roll our eyes because we knew it could make us a little late or because we really wanted to be headed somewhere else. But she knew she was teaching us an important lesson about looking out for people who needed a hand.

She also used to patrol grocery store parking lots in some of the rougher parts of town to make sure that the families who were there doing their shopping would be safe as they walked to their car. It wasn't part of her regular patrol—it wasn't anything she had to do. But she recognized a need and she acted on it. That's just the kind of person she was. My grandmother is the same way—it seems like she is always cooking for people or giving them a place to stay or helping them make ends meet. I guess Mom learned from her, and then wanted to make sure that we learned the same lesson.

Mom worked for everything she ever had, and she was never working for herself. It seemed like everything she did was for other people, but she never tried to call attention to herself—she wasn't interested in that and, ironically, that was what seemed to make her stand out in everyone's mind. She was just a generous, unassuming, down-to-earth, selfless person.

Carl Dehon was a Baton Rouge police officer with my mom and always admired her spirit and strength. After her death, his words of remembrance meant a lot to us, to know how she was seen by other people. "She was always a real polite person. She made an instant impression on you. It was a good thing. It was a good thing with Betty," Carl told me, recalling her work around the city.

"I think about her all the time because of the kind of person she was. You know, she was sweet. She was sweet to anyone. She was a lady. People would speak kindly of her. She would help bag your groceries, I mean, she was just that type of person, always willing to help . . . I have heard about her, no one had a negative word to say about Betty Smothers. Everyone is always impressed by her attention to her kids. Everything in her life was her kids. Probably when she went shopping, it was for her kids. When she went to work, it was about her kids. That's just how she was. She did what she had to do to take care of her children. That's just how she was."

Another officer who felt the impact of Mom's kindness was Murial Hall. Murial thinks it was because she was first and foremost a mother that my mom took an interest in him and took over his training and mentoring when she felt it wasn't meeting "Junior's" needs. "She took me in," he said. "We were real close, spent a lot of time at her home, got to know her kids." Mom even invited him over for meals on his days off, just to check on him and see how he was doing. She was always looking out for people like that. She hated to see anyone slip between the cracks.

Daryl Cornelius had gone to high school with my mom, and later was her riding partner on several shifts with the police department. He was always moved by her dedication to see the best side of people—to try to give them a chance. Her goal was always to help people work through the situation before having to resort to arrest. "She'd try anything to talk a person out of going to jail. I mean, she was more of a person that would try to talk the situation out over there. And I was kinda like, 'God, don't waste the time, I'll put them in jail,'" he said with a laugh. "She would basically try to talk you out of putting people in jail. I mean, she'd give the shirt off her back. That's why I don't understand those idiots who shot her. I mean, she wasn't that type of person. I just remember her being a hard-working individual, trying to provide for her kids."

Her friends on the force really felt the impact of her death, too. They all understand the inherent risks of their job, but no one seemed to grasp at first that it had been my mom, of all people, who had been murdered. "She had a beautiful smile," Carl remembered.

"Her personality was awesome. It was just awesome. Like I said, it was a horrible situation for anything like that to happen to anybody, but especially to Betty, that made it even more hard for us.

"When they told me what happened to Betty . . . I just couldn't sleep the rest of that night. It's just a painful thing, especially to hear that about Betty, or any police officer—it's just a horrible thing to hear. It just really broke my heart, but especially about Betty because she was probably one of the nicest persons I had ever met on the police force. Everybody loved Betty, everybody, even the people that worked there. The night she was murdered, I mean, it was just a horrible thing. Horrible thing."

Keith Bates, another officer, recalled the feeling across the force when they arrested the suspects: "I tell you, we knew the burial was that day, but we picked up the suspects—when we made the arrest, the sun was shining for the first time." He felt they were able to honor her memory by continuing to fight crime and by protecting the community she had given her life to guard.

"It was a sigh of relief," as Daryl described it. "I mean, there was a lot of tension at the trial. There were a lot of angry police officers that probably had to restrain themselves."

Carl said that he had mixed emotions. He was angry about her death, but he was also moved by Mom's undying grace. "At the time she was murdered," he said, "she was already working an extra duty trying to take care of her family. You've got some scumbag that just walks up to her and shoots her down like he did like a savage, that tried to kill her, just to get a bag of money. You got to be just a ruthless savage to murder somebody like that, especially a lady. And Betty Smothers was a lady. She wasn't a just female or woman, she was a lady."

Carl also often worked an extra-duty shift at the Piggly Wiggly store and, like my mom, drove night manager Kimen Lee to the Citizens Bank & Trust to make a store deposit. Carl didn't feel comfortable with the bank's layout, especially at night. The night deposit box was on the back wall of the bank, which was nearly encased by bushes and trees. While Mom pulled her marked vehicle into the exit lane so her passenger was next to the night deposit box, Carl often parked in front of the bank and walked around.

"I went there a couple of times and I looked at it and the first thing that came to my mind was, this is an ambush territory," Carl said. "It was a bad situation to be in. Everyone had their own way [to make a deposit]. I'd do a general walk-up and then I would stand and face out while she put the money in, because if anybody would walk up on us, it would give me a fighting chance. Sitting in that car, man, you didn't have a chance. Betty did not have a chance."

While many police officers believed the shooting highlighted glaring problems in the justice system, such as the lack of adequate funding for public safety and the prison system, Mom's murder also raised another sticky issue—that police officers needed to work a second job to supplement their incomes.

Skipper Jones, co-owner of ten Piggly Wiggly stores in Baton Rouge and Lafayette, was at the Piggly Wiggly store earlier the night Mom was murdered. He remembered Mom laughed and said she wasn't going to make any money on her shift because she had to buy groceries for us. In fact, bags of groceries were in the backseat of her marked police vehicle when Mom was ambushed. Jones called Mom the perfect ambassador for his store because she talked to everyone and knew everyone. Jones said Mom was quick to pull out our family photograph. "That's all Betty really wanted to ever talk about—her family," Jones said. "She was sort of a person that made you feel like you wanted to know her family."

And from the family's point of view, it was just incredible to see support from the community—and not just Baton Rouge. There were donations coming in from all over the country, from as far away as Connecticut. Even those who hadn't known her were touched by the testimony of her life of service.

On June 7–8, 1996, the K-Y Track Club even hosted the Betty Smothers Track and Field Classic at Southern University's A. W. Mumford Stadium. It had about 1,800 participants from Louisiana, Mississippi, Alabama, Tennessee, Florida, Texas, and Oklahoma. The meet began on Friday, but the events on Saturday opened with a ceremony in honor of my mom.

There were guest speakers, including Rodney Milburn, a former Southern coach who had won gold in the hurdles—Mom's event—at the 1972 Munich Olympics. I came back from FSU for the weekend, too, so that I could be there for the meet. It was so wonderful to see proof that almost three and a half years after her death, my mother was still being remembered and honored by the community she had served.

Mom was the second female officer in Baton Rouge to be slain in the line of duty and the seventeenth overall as of late 2006. The first woman to lose her life was Police Officer Linda A. Lawrence, who was killed in 1977 at the age of thirty. Officer Lawrence, who had been on the job only four months, was shot and killed while she and her training officer were at the scene of a residential burglary call.

The Officer Down Memorial Page, Inc., is an Internet site that honors and pays tribute to law enforcement officers who made the ultimate sacrifice in the name of justice. Mom is listed among the seventeen Baton Rouge police officers who have been killed in the line of duty. A short biography of Mom and the details of her death accompany a reflection page that allows visitors to write a note to Mom and shows that people still think about her. Here is a sampling of the reflections that have been posted over the years.

Your death came at a time in our history when we were trying to find ways to work together in a community divided. You were the conduit through which all of us came to see each other as one.

Your contribution to the department went way past the things you accomplished. Your legacy will be remembered by the love you had for all of us. Rest easy your work was done here.

Major GARDINER
COWORKER

Ms. Smothers,

In the past 24 plus years, I have lost many friends on our department, I lost one of my closest cousins as he was killed in the line of duty in 1973 in Springfield, MA. I never knew you, but following many ESPN Christmas airings with your son who I am sure you are extremely proud of, I felt it necessary to thank you for putting your life on the line as all 740,000 officers in the United States do everyday. And Mr. Dunn, Romans 13:1–4 tells us that *The authorities that exist have been established by GOD . . . * we are in law enforcement for a purpose. I lost my mother Mar 1, 2003, as the oldest son, no interview will ever explain how that loss has affected my life as I make sure that my family is cared for.

As for the Baton Rouge City Police, any loss of life within our ranks is crushing, we are family, all across this nation. My mother always reminded me *Tough times never last, but tough people do.*

God Bless all of you in Baton Rouge and God Bless you Mr. Dunn as you and your family celebrate this holiday season.

DETECTIVE GARY VIGNEAULT
PHOENIX POLICE DEPARTMENT

I have had the pleasure of knowing a couple of your children on a personal level and I must say that I am sure you would be very proud of them. I lost both of my parents also and I know how hard it is but I just keep telling myself that they would want me to go on and do well for myself. Your son Travis is a riot, just full of laughs and Warrick is one of the nicest guys you could ever hope to meet. I know you would be very proud of all of your children. Rest in peace Betty because your family will be just fine.

MAURICE BOONE

Betty,

I remember the night that you were taken from us as if it were last night. I remember the rain, tears mixed with the rain as officers gave you CPR, driving the ambulance to the hospital, the sad look on the doctor's face as the sheet was pulled over your body, and the officers in the pouring rain surrounding the hospital to protect the lone surviving witness. The 23 Psalm as your body was carried into the Centroplex for your funeral. The miles and miles of police vehicles, EMS trucks, fire trucks, and thousands and thousands of citizens.

You will never be forgotten, nor will your ultimate sacrifice be forgotten. Rest in peace until the last day when we will all be raised up for the final roll call.

LT. STEPHEN JACKSON
BATON ROUGE POLICE DEPT

CHAPTER 5

EARLY YEARS

THE LAST HOUSE WE LIVED IN WITH MY MOTHER WAS on in the corner of Bradley Street and Addison Street in East Baton Rouge. It was a great house, mainly since afternoons at our home were crazy fun. I say crazy fun because when you had six young children under one roof and your mom was always away working, something was usually going on. And in our house, that something revolved around sports. Track, football, basketball, baseball, you name it, and we played it, inside and outside.

Other children in the neighborhood met at our house each afternoon. With six kids—four boys and two girls ranging from nine years old to eighteen years old—it was the place to be, the center of activity. We didn't have a lot, but nobody cared. We shared what we had. Our front door was always open, and that was a good thing, especially if a football, basketball, or baseball slipped from your hand.

Of all the events that we held at our house, inside or outside, the track meets had to be the best. Our life revolved around track. Mom ran track in high school and college, at Southern University. All six of us were members of the local K-Y Track Club. Mom was the club's vice president, and it seemed we ran in meets somewhere every weekend during the summer. Everyone in our family, no matter their age, was fast. Of course, since I was the oldest, I was the fastest under any condition, rain, wind, or sunshine, and on any surface, cement, carpet, or grass.

Our indoor track meets took the most ingenuity because, let's face it, a quick lap around the living and dining rooms didn't provide a lot of wiggle room to maneuver and kick it into high gear. The starting line usually was in the kitchen or in the bathroom at the end of the hall. I'd grab bricks from the front yard and use them as starting blocks. We pushed furniture against the wall to clear space for, say, the shortened 100-yard or 200-yard dashes, or we used the sofa and easy chair as hurdles.

We lined up two by two, elbow to elbow, jaw to jaw, since somebody—even the girls, Summer and Samantha—would be talking smack. We timed each race with a stopwatch, and the best times were recorded on paper and considered world records, most of which I owned, I might add. If we switched and played football in the house, we fell to our knees in the living room and got after it, everyone piling on one another. Nobody cared about carpet burns on their knees, elbows, or noses.

Our home on Bradley was great to grow up in, especially since we moved around a lot when I was young. I was born in New Orleans on January 5, 1975, but I only lived there long enough for Mom to change my diaper before we moved back to Baton Rouge. Mom always wanted to make sure we lived in nice, safe neighborhoods. As our family grew, we moved from apartment to apartment, rental house to rental house, trying to stay a step in front of any potential problems. Like I said, we didn't have much, but nobody complained. We tried to make the best of our situation and have a little fun, too.

A drainage ditch in the Scotlandville neighborhood where we once lived always overflowed when it rained, so guess what? Say hello to the Dunn Swimming Hole. But you also had to be careful with no lifeguards on duty. I cut my left knee on a broken toilet bowl that was dumped in the deep end of that ditch and needed stitches. Our family landed on Bradley Street when I was twelve years old. Mom, a single mother and police officer, had to rent because she never made enough money to purchase her own home. Mom wanted it to be different and often talked about owning her own place. But we had food, clothes, and a roof over our heads, so we were happy.

Best yet, we had one another.

My father was never a part of my life. I knew he lived somewhere in Texas, but he could have lived on the moon for all I cared. Derrick's father, Carlton Green, lived in Baton Rouge, and he was around. Carlton was head of security at Southern University, so we'd pile into his car and he would take us to Southern football and basketball games. Derrick was fortunate that if he needed something, he could always call his father. I had no desire to telephone my father. Frank Smothers, father to Summer, Bricson, Travis, and Samantha, made it a trifecta for absentee fathers in our house. Honestly, we didn't think much of it, and it didn't bother us. Mom was the family patriarch.

Our home on Bradley Street was a blessing because Mom didn't have to search high and low for us. As kids, we didn't try sneaking around when Mom was at work. Sure, there was a time when I wanted to run the streets and act wild like some of my other friends. Plus, trouble was right around the corner if you looked hard enough for it. But as the oldest, I knew I had to help Mom and make sure my brothers and sisters stayed out of trouble. I cleaned, cooked, and made sure everyone stayed on top of their schoolwork and went to bed at a decent hour. Mom was the law, in more ways than one. But if somebody got out of line, I laid down the law when she was at work. Mom needed me and, really, it was a matter of our survival. We weren't perfect, but most times we were right there at our house,

playing, goofing off, and having fun with the rest of the neighborhood kids. We also paired off if one of us had to run an errand or
went to play. When the streetlights came on at night, or when you
heard a parent's whistle, everyone knew it was time to call it a day
and head home.

While East Baton Rouge Parish was nearly 60 percent white, our
house on Bradley was in a predominantly black neighborhood located off Interstate 110 and Winbourne Avenue. It wasn't the best of
neighborhoods, but it wasn't the worst, either. I knew what areas
and people to stay away from. We had a three-bedroom, single-story
home. It had a kitchen, dining room, living room, and one bathroom
that everyone shared. Mom had her own bedroom. Summer and
Samantha shared one bedroom, while I shared a bedroom with Derrick, Travis, and Bricson. Space was tight for us boys, but it wasn't
that bad because we had bunk beds—I had a top bunk, which I
loved. Our family pet, Nicki, an overweight chow, usually strolled
through the house like she owned it.

Our house was painted yellow and trimmed in white. We had a
small front yard with two large oak trees near each other, guarding
the entrance. The backyard was a strip of grass between our house
and the house behind us, which was separated by a chain-link fence.
A carport was on one side of the house. Traffic wasn't an issue, but
you still had to be careful when you pedaled your bicycle around
the block or you wanted to play catch with the football in the street.

As I said, there was plenty to do at our house. Foot races or bicycle races around the house included circling the trees once, twice, or
three times. When we played baseball and football in the front yard,
you quickly learned that those big oak trees didn't budge when you
smacked into one. We also set up a miniature basketball goal and
pretended we were the LSU Tigers playing in the NCAA tourna-
ment. Our poor front yard was so worn out by games twelve months
a year that it was more dirt than grass. And we shattered our share of

windowpanes with flying footballs, baseballs, and basketballs. Mom was always a good sport about it, though. We taped over the hole and eventually replaced the broken glass, but we never let it interfere with our games.

We also played football next door at Philson Stadium. That's what we called the open, square-shaped yard on the side of our neighbor's house. Audra Philson didn't mind our football games, and there were days when thirty kids gathered in Philson Stadium. We thought that field was one hundred yards long and one hundred yard wide, it looked so big. It was actually just a large yard with grass, no trees, and plenty of room to run a toss sweep or throw the football long.

As far back as I can remember, our football games were physical, too. It didn't matter if we were at Philson Stadium or on the street. One time I tackled my brother Derrick and my front tooth lodged in Derrick's thigh. Derrick ended up in the hospital for days because the wound became infected, and I ended up with a false tooth. There was also a small Boys and Girls Club at the end of our block on Bradley Street that had a regulation basketball goal in the graveled parking lot. We spent many days and nights playing hoops at the club. It was just great to be outside, running around, sweating, and getting funky with our friends.

My football career officially started at the age of seven in neighborhood streets and yards with friends. The first time I played organized football was at nine years old with a local team in Scotlandville, but it didn't pan out. I guess our team was so bad that it folded after a few games. The next year, when I was ten, Maelen "Choo Choo" Brooks, a youth coach with the Rams organization and a former football player at Grambling, saw me run at a K-Y track meet against bigger and older kids. I am not sure of Coach Brooks's initial impression, but he told me he thought I would make a good football player because of my speed. Naturally, I was the smallest player on the football field and weighed all of fifty pounds soaking wet, or bone dry, for that matter. And this marked the first time in a journey that has continued until today, where I had to prove myself because of my size.

The Rams' youth league was divided into divisions by age brackets. I was on the Pee Wee team for nine- and ten-year-olds. However, my coach didn't want to give me a uniform because he thought I was too small to play football. Choo Choo, who coached the junior Rams for eleven- and twelve-year-olds, stepped in and told the coach to give me a uniform. Yes, I was small. But I was fast, too. Many coaches over the next few years told me I was too little for football, but I didn't listen. In fact, I told everyone who listened that I didn't have to be big to be a good football player. I was faster than everyone. My running style wasn't a secret. No sir. I ran for my life when I had the football in my hands because I didn't want to get tackled or hit.

Track, of course, was far safer and just as much fun. We stayed busy with the K-Y Track Club. I was "discovered" as a nine-year-old by Coach Willie Williams, who scouted Baton Rouge neighborhoods for kids who could run fast. We were living in The Avenues when Coach Williams walked in my backyard one day during one of our basketball games. We had a regulation basketball, but our goal was a bicycle inner tube that we nailed to a tree. I had fractured my right elbow when I fell off my bunk bed and my arm was in a cast, but that didn't stop me from a hoops game with my friends. Coach Williams introduced himself and asked me if I was Warrick Dunn. He said he had quizzed the neighbors and other kids and was told I was the fastest dude in the neighborhood, and he wanted to know if I was interested in running track on his team. It sounded good to me. Mom had arrived home by that time, and she thought it was a great idea, too. The next day I attended my first practice with the K-Y Track Club at the Southern University track.

Coach Williams needed me to fill out his 4×100 relay team, which also included his son Marquis Williams. The club was headed to Miami for a summer meet, and Coach Williams wanted to compete in the 4×100. Though we didn't win in Miami, we continued to get better in a hurry. K-Y was a great time. I took my first airplane ride when I was ten years old to the Hershey Relays in Hershey, Pennsylvania. Five years later we traveled to Los Angeles, and we returned home West Coast–style cool—Mom saved enough money to buy me a polo shirt, baggy shorts, and a hat.

K-Y held car washes, cookouts, raffles—anything we could think of to help raise money to offset the cost of travel. Mom handled the club's paperwork, helped with fund-raising, and chaperoned on team trips. We traveled to Florida, Mississippi, Texas, and Alabama for age-group meets. I ran sprints and relays. Mom eventually became the first female vice president of the K-Y Track Club, and she paid the $100 dues for each of us. Mom's good friend Greg Brown was the club's longtime president. He also was an aide to Baton Rouge mayor Tom Ed McHugh. Mom wasn't bashful about bursting into meetings between Brown and the mayor when it concerned issues about K-Y, and Mom would tell the men to flat-out get lost if they disagreed with her. K-Y's reputation and success grew over the years. As a high school sophomore, I traveled to Hong Kong for a meet where I competed against men eighteen, nineteen, and twenty years old. It was crazy.

Naturally, school came first with Mom. I attended a number of different schools, since we moved around so much. I went to preschool at First Christian Academy. Then I went to Crestworth until the fourth grade. I attended Episcopal, an all-white school, in the fifth grade and Westdale Middle School in the sixth grade. I went to Prescott Middle School for seventh and eighth grades before I made the move to Catholic High as a freshman in 1989. I was zoned for Istrouma Senior High School, but the best education and best athletic teams were at Catholic High. It was an easy decision for Mom. She wanted me to be a Catholic High School Bear.

Attending Catholic High School was, to say the least, a culture shock.

Catholic High is an all-male, predominantly white, Catholic college preparatory school run by the Brothers of the Sacred Heart. It has grades eight through twelve, with around 750 students at the time. We had a dress code and requirements for community service, plus we had to attend a yearly retreat. The yearly tuition was just under $6,000, which my mom couldn't afford, but she paid as much as she could when she could. Catholic had teams in all the main sports such as football, basketball, baseball, track, and wrestling. The all-girls Catholic school, St. Joseph's Academy, was a block away. But, of course, my focus was supposed to be on academics and athletics, in that order. Man, I messed that up my freshman year.

Aside from the fact that there were no girls at Catholic, the biggest difference between Catholic and public school was the homework. I actually had to study at Catholic. Students had to have a C average to be eligible to participate in sports, and my average hovered around a D, if not below, my first nine weeks as a freshman. Now, D wasn't for dummy in my case. D was for doggone lazy with a capital D.

Mom used to wonder how I made good grades in public school because she never saw me bring home any books. When I first went to Catholic, I didn't know if I could take it. There were no girls to talk to or flirt with, and I had a test every day and homework every night. Needless to say, I spent more time in the offices of athletic director Pete Boudreaux and varsity football coach Dale Weiner than I did on the football field and track because of my grades. Coach Weiner told me Catholic was a graveyard of athletes. The school's fields had sun-bleached bones of talented players who didn't work hard in the classroom. Coach Weiner said if players didn't make it academically, they didn't make it, no exceptions. I wasn't an exception, either. I was ruled ineligible for the final few games of my freshman football season and didn't run track that spring because of poor grades.

That was the worst feeling ever, not playing the game I loved. I started at quarterback and our team was undefeated. I thought I was Tony Rice behind center, running the option, just like the athletic Rice did at Notre Dame. Mom didn't scream, smack, or punish me when she found out about my grades. Mom was more reasonable than emotional. She simply asked me what I planned to do. Was I going to show people at Catholic that I could make good grades? Or did I want to head back to public school and save her the money she didn't have? Mom challenged me to prove I was different, that I had the discipline and determination to succeed in the classroom. There were other athletes in the same boat with me who decided to jump and leave. Mom, of course, was right. I stayed.

I got in my mind that, okay, there are no girls, I have to wear khakis, loafers, and a collared shirt every day, and I can't play sports because I was too lazy in the classroom. I used reverse psychology on myself, and that made me hungry. I buckled down in the classroom and slowly dug myself out of deep, deep trouble. My grade point average went from a 1.0 that first nine weeks to 2.4 by the final nine weeks of my freshman year.

I had three people to thank for my improvement—Mom, assistant football coach Sid Edwards, and Coach Edwards's wife, Beanie. Mom, of course, set the tone. She was my best friend and I didn't want to disappoint her. Coach Edwards cared enough about me and other students that we met nearly every day after school to study. Beanie also would help tutor me at night. Coach Edwards told me that I had a great opportunity at Catholic, and he thought I was talented and smart enough to succeed. Coach could relate to what I was going through, and his approach made sense to me. When it was time to take a test, I was prepared and my grades gradually improved. I was determined to stand out in the classroom and on the athletic field.

I stood out at Catholic for another reason, too. I was one of only a handful of African Americans enrolled in the school. Students were friendly and cordial and there really wasn't any tension, but we dealt with racism, too. One morning, one of the black students opened his locker in the hallway and found a picture of a black man hanging from a tree. We never found out who left that picture. Most of the time, whites and blacks sat at separate tables during lunch hour. I was shy, bashful, and nonconfrontational. I barely said three words to anyone, so it was easy for me to fit in because I didn't stand a chance of ticking anyone off. Plus, I knew when it came to sports, nobody in my class was better than me. That was my mentality. There was that camaraderie on the field between whites and blacks. Many of the white players were great guys and I considered them friends. There were times on Thursday nights before our games on Friday when we ate at restaurants owned by the parents of white players. It was fun. We had all-you-can-eat pizza one night and steaks at Western Sizzlin' another night. I had a chance to see their world, but my white teammates never had a chance to be in my world. It just didn't happen.

My two closest friends at Catholic were Cory Gaines and Kevin Franklin. They were African American and great athletes, too. We became instant friends and went everywhere together. We sat at the same lunch table in school with buddies Steven Sterling and Reggie Owens. When we were old enough to drive, we would pile into one of our cars and head to New Orleans to meet girls, kick back, and have fun. It seemed like we attended a college football game every Saturday, be it at LSU or Southern. Mom even got us into an MC Hammer concert at the Convention Center when she worked extra security at the event. Everyone was wearing those baggy Hammer pants and singing "U Can't Touch This." It was crazy.

Kevin and I were in the same grade, but Cory was a year behind me. When Cory and I first met during my sophomore year, he said it looked like I had the calf muscles of a 250-pound man on a 150-pound body. I might have been small at five feet seven, but I had a muscular lower body from all those years of running track and running around our house and neighborhood.

Kevin, however, was bigger, stronger, and fast also—the perfect combination on the football field. And it was Kevin—not Warrick Dunn—who was the featured tailback at Catholic. I admit that didn't sit too well with me. I was a jack-of-all-trades my sophomore and junior years and played primarily quarterback my senior year. Coach Weiner wanted my versatility at quarterback because we ran the option offense, which mixed running, pitching, and throwing the football. I didn't have a great arm, but I guess I had enough overall talent to make the offense work and throw the football when I needed to. But I wasn't a happy camper. My first love was to play at tailback, but it was Kevin who got all the love there.

During our sophomore season Kevin was promoted from the junior varsity team to the varsity early in the season because one of the older tailbacks was injured. That was tough, watching Kevin excel on varsity while I remained behind on junior varsity. I was mad and frustrated as hell and really wondered why I was even playing. It took time for me to cool down. Thankfully, it wasn't much later when I was also promoted to the varsity. Both Kevin and I helped the team reach the 1990 Class 4A state championship game. I started at fullback—yes, fullback—and Kevin at tailback, but we lost to Ruston High 52–10 in the Louisiana Superdome.

I started at cornerback my junior season and switched to quarterback as a senior. Actually, I played quarterback, fullback, receiver, and cornerback and returned kicks my senior season. Kevin was our starting tailback again, but I was cool with it. Kevin and I competed against each other, but we were good friends, too, no matter what happened on the field. We each rushed for 1,500 yards during our senior seasons, and I averaged 10.2 yards per carry. Cory also got into the act, and there were many games when Kevin, Cory, and I were lined up in the backfield at the same time. We talked in the huddle about whose turn it was to run the football.

I was soft-spoken off the field but fiercely competitive on it. I got pretty hyped, too. Our senior season we fell behind rival Glen Oak High School, a public school where a lot of my good friends played. We trailed 13–0 early but battled back, and I scored on a long touchdown run late in the game. I was jumping up and down in the end zone celebrating, and one of my offensive linemen picked me up over his head and squeezed me. That's the last thing I remember because I passed out. My teammates didn't even realize it because they had sprinted off the field. There I was, sprawled out on the ground. Thankfully, my teammates came back out, got me to my feet, and helped me to the bench.

While I was extremely close to Coach Edwards, Coach Weiner was a good coach and a good guy. Sure, there were times when I was upset with him. He pulled me from quarterback during my senior season if I made a mistake and switched me to another position like receiver or cornerback. But Coach was cool. He used to drive a bunch of players home after games. We sat in the back of his car and laughed as we listened to him sing to 1950s music that blared from the radio. If he wasn't singing, he would be thumping his hand on the roof of the car to the beat of the music. Coach always seemed to be in a good mood. But he learned about my competitiveness my sophomore season. I was the last player he dropped home after a game we lost, and I didn't say a word during the entire drive. He asked me what was wrong, and I told him that was the first football game I had ever lost in my entire life. From youth leagues to my freshman season at Catholic, I never played on a team that lost a game. It was a horrible feeling.

But I got used to winning at Catholic.

We won state track titles in my sophomore (indoor and outdoor) and senior (outdoor) seasons. Coach Boudreaux had me run the lead leg on our 4×100 relay team, which set the school record with a time of 41.7 seconds. As a junior, I finished third in the Louisiana state track meet with a 10.5 in the 100 meters. I also finished second in the 55-meter indoor state championship with a 6.40 clocking.

One of my best performances on the football field occurred during my senior season when I rushed five times for 196 yards and three touchdowns out of the option offense in one game. It was crazy—I averaged 39.2 yards per carry! Plenty of college football recruiters and coaches visited our school, and most showed up to watch Kevin and myself. They were from schools such as Florida State, Texas, LSU, Alabama, Southern Cal, and Tennessee, just to name a few. It was exciting to be wanted by these major programs, and Mom and I often talked about each of the schools. Our plan was to take the recruiting trips together because we were a team. Mom was my biggest fan and she attended all of my sporting events. I looked in the stands and saw her, usually dressed in her police uniform.

Although we lost in the playoffs my senior year, I couldn't have asked for a better season. I had 1,541 rushing yards on 155 carries and scored 21 touchdowns. I also passed for 701 yards and four scores. On kickoff returns, I averaged 27.7 yards per return. I also had 27 tackles and three interceptions on defense. I made every All-State team in Class 5A, Louisiana's largest classification, and was named Co-MVP of my district and parish along with Kevin. While Kevin was named a first-team *Parade* All-American, I was voted Honorable Mention All-USA by *USA Today*. I was regarded as the nation's ninth-best tailback by recruiting analyst Tom Lemming. Max Emfinger described me as an athlete, where he ranked me third nationally. I was voted the state's tenth-best prospect by SuperPrep.

When Coach Weiner talked to the media or recruiting analysts about me, he said I was a legitimate game-breaker. What the statistics didn't say was that a lot of my big plays and long runs came at critical times in the game. Coach thought my best physical attribute was my change of direction and balance to go with my sprinter's speed. Coach Weiner liked to say that a defense couldn't catch me in a phone booth. Best yet, Coach told colleges he played me out of position and I was best suited at tailback, which is where I always wanted to play.

When our football season ended, Mom and I couldn't wait to see where my next step would take me.

Little did I know.

CHAPTER 6

LIVING WITH CHARLIE

IT'S AMAZING THAT A FORTY-MINUTE TELEPHONE CALL can forge an immediate bond between two guys who had never met face to face. But that's what happened when Charlie Ward and I talked to each other for the first time on the telephone. I had signed with Florida State a few months earlier, in February, and I was headed to Tallahassee from Baton Rouge, Louisiana, to take the first step of my freshman season with the Seminoles.

Charlie and I were roommates. That's why I wasn't surprised when Charlie saw me break open in the flat at Florida Field. We had that connection between us. I really can't explain it other than to say it was special. We were a lot alike. We were more interested in hanging around our place in Burt Reynolds Hall than going out and socializing. That first telephone call between us would have stunned people who thought we were two reserved, soft-spoken guys who didn't say peep to anyone. We had grown so close so quickly that we knew each other's thoughts and actions on and off the field.

The Gators never knew what hit them.

Charlie was flushed from the pocket as I floated to my left into the flat. It was that kind of season for Charlie and Florida State in 1993. Charlie was a senior and our star, one of the most exciting players in the country, who had emerged as the leading candidate for the prestigious Heisman Trophy. I was a wide-eyed freshman who had worked my way up the depth chart since preseason drills and had contributed in key spots in the run and pass games. Despite a 31–24 hiccup at Notre Dame a few weeks earlier, we still controlled our national title hopes as the country's second-ranked team. But we needed to beat archrival Florida in Gainesville in our regular-season finale, Saturday, November 27, to ensure our title hopes.

Leading 27–21 after UF marched 94 yards for a touchdown, we took over at our own 21 with 5:52 left in the game. Two consecutive passes from Charlie were swatted away at the line. UF suddenly had all the momentum on its side. Even Gator defensive end Kevin Carter felt that UF would score again to win the game if it could stop us on this key third down. That's when the record crowd of 85,507, which had been relatively quiet for much of the game, exploded into life. UF coach Steve Spurrier said afterward that moment was "without a doubt the loudest I have ever been in at a football game. In fact, I found myself covering my ears a little bit."

The UF crowd was forced to cover its eyes, too.

Faced with third-and-10, Charlie was flushed from the pocket on a play-action pass and was nearly dragged down by Gator defensive tackle Ellis Johnson. I floated to my left into the flat, where I was isolated on UF linebacker Ed Robinson. Charlie spotted me and lofted a pass over Robinson and over my right shoulder. I caught the ball in stride toward the UF sideline close to a first down. Receiver Tamarick Vanover made a great block to free me off the corner, and UF safety Michael Gilmore couldn't head me off as I sprinted down the sideline. I took a few chop steps to make sure nobody nipped at my heels as I raced in for a 79-yard touchdown that sealed our 33–21 victory. Man, what an incredible feeling.

When I scored, Florida Field went stone-cold quiet. UF fans were stunned and shell-shocked. FSU's faithful erupted in cheers and applause from the end-zone corners of the stadium. The play, called 344 Takeoff, was designed to go to receiver Kez McCorvey. When McCorvey was covered, Ward, like he had done all season when under pressure, improvised. We had precise routes to run, but Charlie always told us to just get open when he was forced to scramble. Charlie scrambled and I got open. Coach Bobby Bowden wasn't sure I would score when I caught the ball. He was thinking, *Get the first down, get the first down*.

I got the first down, and much more.

Honestly, the game shouldn't have been as close as it was. We outgained Florida in total yardage, 556 to 374. Charlie threw for 446 passing yards. But we also suffered two turnovers inside the UF 10-yard line, and two other times we settled on Scott Bentley field goals. Still, it was a sweet, sweet win, since Coach Spurrier entered the game 23–0 at Florida Field. And unless there was a major shift in the polls, the victory assured us a spot in the national title game on New Year's Day in the Orange Bowl against Nebraska. In the all-important Bowl Coalition Poll, which combined the Associated Press and the CNN/*USA Today* polls, the 11–0 Cornhuskers stood first and we, at 11–1, were second in front of undefeated Virginia Tech. It didn't seem like we had time to catch our breath. It was already the first week in December, and we had a chance to win the program's first national title. It didn't seem that long ago when we had started preseason drills, and I wondered exactly what backfield I would fit in—running back or secondary?

We were loaded at running back entering August's preseason drills. Sean Jackson was penciled in as the starter, Tiger McMillon led all Seminole rushers in 1992 with 597 yards, and Marquette Smith looked better than ever after a redshirt freshman season. Although I was recruited as a cornerback, Bowden promised me an early look at tailback, where we also added fellow incoming freshman Ricardo "Rock" Preston. Rock had the great nickname, but our physical stature was similar—I checked in at five feet eight and 172 pounds for freshman testing, while Rock was five-eight and 176 pounds. Rock and I had to learn the offense as quickly as possible if we wanted to contribute. And I wanted to contribute.

As fate would have it, I was elevated to first-team offense by the end of the first week of practice. Of course, it had more to do with injuries than any amazing ability on my part! Jackson and Smith were sidelined by mild ankle sprains, and Tiger suffered a bizarre kneecap injury when he caught his foot while he was leaping and twisting to catch a pass in a noncontact receiving drill. Tiger was ruled out for the year with a torn patella tendon.

In our first preseason scrimmage inside Doak Campbell Stadium, I carried the ball ten times for 43 yards behind the first-team offensive line and caught a pair of passes for 29 yards and a score. The touchdown came on a screen pass, where I scored before anyone knew I had the football. I also beat the defense in goal-line drills when I easily outran everyone to the corner on one play, then weaved through traffic to score on another. Plus, I had a 28-yard touchdown run that was whistled back due to penalty. Linebacker Derrick Brooks ripped off his helmet and took a knee. He couldn't believe a little ol' freshman had easily run past his defense that was noted for its speed and physical play. That just didn't happen in practice.

Assistant coach Jimmy Heggins, who recruited me out of Catholic High School, telephoned my head coach at Catholic, Dale Weiner, to remind him of a conversation they had about me earlier that spring. Coach Weiner implored Jimmy and FSU to give me an opportunity at tailback because Weiner said a defense couldn't catch "that dude" in a telephone booth. Coach Heggins called Weiner after that scrimmage to tell Weiner he was right, our defense couldn't catch me in a telephone booth. It's funny how it worked out because Coach Bowden nearly made a call of his own earlier in the week. Coach Bowden indicated to his staff that he was close to moving me to the secondary because of season-ending knee injuries suffered in practice to Corey Fuller, our top backup at cornerback, and Steve Gilmer at free safety.

Running backs coach Billy Sexton was happy with my scrimmage performance and compared my strength and quickness to former FSU backs Rosie Snipes and Homes Johnson. I wasn't intimidated on the field or by the surroundings. I just wanted to contribute, and Sexton told all the running backs to be ready and prepared as drills winded down. We were ranked Number 1 in the country and boasted the nation's most difficult schedule, which started against Kansas in the Kickoff Classic at the Meadowlands on August 28.

I was one of nine true freshmen who played in our opening 42–0 victory over the Jayhawks. I went 18 yards on my first collegiate carry after breaking a tackle in the backfield. I ended with 45 yards on seven carries. Since our plan was to pressure Kansas's defense from the game's opening play, we went without a huddle for nearly the entire game but often shifted into the I-formation from an initial gun/split-tackle set. It was so cool to finally be playing at Florida State. It's something that I always wanted to do, and here I was, fulfilling a dream that my mother and I shared.

We rushed for 248 yards, and Marquette Smith led the charge with 105 yards on just eleven carries. The game also featured a twelve-play goal-line stand by our defense that preserved the shutout. It was an incredible experience to play at Giants Stadium, and it was hot as blazes—a field-level thermometer read 120 degrees. But my collegiate career and our season were off to great starts. All was going well off the field, too, in large part because of my roommate.

I learned so much from Charlie. I mean, how can you not learn from the guy? Here I was, a freshman watching a superstar in action. He was like my big brother. I just watched the way Charlie handled his life. He was graceful, he was professional, he was courteous. Charlie could have had anything he wanted his senior season, it was all there right at his feet. But Charlie respected people. I kept thinking, *Wow, you can still be a superstar and a class act, too?* You didn't have to be an A-hole. That taught me a valuable lesson: I promised myself that if I was ever in Charlie's position, I would be a good guy, too.

Charlie did not have an ego. Late in the season, at Notre Dame, Irish fans wanted Charlie to strike a Heisman Trophy pose—you know, the ball tucked underneath your left arm, your right arm extended out—but he just smiled. Charlie was so humble. He worried only about his team. Charlie was a regular guy, too. We spent any extra time we had at Charlie's home in Thomasville, Georgia, which was about a thirty-five-minute drive from Tallahassee. It was great to get away and relax. I had Thanksgiving dinner with Charlie's family. And if we had a free weekend, we'd jump in my car and head to Baton Rouge to catch a Catholic High football game. We'd just hang out and talk with the players, then head to my house to visit with family and friends. We'd bring back a cooler of crawfish for our FSU teammates, and my grandmother made sure we had plenty of cooked food and canned goods crammed into the trunk. Charlie was as unassuming as he was famous, if that makes sense.

My brother Derrick joked that Charlie was quieter than I was, if that was possible. Derrick also believed Charlie made a positive impact on my life, that hype doesn't have to cloud your judgment. We all have special gifts, but at the end of the day, we are each just one person, and it's up to each of us to help make a difference in our lives and in the world. As I studied and watched Charlie, I thought we were alike in many ways. We were both confident and goal-oriented, but we didn't have to shout it from atop the courtyard steps. We also loved to compete and wanted to be the best.

My high school coach, Dale Weiner, said he had never met a true competitor who didn't care if he was the best or not. A true competitor, in his heart, wants to be the best, Coach said. Well, I wanted to be the best, but I wasn't going to sit there, holler, and draw attention to myself. Charlie wasn't that way, either. You know when sometimes things are meant to be and you really can't explain it? That was the friendship that Charlie and I shared. We both enjoyed the same television shows and shared the same interests. Many nights we sat in our living room with the lights turned off and talked about school, life, and football. And we fell asleep right there where we sat.

Charlie had a way of making me see what's important in life and helping me remain focused. And as the season progressed and the Heisman Trophy talk surrounding Charlie increased, he spent a lot of time dealing with the media. Our telephone rang constantly and somebody always knocked on our door. Finally, I put a sign out front that simply read: CHARLIE AIN'T HERE.

Charlie and I were set up as roommates. You could say tragedy and former Washington Redskins quarterback Doug Williams technically brought us together at FSU. Williams, a Louisiana native, had known my mother since they were teenagers growing up outside Baton Rouge. Williams had met Charlie in an airport two years earlier when the FSU basketball team was on a road trip—Charlie was the starting point guard for the Seminoles. Charlie and Doug became fast friends, and Charlie even sported jersey number 17 because Williams had worn that number while passing the Redskins to victory over the Denver Broncos in Super Bowl XXII. Charlie and Doug remained in touch, and Doug even showed up at FSU to watch Charlie play football during his junior season. When Doug learned that I had signed with FSU, he immediately telephoned Charlie and asked a favor: would he keep an eye on Warrick? Charlie did better than that. He had Doug ask me if I wanted to be his roommate.

At first, I thought it was kind of weird that a senior wanted to be my roommate. Coach Bowden had okayed it, but I figured maybe Coach and FSU wanted somebody to watch over me and make sure I didn't do anything crazy, since I had just lost my mother. But it wasn't like that all. Charlie and I hit it off immediately when we talked for that first time on the telephone. Charlie understood that I cared about my brothers and sisters and that it was my responsibility to watch over them. So the last thing I was worried about was myself and if I was going crazy or not. I felt like my purpose in life was my family, and I couldn't let anything separate us. I had to do everything in my power to make sure they were okay, and Charlie understood.

When my mom was murdered, I thought about staying home and attending LSU. It would have been easier on my family, but I also had to do what was best for me. The opportunity to play college football was a dream that my mother and I shared together, and I wanted to fulfill our dream. Sure, many locals thought I needed to stay close to home, and many pointed out that it was my obligation since the community had rallied behind our family following my mom's murder. I didn't let that way of thinking enter my mind. All the coaches at Catholic High—Coach Sid, Coach Weiner—encouraged me to do what was best for me and select a school where I would be the happiest. My grandmother, brothers, and sisters all said the same thing.

I visited both Florida State and Alabama following Mom's death. Greg Brown, a family friend, made the trip to Tallahassee with me a week after my mom's murder. When I sat in Coach Bobby Bowden's office for the first time, I knew FSU was where I wanted to go. I just felt it inside. Coach Bowden also took an immediate liking to me. Coach knew what had happened to my mom and understood the responsibilities I faced as an eighteen-year-old. Coach was amazed at how I handled myself and was impressed by my character and maturity. A few days later Coach, who admitted he had to be careful about liking one player more than another, penned me a handwritten letter and told me he would take care of me over the next four years. He said that was the first time he had done that with a recruit. It meant a lot to me, and I committed to the Seminoles four days before National Signing Day in February.

I tried not to talk about the past too much that season, even with Charlie at the beginning, but a day didn't pass when I didn't think about Mom. I still had Mom's pearl earrings, the ones stained with her blood from the night of her murder, and kept them in a box on my dresser. Charlie was a great friend and roommate, and he was there when I needed him. There were some nights when I shared my most personal feelings about my mother with Charlie. As we became closer, we talked even more. I think that's natural. But I also cried myself to sleep many nights. I was sad, depressed, and lonely. I also had to head back to Baton Rouge to make sure all was well with my brothers and sisters. Mom's murder was an emotional, open wound for all of us. Outside of Charlie, I really didn't get to know people or let them know me.

Thankfully, football helped me keep my mind on the task at hand.

I became more a part of FSU's offense as the season went on. My first collegiate reception went for 57 yards against Duke in the season's second game. I also turned in a big play against Miami in October. We led 14–7 early and were faced with a third-and-7 from the UM 43-yard line. We lined up in the shotgun formation and hinted pass. Lined up next to Charlie, I took the direct snap and sprinted 27 yards to keep a drive alive that ended in a 2-yard scoring run by Charlie. I busted free on the same play later in the game. Our offensive coordinator, Brad Scott, complimented me on my poise, saying I had to grow up faster than most kids my age and that I had been "an inspiration to the team."

I just wanted to keep winning. We beat Virginia 40–14 at home in a game where Charlie took a giant leap into the Heisman Trophy race. Scrambling toward the goal line, he was at the 5-yard line when Virginia defensive back Percy Ellsworth dove to block Charlie's path. Charlie calmly jumped Ellsworth like a hurdle into the end zone. Our defense recorded its fourth shutout of the season with a 54–0 victory over Wake Forest, but we also survived a scare when Charlie suffered bruised ribs when he was sandwiched by a pair of defenders as he scrambled. We clinched the Atlantic Coast Conference title and New Year's Day bowl bid the following week without Charlie, who rehabbed his injury as we beat Maryland 49–20. But we also lost tailback Marquette Smith to a knee injury in practice prior to playing the Terps.

The win over Maryland set the stage for our Number-1-versus-Number-2 showdown at Notre Dame on November 13. It was a great game, but we lost 31–24. Charlie's last-gasp pass with three seconds remaining hit Irish cornerback Shawn Wooden in the chest. Even before the football hit the ground, thousands of fans stormed the field to celebrate. It was a frustrating loss.

We worked almost exclusively from the shotgun formation and threw fifty-three passes, which tied for second most in FSU single-game history. Charlie's thirty-one completions also tied a second-best mark. I only had three rushing attempts for 8 yards, but I did score on a 6-yard swing pass from Charlie. The good news was that we only fell one spot to Number 2 in the Bowl Coalition Poll behind Notre Dame, which meant we would face the Irish in a rematch for the national championship in the Fiesta Bowl if both of us remained 1–2.

We made easy work of North Carolina State the following week, 62–3, but who would have thunk it? Boston College upset Notre Dame, which put us back in the driver's seat in the national-title race. But we knew we couldn't really celebrate, not with rival Florida up next in our regular-season finale on November 27 in Gainesville. Of course, we felt right at home in the Swamp. Because of our connection as friends and roommates, Charlie and I connected on that 79-yard touchdown pass the helped us quiet Florida Field and beat the Gators.

Charlie, meanwhile, had all but run away from his competition in the Heisman Trophy race, too. Assistant athletic director Wayne Hogan joked before the presentation in New York City on December 11 that "Charlie will finish first, second, and third." Well, Charlie finished where it counted, first, and beat out Tennessee quarterback Heath Shuler and Alabama all-purpose back David Palmer. Charlie was also honored by FSU in a special presentation at Doak Campbell Stadium that attracted more than 15,000 fans on a cold but wonderful night that featured a laser show and fireworks.

Best yet, our athletic director, Bob Goin, announced that Charlie's number 17 jersey would be retired—Fred Biletnikoff (25), Ron Sellers (34), and Ron Simmons (50) were the only previous Seminoles so honored. Two large screens also flashed taped congratulations to Ward from such notables as Spike Lee, Michael Jordan, Warren Moon, and Clyde Drexler. The closest any Seminole had come to winning the Heisman Trophy prior to Charlie was Casey Weldon's second-place finish to Michigan's Desmond Howard in 1991. Charlie had placed sixth in the voting in 1992.

The bowl picture had also cleared itself during this time, and we were penciled in to face Nebraska for the national title on New Year's Day. We were tabbed a 17-point favorite over the Cornhuskers, but we knew better. While FSU had beaten Nebraska 27–14 in the Orange Bowl a year earlier for our eighth consecutive bowl victory, fans, of course, talked about FSU's inability to win "the big one" under Coach Bowden. Bowden, however, always had a quip ready, and he had one this time, too, since Nebraska's coach, Tom Osborne, had never won a national title, either. "I've never won one. He's never won one. And unless we tie, one of us is fixing to get one," Bowden said of the national crown. He later added, "I'd like to have any part of a championship I could get. That way, I wouldn't have to go to any grave and have y'all say I didn't win one."

If that wasn't enough, we had other distractions on our table. Offensive coordinator Brad Scott had accepted the head coaching position at South Carolina following the Florida game, becoming just the second full-time coach earmarked to leave Coach Bowden's staff in the last nine years. Scott, who announced he would remain with us through the Orange Bowl, also offered jobs to quarterbacks coach Mark Richt and linebackers coach Wally Burnham. Richt later opted to remain at FSU, while Burnham joined Scott at South Carolina. Receivers coach John Eason also turned down a job at Florida A&M, his alma mater, to remain at FSU. However, Coach Eason later joined Scott at South Carolina as well. A coaching staff that talented was bound to split up as other schools tried to hire different members away. But despite pending changes, we still had one game to tackle together.

I was pleased with my contribution to the team. I gained 511 yards—second on the team behind Sean Jackson—on just sixty-eight carries (7.5 yards per carry) and also caught twenty-five passes for 357 yards. We knew we would have our hands full with Nebraska's defense, which was led by outside linebacker Trev Alberts, and had totaled 44 sacks (4 shy of the school record) on the season. Alberts had twelve tackles, a sack, and two tackles for loss against FSU a year earlier in the Orange Bowl. Offensively, Nebraska was paced by quarterback Tommie Frazier and I-back Calvin Jones. Frazier, a Floridian with 4.63 speed, had 704 rushing yards and 1,159 passing yards out of Nebraska's I-back/option attack, while Jones was the team's leading rusher with 1,043 rushing yards.

Of course, nothing is ever easy in big games.

It was a tense, excruciating finish, but we beat Nebraska 18–16 to win the school's first national title. The outcome wasn't clinched until Nebraska kicker Bryon Bennett's 45-yard field-goal attempt for the victory sailed left as time expired. We thought we had won the game moments earlier when Derrick Brooks tackled Trumane Bell at our 28-yard line following a pass reception from Frazier. The scoreboard clock at the Orange Bowl read zeros and our sideline poured onto the field in celebration. Coach Bowden also received a congratulatory Gatorade bath from quarterback Danny Kanell and kicker Scott Bentley that nearly knocked Bowden's glasses from his nose.

Not so fast.

Officials frantically cleared the field and put one second back on the clock, just enough time for Bennett to attempt his field goal. Clifton Abraham got a great jump from the outside and said he felt the ball barely graze his left hand. Bennett's kick hooked wildly to the left, and FSU had its first national football championship in school history. It wasn't the blowout that the media and fans predicted, but it was just as sweet. Bentley, a fellow freshman who appeared on *Sports Illustrated*'s preseason football cover, nailed the game-winning 22-yard field goal with a mere twenty seconds left in the game before Bennett's shot sailed wide left. Bentley also made field goals of 34, 25, and 39 yards to help our cause. Charlie, who was slowed by a head cold and a fierce rush paced by Alberts, threw for 286 yards and was named the game's MVP.

While I only rushed one time for 3 yards and had two receptions for 30 yards—Nebraska did a great job in its coverage schemes—it was an incredible feeling to win a national title. As we poured into the locker room, it was great to share the moment with your teammates.

And, of course, I knew exactly where to look for Charlie.

We had that connection.

CHAPTER 7

DEALING WITH TWO LOSSES

I T WAS NOVEMBER 3, 1995, AND I WAS IN CHARLOTTES-ville, Virginia, with my Florida State teammates. When you travel to away football games as a player, you really don't have any free time to catch the sights, except for maybe what you see from your hotel window or from your seat on the bus ride to the stadium and airport. All I knew about Charlottesville was that it's a beautiful city in the foothills of the Blue Ridge Mountains.

It was a Thursday night, and we were set to play Virginia in an important Atlantic Coast Conference game being broadcast on ESPN. It was my junior season, and we entered the game undefeated (7–0) and ranked Number 1 in the country. We were 18-point favorites, and a victory would keep us in the national-title race with Nebraska, Florida, and Ohio State.

Virginia, of course, didn't have to look very far for incentive. We had won twenty-nine consecutive ACC games since we began playing for the league championship in 1992, and many football fans around the country mockingly called the conference "Florida State and the Eight Dwarfs" because of our domination. But we knew

Virginia was ready; they were jacked to play us. Virginia had dropped two games earlier in the season on the game's final play, and George Welsh, in his twenty-third season as a Division I coach, had a team with plenty of star power in Tiki and Ronde Barber and Anthony Poindexter.

It was a cool autumn night, and the overflow crowd of 44,300 at Scott Stadium was excited. The game opened with Virginia's traditional cannon shot out of the north end zone, and it was a battle from start to finish. We led 7–0 and 14–7 early, but trailed 33–21 late. We couldn't stop Tiki, who finished with 311 all-purpose yards, and our offense, which averaged 56.1 points per game, was slowed by our own mistakes. But we never stopped working.

I scored on a 7-yard sweep to cap a four-play, 88-yard drive with 6:13 to play. Down 33–28 with possession at our own 20-yard line and 1:37 remaining, quarterback Danny Kanell moved us across midfield to the Virginia 11-yard line with 13 seconds left. Kanell spiked the ball on first down to stop the clock, but the Cavaliers were whistled for having too many men on the field. That gave us possession at the 6-yard line. Kanell threw out of the end zone on the next play.

With four seconds left, we had time to run one last play. I stood next to Kanell in the shotgun formation, and center Clay Shiver, on a designed play called a direct snap, snapped the ball to me instead of Danny. I was surprised when the play was called in the huddle, but I thought it could work. It looked like we had Virginia's defense sealed off. I sprinted off right tackle toward the end zone. I thought I scored the winning touchdown on the play, but officials ruled that I was stopped inches shy of the goal line by Poindexter and safety Adrian Burnim. Virginia cornerback Ronde Barber trailed the play and was told by an official near the play that the ball had touched the ground before I crossed the goal line.

My upper body was actually in the end zone, but the ball, knocked loose as I was tripped at the last second and lunged forward, was near my waist. Virginia's crowd erupted, and it seemed like everyone rushed the field. We just wanted to get off the field as fast as we could so nobody got hurt. Fans tore down the goalposts and carried them above their heads and out of the stadium. Our locker room was so quiet you could hear a tear drop. And there were plenty of tears. Shiver and fellow offensive lineman Chad Bates held hands, prayed, and wept. I sat in front of my locker and stared blankly into space. Running backs coach Billy Sexton patted my shoulder pads and told me he thought I had scored, too. We were deflated. Our national championship hopes were back out on the field. I was sad, upset, and frustrated because I knew I had scored. I knew it.

But I also had other thoughts on my mind, and they had nothing to do with a football game.

Less than twelve hours later, I was in the Baton Rouge, Louisiana, courtroom of Judge Ralph Tyson. It was Friday, November 4, 1995, and I was there to testify in the sentencing phase in the trial of Henri Broadway. A month and a half earlier, Kevan Brumfield, who shot and killed my mother, and was Broadway's accomplice in the crime, had been sentenced to death. While I was playing against Virginia the night before, a jury convicted Broadway for his role in my mom's death. Following eight days of testimony, the jury deliberated for ninety minutes and returned the guilty verdict at 10:05 P.M. At 1:00 P.M. on Friday, I was in the courtroom to tell the jury about my mother, a fourteen-year police veteran who always worked a second job in order to provide better for her children.

Honestly, I was reluctant to testify. I told Assistant District Attorney Prem Burns, who successfully prosecuted both the Brumfield and Broadway cases, that I didn't want to be exploited and put on the witness stand simply because I was known in the community as an athlete. Ms. Burns offered sound reasoning why I should testify. She said I was Betty's son, and that I would represent my mother as her son—and not as an athlete—on the witness stand. It made sense to me, so I decided to speak out. Ms. Burns called me to the witness stand and we talked about Mom:

Q: *Please state your full name for the jury.*
A: *Warrick De'Mon Dunn.*

Q: *Warrick, how old are you?*
A: *I'm twenty years old.*

Q: *And are you Betty Smothers's eldest child?*
A: *Yes, ma'am.*

Q: *I am going to ask you, if you would, to tell this jury who your brothers and sisters are?*
A: *That's Derrick Green. That's Travis Smothers, that's Bricson Smothers, Summer Smothers, and Samantha Smothers.*

Q: *I'm going to ask you to tell this jury what kind of a relationship you had with your mother?*
A: *The relationship with my mom was more like a best friend type, brother/sister. It wasn't just a mother/son type of relationship. I mean, we were closer than anything can ever be closer in the world. And you can tell. Any time I was hurting, she hurt. Any time she hurt, I was hurting. We just felt that. That's the type of feeling we had for one another.*

Q: *What type of values did your mother teach you to value as you were growing up?*
A: *Well, to be honest, I had to babysit a lot. She disciplined me to take care of them while she worked. I mean, my life changed. I really couldn't go out or anything. I'm used to that now. I guess I was more like a father figure. I had to grow up when I was,*

say, fourteen, thirteen years old, and act like a young man. She
taught me to do that.

Q: What did she teach you about your studies and about athletics? Did she feel that those were important?

A: She felt athletics would keep us out of trouble. The only way
we can play athletics is make the grades. You have to do well
academically. So all that played in hand. And once—if we
made mistakes academically, she was like, well, the choice is
yours. I mean, she didn't put any pressure on us. The choice
is yours. You're going to have to do what you want to do.

Q: Would you put the pressure on yourself then?

A: Yes, ma'am. I mean, I'll take it in my hands in order to prove
her wrong and everyone else wrong that I can make it.

Q: Tell me the kinds of sports that you played as you were going
through high school that your mother may have been involved
in with you.

A: Well, track, track and field, football. I played a little basketball.

Q: Would your mother go to your games, your meets?

A: She would make the games. She would try to—even if she was
at work, she would try to make it. I mean, say she was supposed to be on the other side of town, she would have been
watching me play on Friday nights. So, I mean, that was real
important to her that she was there supporting me.

Q: And she tried to make those games even when she was working
two jobs?

A: Yes, ma'am. No doubt about that. I mean, anywhere that we
played, she was going to try to be there. She didn't want to miss

any part of the game. I mean, that's just the type of mother she was. She was trying to support all six of her kids.

Q: And did your brothers and sisters play in any sports as well?

A: Yeah. My whole family runs track. My brother plays football. My little brothers play football, basketball. My sister plays volleyball. I mean, everyone is real involved in athletics.

Q: As you were growing up, do you always remember your mom as working that second job besides being a full-time police officer? Was she always doing as much as she could for the rest of you?

A: You can say for us and everyone else. She went the extra yard for everyone, not just for me.

Q: Did she coach other children?

A: Yes, ma'am.

Q: Did she enjoy that kind of work?

A: She loved it.

Q: I'm going to ask you how you found out that your mom had been killed?

A: Well, police officer Theodore Jordan called me around 12:30, told me that my mom had been shot. I thought he was joking. And he told me he wasn't. He say don't wake up anyone, just get dressed and I'll meet you outside, and he came and picked me up and took me to Our Lady of the Lake.

Q: How has your life changed and the lives of your brothers and sisters since your mom has been taken away?

A: It's changed dramatically, greatly. To say now that I'm in college,

I see other guys on the team, you know, they're talking to their parents, their moms, calling their mom. I can't do that. I have no one else to call. I mean, I call home. I call my grandmother, but it's not the same. I mean, it's just something that is missing. And I know my five brothers and sisters, they're going to miss that, too, because they haven't experienced the same things I experienced with her, knowing that they were going to get their chance when I got out of the house.

Q: They never had her there for as long as you did, so maybe in a way you were the luckiest one?

A: I was lucky in the sense where she taught me enough things, I guess, to pass along in case something like this would happen because I guess she was prepared for this day, that day.

Q: And she accepted that risk when she became a police officer.

A: Yes, ma' am.

Q: What types of things do you do for your brothers and sisters even when you're away at school? Do you feel a responsibility being the eldest child?

A: Yes, ma' am. I've always called home. Basically, I call home every day to see how they're doing academically, do they need anything, they have problems, call me. I mean, I try to come home as much as possible. And if they need shoes, clothes, I mean, I try to do that for them. I'm the only one they really have. I'm like their father. I treat them much better than anyone else is going to treat them.

Q: I'm going to ask you to—what would you want your mom to know about the six of you right now, how your lives have gone?

What you're feeling? What would you like to tell her if you could tell her something?

A: *I mean, I really don't know what to tell her. Probably, that we love you. I mean, that's probably most important. That all through this, we are making it. Taking it day by day. Everyone is growing up, getting mature, getting older. It's just something we have to accept, something we have to get used to. And that I know that no one in this family is going to want to do that to their kids. They're not going to want to leave their kids when they have kids. So we just have to take it in stride.*

Q: *Are you looking forward to having a family of your own one day?*

A: *One day. I mean, in the future. No time soon. I mean, that would be nice. That's something that I would like to experience, pass on to my kids.*

Q: *Do you think you would want the same relationship with your children that you had with your mother?*

A: *No doubt about it. I mean, I plan on being home all the time. I'm used to being at home. I want to be close to my family.*

Q: *You want to be with them as long as you can?*

A: *As long as possible.*

Q: *Because you know how that feels not to have somebody there?*

A: *Yes, ma'am.*

Q: *I am going to ask you to look at a picture that I've marked as State [evidence exhibit] 160 and tell me do you remember that picture?*

A: Yes, ma'am.

Q: *Tell us when that picture was taken and what you remember about all of you being together.*
A: *That was roughly, what twelve, thirteen years old. If I can remember correctly. This is everyone trying to wear the same outfits. We were trying to dress all alike. You could tell who the oddballs in the picture are. But that's just something that brought us closer together as a family because we were always going in different directions. That picture, that time right there just brought us closer together.*

Q: *Took time out of all your busy schedules and all your personal things to be together?*
A: *Yes, ma'am. She definitely took time off to have that picture taken.*

Q: *Thank you.*
Ms. Burns: *I would move 160 into evidence, Your Honor.*
The Court: *Objections?*
Mr. Kroekne: *No, Your Honor.*
Ms. Burns: *Ask that it be shown to the jury.*
The Court: *All right, be admitted. [The jury viewed evidence at this time.]*
Ms. Burns: *The state tenders the witness.*
Mr. Kroekne: *No questions, Your Honor.*
The Court: *Thank you. You can step down.*

Earlier in the week, I told a Florida sportswriter that football didn't amount to anything with what I had been through the past two and a half years. If I could have my mom back, if I could have the day back when she was murdered, I'd give up football in a heartbeat. I'd give up college in a heartbeat. I'd give up everything in a heartbeat to have her back.

But that wasn't possible—that's why we were in court today.

My brother Derrick was called to testify after me. We decided that Derrick and I would be the only two siblings to testify, since we were the two oldest. Ms. Burns did not want to parade the entire family in front of the court, including our grandmother, who also watched from the front row in the courtroom. When it was Derrick's turn to sit on the witness stand, his hurt, anger, and hatred bubbled to the surface. The trials had gnawed away at Derrick's heart and soul.

Derrick told Ms. Burns how he was looking forward to spending more time with Mom, since I was headed to Florida State following high school. But with me in Tallahassee after Mom's murder, Derrick was in charge of our home. He explained how, as an eighteen-year-old senior at Catholic High, he helped his brothers and sisters with their homework and chores and also juggled all that with his football and schoolwork. Derrick also said he often visited Mom's grave in St. Francisville, where she was born, and his thoughts dealt solely with the payback he planned to give Broadway and Brumfield for the murder. When asked by Ms. Burns if he still felt a lot of anger, Derrick, who glared at Broadway during the questioning and stared straight through him on this one, answered, "Yes. You just don't know."

Broadway's mother, Debra Odom, tried to convince the jurors to spare her son. She said she felt sorry for our family but insisted that her son was innocent. Ms. Odom said she had suffered, too, saying people she's known for years stopped talking to her after her son's arrest. She begged the jury to let her son live.

The jury took less than an hour to return the death penalty against Broadway. I sat next to Kimen Lee, who had her arm around my shoulder. We helped comfort each other. Lee said she made a promise to Mom that she would see this through and not quit. I was grateful because this had turned Ms. Lee's life upside down as well. She often asked what she and my mom did to be ambushed.

I will never know.

In a few days I returned to Tallahassee, where football fans were still dissecting our defeat at Virginia and calling it a heartbreaking loss. My heart had been broken two years earlier and all I felt was emptiness.

But life continues for everyone. My circumstances were different from everyone else's, and I had to deal with them.

I was back on the practice field with my teammates in preparation for Saturday's game at North Carolina.

CHAPTER 8

CRIMINAL TRIALS

W HEN TASK FORCE MEMBERS ARRESTED THE SUSPECTS involved in my mom's murder, police detective Keith Bates, a member of that task force, recalled how the sun finally peeked and smiled from behind rain clouds that had covered Baton Rouge for nearly a week. Bates believed it was God's way of recognizing the good in my mother and that justice would prevail in this case.

In separate trials more than two years after my mom's murder on January 7, 1993, God was back at work and justice prevailed.

Kevan Brumfield and Henri Broadway were each convicted of first-degree murder in my mom's death and sentenced to death by lethal injection under Louisiana law. West Paul, the getaway driver in the killing, was sentenced to twenty-five years in prison as part of a deal with prosecutors. Both the Brumfield and Broadway trials were held in Baton Rouge despite motions filed by defense attorneys that requested a change in venue due to massive amounts of pretrial publicity.

I was at Florida State for the two years following my mom's murder until the start of the trials. That was a good thing, because it helped keep my mind off the trials. I would have been so focused on everything back home in Baton Rouge that I might not have known which way to turn. Football and schoolwork kept me occupied. I tried to get home as much as possible, but my family updated me on the details involved in the cases.

Brumfield was the first defendant to go on trial, in June 1995. After four days of testimony, a jury deliberated for around two hours and convicted Brumfield of murdering my mother. A day later, that same jury rejected a defense argument that two wrongs don't make a right. The jury deliberated for a little more than an hour and chose a death sentence over life in prison for Brumfield.

I was in the courtroom both days, and I really wasn't sure what I wanted—death or life in prison for Brumfield. I decided to leave it in God's hands. And, when it was all said and done, I thought God and the jurors made a good decision. On September 19, 1995, Brumfield was formally sentenced to death. Judge Ralph E. Tyson told Brumfield that his actions broke the heart of a city and that Brumfield had carried out a "cold, calculated ambush" and deserved death.

Less than two months later, it was Broadway's turn to face justice.

On Thursday, November 3, 1995, while I was in Virginia with my Florida State teammates, a jury convicted Broadway of first-degree murder. The jury rejected Broadway's claim that he played no part in the ambush of my mother and Piggly Wiggly night store manager Ki-men Lee, who survived the attack. Broadway also claimed in testimony that the attack must have been an "inside job" and believed Lee helped plan the ambush.

On November 4, after I returned to Baton Rouge following our football game and testified in the sentencing phase, the jury returned the death penalty for Broadway in slightly less than an hour. It was the first time in the parish that a jury had chosen execution for someone who wasn't the gunman in a murder. Under Louisiana law, however, people who play the type of role Broadway did in a murder are as guilty as the person who did the actual killing. On February 2, 1996, Broadway was formally sentenced to death by Judge Tyson, and he joined Brumfield on Death Row at Angola State Prison.

A week later, following Broadway's trial, on November 9, 1995, Paul was sentenced to twenty-five years in prison as part of a deal with prosecutors. Paul pleaded guilty to attempted armed robbery for his role. He cut a deal with prosecutors shortly before Broadway's trial, taking the stand and identifying Broadway as one of the two gunmen.

Baton Rouge assistant district attorney Prem Burns called the murder of my mother one of the most heinous she had prosecuted in twenty-two years as a prosecutor. Ms. Burns was a great choice to handle Mom's case. Prior to my mother's murder, Ms. Burns was the prosecutor in the most recent trial involving the death of a Baton Rouge police officer, Sergeant Warren Broussard. Broussard was shot and killed in June 1988 while questioning a pair of burglary suspects. A mistrial was declared in October 1991 when jurors were unable to reach a verdict in the first-degree murder case against Kermit Parker. But Parker was convicted of second-degree murder in January 1992 and received a mandatory life in prison sentence. While Ms. Burns openly criticized the city police investigation of Broussard's death, she praised the city police investigation that resulted in the arrest of four suspects in my mom's murder.

Ms. Burns, a New Yorker, was born in Queens. She was educated in the Boston area, graduated from Wheaton College, and arrived in Baton Rouge in 1970 with her husband, who was hired as a French professor at Louisiana State University. Although Ms. Burns had an undergraduate degree in foreign languages, she decided to attend law school at LSU and graduated in 1974. There were not many women practicing law in Baton Rouge at that time. Only eight of the thirty women enrolled in her class graduated, but Ms. Burns was hired by the district attorney's office in 1975 to help prosecute in family court. Ms. Burns wanted to make more of a difference and requested a switch to criminal cases two years later, in 1977.

After handling misdemeanors for three months, Ms. Burns became the first woman in the history of the parish to prosecute a jury trial. It wasn't an easy step. Here was a woman, a Yankee, mind you, standing in front of a Southern jury. Ms. Burns said she worried about the smallest details, from the color of her suit and fingernail polish to the amount of jewelry to wear. To demonstrate stability for the jury, Ms. Burns continued to wear her wedding ring even though she had been recently divorced.

Ms. Burns won her first case in fourteen minutes, and soon thereafter became the first woman promoted to section chief in the district attorney's office. By 1993, Ms. Burns had handled more homicides than any one prosecutor in her office, and she figured eighty of her one hundred jury trials were murder cases. Ms. Burns was considered Top Gun in the district attorney's office, plain and simple.

My brother Derrick worked closely with Ms. Burns, since I was away at Florida State, and the two forged a strong bond and friendship during that time. Derrick kept me updated as best he could as Ms. Burns prepared for trial. I actually didn't meet with Ms. Burns until we reached the sentencing portion of the Brumfield trial. Ms. Burns didn't know my mother, but as the assistant district attorney, she was involved in the case from start to finish.

Ms. Burns was off the day my mom was murdered, but she hurried into the office that morning when she received the news in a telephone call from her secretary. There wasn't any hesitation by Ms. Burns. This was her case, win, lose, or draw. Ms. Burns felt that unless she really messed up when it came time to pick the jury and prosecute the case, she believed the evidence was there for the jury to convict. She felt that any reasonable jury would come to that conclusion because it was such an egregious crime, one that was preplanned and one that involved a police officer.

Ms. Burns felt that the case cried out for the death penalty.

Getting to trial was a long and difficult road.

Captain Don Buller, chief of city police detectives, led the task force that was formed immediately following my mom's murder. Police detectives struggled initially to find a suspect in the case. It was reported by the media that Mom was "ambushed" along with a grocery store night manager as the two made a store deposit at a Jefferson Highway bank in the early morning of January 7, 1993. Corporal Don Kelly said it was an absolutely planned ambush and that my mother never got her gun out of her holster. Police Chief Greg Phares said it was one of the boldest crimes he had been involved with in his twenty-one years on the police force.

Two days later, on that Saturday, the Baton Rouge Police Department released a composite drawing of a suspect. The police also said they were almost certain the shooting was committed by two people. The wounded store manager, Kimen Lee, who survived the attack, saw only one of the gunmen and described him as a black male, possibly twenty-five to thirty-five years old, between five feet six and five feet ten inches tall and weighing between 170 and 185 pounds.

The task force's big break came on Sunday, January 10, when police dispatchers received a telephone call from a man, later identified as Eddie Paul, who lived in an apartment on Prescott Road. The man told dispatchers that there was a disorderly person there and police officers were needed. During radio dispatches between uniformed patrol officers, detectives overheard the name of the disorderly person—Brumfield. Brumfield turned out to be Kevan Brumfield, the same name the task force had heard from a confidential source a night earlier. When officers arrived at Paul's apartment, Brumfield was gone. However, detectives instructed the officers to bring in Paul, who began to tell a story about my mom's murder. Paul told investigators that his cousin West Paul, Brumfield, and a man named "A.J." or "Ray Jay" had been inside his apartment plotting the murder and robbery of a police officer a week before the shooting.

On Monday, January 11, the task force met in the conference room in Chief Phares's office. The group reviewed the evidence and discussed the best way to pick up the suspects, who were considered armed and extremely dangerous. Burns said the task force was determined to get the suspects to trial and prevent the take-care-of-them-on-the-street attitude held by some citizens and some officers in the department. Task force members were constantly watched to make sure they didn't become too emotionally involved in the case. Task force members discussed the need for complete surprise and decided not to use police radios when they executed the arrest warrants, signed by District Judge Carl Guidry, so total secrecy could be maintained.

Within ninety minutes, agents located Brumfield, who was arrested without incident and tossed away a .357 Magnum pistol as police approached. Shortly after midnight, agents knocked on the door of Horace and Elouise Belton, the grandparents of West Paul, who was in his room watching television. After police questioned and released a man they thought was A.J., the detectives identified the correct A.J.—and that was Henri Carity Broadway, who lived at his mother's house on Heidel Avenue.

Family members said Broadway was asleep when detectives knocked on the door at about 4:30 A.M. When Broadway saw the detectives, he said he had been expecting them and "I didn't shoot the police officer." On the way to the police station, according to court documents, Broadway said that he had nothing to do with the killing of the police officer and nothing to do with Brumfield, although police did not mention either the murder or Brumfield.

Shortly after 4:30 A.M. on Tuesday, January 12, police had all four suspects in custody—Kevan Brumfield, Henri Broadway, West Paul, and Eddie Paul. Police also took extraordinary security measures for the four suspects. Detective stretched yellow police line tape across the entrance to the office, and armed detectives stood guard at the door. Even police officers weren't allowed inside unless they had business there.

The day my mother was buried—Tuesday, January 12—it was announced that four men had been arrested for the slaying of my mother. Police said the men plotted in a north Baton Rouge apartment a week earlier to "murder and rob a Baton Rouge police officer." Three of the men were accused of carrying out the alleged conspiracy, while the fourth man remained at the apartment where the murder had been planned. The three men who were accused of taking part in the murder were Kevan T. Brumfield, twenty, who had a previous warrant out for his arrest; Henri Carity Broadway, twenty-two; and West Paul, twenty. Paul's cousin, Eddie Paul, forty-nine, was also arrested. Police said Brumfield allegedly fired the shots that killed my mother; Broadway allegedly fired the shots that wounded store manager Kimen Lee; and West Paul was the alleged driver of a getaway car parked nearby.

Bond was denied on the first-degree murder charges against Brumfield, Broadway, and West Paul, and it was denied to Eddie Paul on the principal to first-degree murder charges. Burns said each of the suspects provided investigators with taped statements in which they admitted their involvement in my mom's death. First-degree murder is punishable by death by lethal injection or life in prison, and Burns said she wanted to seek the death penalty against Brumfield and Broadway.

It was also announced that Baton Rouge police had stopped Brumfield and West Paul a day before my mom's murder when they were pulled over during a routine traffic stop. Officers stopped their vehicle because it had an expired license plate and a taillight out. As officers questioned the driver and passenger, both fled and escaped on foot. They also confiscated a .44 Magnum. Brumfield told police he ran because he didn't have a driver's license, but police believed he ran because of a previous warrant that had been issued for his arrest. At the time of the January 6 stop, East Feliciana authorities already had issued a warrant for Brumfield's arrest in connection with a December 25, 1992, armed robbery near McManus.

In early February, a grand jury returned first-degree murder indictments against Brumfield, Broadway, and West Paul. The three pleaded innocent to the charges. While authorities said the defendants provided police with audio- and videotaped statements in which they admitted their involvement in my mom's shooting death, defense attorneys for two of the accused—West Paul and Kevan Brumfield—said their clients were threatened by investigators and that taped statements by police were "not freely given."

In a pretrial hearing in March, Brumfield told authorities he was sorry that my mom was killed and that he visited the funeral home where her body lay. The *Advocate* reported that Brumfield said, "I'm real sorry for what happened and I'm still sorry. If I could do anything to bring Ms. Smothers back, I would." Two contradictory videotaped statements by Brumfield were played on the first day of that pretrial hearing. In one statement, Brumfield said he "started shootin'" when my mom drove up to a night deposit window at the bank. But in another statement a day earlier, Brumfield said he never saw the shooting, didn't know exactly what his co-defendants had planned, and only drove the getaway car. Brumfield claimed in the first videotape that he wanted to do "a hustle," street slang for robbery or burglary. Brumfield said he drove the getaway car and parked it down the street from the bank at a Baskin-Robbins ice cream parlor, where he waited for the others to return.

The *Advocate* reported that Brumfield provided the second tape a day later, following the arrests of West Paul and Broadway. In that statement, Brumfield said he knew in advance that they planned to rob a police officer and the store's manager at the bank of an estimated $10,000 to $15,000. Brumfield said he and Broadway waited outside the bank for ten to fifteen minutes before Smothers and the manager arrived in the officer's patrol car. According to the *Advocate*, Smothers "looked back and I started shootin'," Brumfield said. He said he saw Smothers's city police uniform and recognized her as a police officer. "I started shootin' and Henri started shootin'. He was shootin', too." Brumfield said he was standing slightly in front of the police car when the shots rang out. "I really wasn't shootin' at the police officer," Brumfield said. Brumfield said he was trying to make them lie down in the car, and he did not know where the officer was shot. In December 1994, Broadway claimed that the detectives who arrested him threatened to shoot him after he was apprehended and beat him during an interrogation session. Broadway testified that "I was in pain. Blood was running down the side of my neck. I was saying to myself, 'This is a nightmare.'"

Broadway didn't know the true meaning of a nightmare.

AFTER MORE THAN TWO years of tears from my family, the trial against Brumfield started on Tuesday, June 27, 1995, in the Nineteenth Judicial District Court in the Parish of East Baton Rouge. Ralph E. Tyson was the presiding judge. I asked Clint Purvis, our team chaplain at Florida State, to pray for my family, especially my grandmother, and ask for God's strength. Most of my younger FSU teammates had no earthly idea what I dealt with off the field as we tried to win a second national championship on it. Close to two

hundred prospective jurors were interviewed before twelve were selected. Ms. Burns explained Louisiana law—that Article 30 of the
state's criminal code defines first-degree murder—detailed the case,
and set its tone in her opening statements. Ms. Burns's statements
helped outline the final moments of my mom's life and the callousness of Brumfield in this crime:

> At approximately ten minutes after midnight on what was now
> the morning of Thursday, January 7, 1993, Corporal Smothers
> and the store's manager, a young woman by the name of Kimen
> Lee, got in her full marked police unit and began to drive from
> the store to Citizens Bank and Trust on Jefferson Highway. Ms.
> Lee, the store manager, rode on the front passenger side of the
> marked police unit, and with her was a locked bank deposit bag
> containing $13,338.98 of cash, food stamps and checks. Some
> $4,913.00 of that deposit was cash money. The two rode the 2.2
> miles from the store to Citizens Bank and Trust without any prob-
> lem, using Corporal Smothers' usual route of driving from Florida
> Boulevard onto Lobdell Avenue and finally onto Jefferson High-
> way. And when she got to the bank she used her preferred method
> of going about the making of this deposit, and that was to enter
> through the exit lane of the bank, rather than the entrance lane,
> and she deliberately did this, because by doing so she would pull
> up to the night deposit, which would be directly next to the pas-
> senger side where the manager was seated. And the manager
> could very quickly make the night deposit into the bank without
> ever having to leave that vehicle.
>
> As the car pulled up at Citizens Bank and Trust, neither of the
> individuals noticed anything out of the ordinary. When the car
> stopped at the night deposit, Ms. Lee rolled down the window of
> the passenger side of the car, and she reached out, inserted the keys
> to the bank deposit into the depository itself. But the car was not

quite close enough to allow her to simply turn the keys, open the box and complete the deposit. What she had to do was to get closer. She began to maneuver her body, and in doing so, looked to the rear of the bank near some bushes. She then heard the sound that appeared to be the sliding back of the slide of an automatic weapon. And shortly thereafter from the same area she heard what sounded to her like firecrackers exploding, but were in fact, a volley of gunfire. At that time Corporal Smothers threw up her arms, she gasped, dropped her head to the right with her eyes open. Ms. Lee instinctively reached over Corporal Smothers' body to try to take control of the steering wheel of that car, and as she did so, she came face to face with a caramel-complected black male, wearing glasses, a cap tightly pulled down on his head, a camouflage jacket pulled tightly up at the neck, the sleeves of this jacket extended well past his wrists. And in his hands at his side was an automatic weapon. Kimen Lee looked directly into the face of this individual, and she has never forgotten that individual's face. She managed to take control of the car and in doing so, reaching over Corporal Smothers' body, she hit the pneumatic teller and caused damage to the front panel of the police unit. She managed to get the car to Jefferson Highway and drove four tenths of a mile from the driver side of the car, to the Circle K, with the bank bag, still untouched inside the police unit. At seventeen minutes after midnight on January 7, 1993, a very frantic, panicked 911 call was placed to 911 by an employee of that Circle K and by Ms. Lee, reporting the shooting of Corporal Betty Smothers. And at this point in time, Ms. Lee realized that she, too, had been repeatedly shot throughout her body.

EMS and the police immediately responded to the Circle K on Jefferson Highway. Officer Smothers was transported to Our Lady of the Lake Hospital. She could not breathe on her own; she had no pulse or blood pressure. Her pupils were fixed and dilated. She was essentially dead on arrival, and was officially pronounced dead *at 12:42 A.M. An autopsy of her body showed that she sustained five separate gunshot wounds to her body. She sustained one wound which entered her right forearm and exited through the right forearm causing hemorrhage. A second gunshot wound entered the back of her head, fracturing her occipital bone, and lodging in that area of her head. A third gunshot went behind the left ear of Corporal Betty Smothers, through that left ear, deflecting onto the mastoid bone, the very large bone that we all have behind our ears, and it lodged in the right side of her chest. That gunshot wound perforated, went through both her lungs and fractured her eighth rib. A fourth gunshot wound entered behind her right breast and perforated her aorta, the main artery of the human heart. That was the fatal shot in this case. A fifth gunshot entered her upper shoulder and lodged in the midline of her body. The three bullets that remained in her body, in her head, in her right chest, in the midline, were all removed during the course of the autopsy, and they were sent to the state police crime lab. They were all bullets, .380 caliber.*

Kimen Lee was also committed to Our Lady of the Lake Hospital on the morning of January the seventh, and she was discharged on January the thirteenth, some six days later. She sustained at least four separate gunshot wounds to her body, leaving eleven gunshot holes to her body, which she still has . . .

You will hear testimony also from the ballistics expert that upon examination of the ejection casings at the crime scene and the trajectory of the .380 caliber bullets that entered Corporal Smothers' unit through her police window on her side, that that shooter of these .380 caliber bullets was located on the driver side of the vehicle, on Corporal Smothers' side. And that that person was moving, converging gradually, towards her window at the time that these various shots were fired. And you will hear testimony based upon the presence of gunshot residue on her police sweater, that at least one of these shots was fired point blank from no more than three to four feet from Corporal Smothers' body . . .

You will hear testimony that Kevan Brumfield fired six shots into that car, all six aimed at the car through the driver's window where Betty Smothers sat. And five of these six rounds actually went into her body, one of them killing her. And you will hear that during the course of the first he was three to four feet from Corporal Smothers as he shot her repeatedly. . . . You will hear during the course of this trial the statements made by Kevan Brumfield after this killing. Statements in which he expressed anger over the fact that this whole thing was simply a waste of time. You will hear the callousness of this man who went to Winfield Funeral Home to view the body of Corporal Betty Smothers whom he had just killed . . .

Ironically, you will learn that in this case, January 7, 1993, was the birthday of Kevan Brumfield. And on the day that he was given life, he took the life of a uniformed Baton Rouge police department corporal, who was sitting in a fully marked police unit. A woman who had been a career officer, and who was also the mother of six children. And he did so coldly, deliberately, and without any remorse. For this act of murder and for this act of defiance, at the conclusion of this trial, the state of Louisiana will request that this jury find the defendant, Kevan Brumfield, guilty as charged of first degree murder.

Court-appointed defense attorney Ed Greenlee said in his opening statement that Brumfield was wrongfully charged with Mom's murder. He suggested that a videotaped statement in which Brumfield admitted his involvement in Mom's death was coerced by investigators. He urged the jury:

What I want you to do, and what I think all of you have promised to do is listen to the evidence. And listen to every bit of evidence that you hear. You're going to hear, as Ms. Burns has said, that Corporal Betty Smothers was murdered. There's no doubt about that. Absolutely no doubt. She was murdered. The only questions become whether or not Kevan Brumfield was the person that murdered Betty Smothers. And that's what you've got to listen to. You're going to hear emotional evidence. But you've got to be able to listen to the evidence and decide whether or not the state has proved that Kevan Brumfield was that person that killed Betty Smothers, because I submit to you that by the time we reach the end of the case that I am involved with that you'll find that they have not. This is going to be a case about the murder of Betty Smothers, and about the lack of evidence. Pay very, very close attention to the state's theories about the case. That's going to be important. . . .

Normally, Ms. Burns was telling you about statements that were being made, statements that were made by Kevan Brumfield. In normal situations, what you hear is a recorded statement or oral statements recounted by police officers, but again, I want to point you back to something that Ms. Burns said during voir dire. You're going to have a unique opportunity in this case that other jurors don't usually get, because most of the time when jurors are listening to statements by people who've been charged with a crime they're listening to a tape recording, they're listening to a police officer recount what has been said. You're going to have a unique opportunity. You're going to be sitting in that room along with everybody else. And that's where just as important as Ms. Burns has said earlier, a picture is worth a thousand words, that video tape is going to be worth a thousand words . . .

All we have is a young man who was turning twenty years old the next day and he was out with his girlfriend and his friends having a good time and enjoying himself. But he was not out planning the death of somebody else. Kevan was planning his twentieth birthday. That's what he was doing. Ladies and gentle-

men, please, listen to everything. Listen to what we talked to you about during the voir dire, and realize that it's the state's burden to prove this case beyond a reasonable doubt. And each and every one of you have said if you find a reasonable doubt you're going to find Kevan not guilty. I submit to you that there's a lot more—in this case. There's a lot more and you're going to see it. Thank you very much.

After nearly two weeks of witnesses and testimony, I sat in the front row of the courtroom on Sunday, judgment day. Brumfield was convicted by the jury of first-degree murder. I sat there, my face buried in my hands. Kimen Lee sat next to me, her arm around my shoulders. We helped comfort each other. I knew the result of this case was in God's hands.

One defendant down, two more defendants to go.

On Thursday, October 26, 1995, the case against Broadway started. I was on the football field at FSU, and we had scored 70 or more points in victories over Duke, North Carolina, State, and Wake Forest. But I constantly thought of the trial. Although Broadway wasn't accused of firing the gun that killed Mom, Ms. Burns sought the death penalty for Broadway because he took part in the attack and repeatedly shot Kimen Lee. One of Broadway's attorneys, Fred Kroenke, said that Broadway had an alibi and there was no direct evidence linking his client to the scene of the crime.

In her opening statements, Ms. Burns said Broadway was seen twice in the Piggly Wiggly on Florida Boulevard before the ambush, once just seventy-five minutes before the killing. She also told jurors that Broadway was a former employee of another Piggly Wiggly in Baton Rouge.

One week later, on Thursday night, November 3, while I was in Virginia, a jury took just ninety minutes to convict Broadway of first-degree murder and rejected his claim that he played no part in the deadly ambush. When Broadway took the stand earlier on Thursday, he said he was at home when Mom and Lee were attacked as they made a midnight deposit at the bank. The *Advocate* reported that Broadway also testified that at least six officers physically abused him after his arrest and that one officer took his hand and made him initial several pages of notes. Broadway said police put a clear plastic bag over his head, then tightened or loosened it to control his air supply. He also said they put a picture of Mom inside the bag and made him look at it. The photograph was of Mom lying dead with her head bandaged. Broadway also told the jury that at different times police pulled his ears, repeatedly kicked him in the shins, slapped him, hit him in the mouth, and punched him in the chest. He said they cleaned up blood from a cut inside his lip before photographing him.

In her closing arguments, Ms. Burns called Broadway's allegations of police brutality a "tall tale of abuse" and that several family members who testified that Broadway was at home the night my mom was slain had lied to protect him. In his closing arguments, Kroenke told jurors that the ambush was an inside job and "the mastermind . . . is running loose on the street."

Of course, that wasn't true at all. The guilty persons in Mom's murder were behind bars where they belonged.

IT WAS A CHANCE MEETING when I last saw Kimen Lee in 2003 at Tony's Seafood Restaurant in Baton Rouge. I was on my cell phone and I just happened to turn around. There was Kimen. We hugged each other and chatted. It was great to see her.

While Kimen and I had talked a few times on the telephone while I was at Florida State, it was the first time I had seen Kimen in person since the sentencing phase in the Henri Broadway trial on November 4, 1995—nearly eight years. The only other time I had visited with Kimen at length was when she came to our home on Bradley Street two months after the ambush and Mom's murder in 1993.

Mom's murder obviously changed the lives of many people, but none more so than those of my family and Kimen. Kimen, who was born and raised in Baton Rouge and still makes the city her home, will be forty-six years old in 2008. Kimen was a preload supervisor at UPS and was a contract employee for a vending company, Sweet Things, when she agreed to be interviewed for this book in September 2007.

Kimen said she continues to recover emotionally and physically from the volley of gunfire that killed Mom and seriously wounded her. Kimen was shot at least four times but has eleven bullet holes in her body where the shots entered and exited—three in her left breast, four in her right thigh, and four in her buttocks. The horrific night remains forever etched in her mind.

"As I got my keys in the [night deposit] box, that's when the barrage of bullets just started coming," Kimen said in measured tones. "I first thought it was firecrackers, black cats, going off. I saw sparks and I saw paper. Later I found out the sparks were the fire of the bullet and the paper was the shattering of the glass. You really never know what's going on. It didn't even register what was truly happening.

"It's something that I will never, ever, ever forget. It changed my life in a lot of ways. It weighed me down for years. When Prem [Burns, assistant district attorney] told me that my life would start moving forward once the trials were over, that was so far off that I never could believe that could be so. But once the convictions were in, slowly my life started to move forward. It did start healing—healed but not forgotten. Every bullet that hit me went through me. I have scars where I was shot that will be constant reminders.

"I am the kind of person who used to see a glass half-full. I don't anymore. It has made me bitter. Life has made me bitter and I hate being that way, but my trust level is damaged. I give people one chance with me. If they screw up, they usually don't get a second chance and I know that's not the way to be."

While my therapy for depression came later during my NFL career, Kimen's recovery process included therapy soon after the ambush. A day following the shooting, Lee underwent hypnosis in the hospital to aid police in preparing a composite drawing of the assailant who she had observed at close range. Kimen said she experienced bad dreams and flashbacks and was diagnosed with post-traumatic stress disorder.

As part of her recovery, Kimen's therapist recommended that Kimen visit with my family at our home on Bradley Street in early March 1993, two months after Mom's murder. Kimen said she also visited the Citizens Bank & Trust on a Sunday when the bank was closed, and her journey included a stop at the Piggly Wiggly where she was an assistant night manager and got to know my mom.

Kimen said her grocery career, which included nearly fifteen years at Winn-Dixie and four months at Piggly Wiggly, ended on January 7, 1993.

"I was extremely nervous when I went to Warrick's home with my father and therapist," Kimen said. "I remember it was at night and Warrick was sitting across from me. I tried to answer their questions, but I didn't have all the answers. I wanted Warrick and his family to know that Betty never suffered. She never knew what hit her. Was it good therapy for me? I don't know. It was a long time before I felt better. When I decided to go get help, I had a lot of anger. I went through a lot of guilt, the guilt as why did you take her and you didn't take me? She has a family. Why did I survive? There was a lot of anger, and with that came the anger of why did they [Brumfield, Broadway, and West Paul] do what they did? Just ask for the money and I would have given it to you.

"You can never imagine your wildest dreams . . . the worst part was feeling alone, feeling alone and somebody wanting to hurt you. It's the scariest thing I've ever felt. By the grace of God, I have the will to survive. It [getting shot] doesn't hurt at first. It's the aftermath that really hurts."

Kimen doesn't blame Mom for the ambush and admits she thwarted the trio's plan to have no witnesses when she survived the attack.

"I've heard, 'Why didn't you sue the city?'" Kimen said. "My thoughts were suing the city—that would all come back down on Betty. She already lost her life. I wasn't going to blame her for anything. As somebody said, the logo on the side of the [police] car is to protect and serve. You can't protect and serve when you, as they call it, have been snuck. They snuck two women. They were there to kill the both of us. There wasn't supposed to be anybody who walked away. They knew what was going on. They came to the store. They knew it was us making the deposit and they waited. They had it all planned out. The only plan they didn't have was for me to live."

Kimen can still remember the night in its gory detail. She never lost consciousness during the entire incident, from the time the shots were fired to being rushed into the emergency room at the hospital. Kimen can tell you the clothes she wore. She can still see Broadway as he stood and peered into Mom's police vehicle. She can tell you the look on Mom's face, the way her hands landed when Mom was shot. Kimen can describe the chaotic scene at the Circle K as emergency personnel started to arrive. That's when Kimen first realized she had been shot. Kimen also can tell you the last time she saw Mom as she frantically climbed back into the police cruiser in that store parking lot. She pushed on Mom's chest, checked for a pulse, and told Mom help was on the way. Kimen was unable to attend Mom's funeral and burial as she recovered from her wounds in the hospital.

"I never got to say goodbye to Betty," Kimen said. "I went to Betty's grave on that first-year anniversary and probably went for the first six or seven years. It's an old little-bitty church with a fence around it. There were times I jumped the fence because nobody was there. I would spend some time there and bring some flowers. I try not to be too bitter. One way, you try to learn and pick up the pieces and not make the same mistakes. My other outlook is, if it's going to happen, it's going to happen. Look, I was with a uniformed police officer in a marked car and look what happened. If somebody wants you, they are going to get you."

Kimen also has fond memories of Mom from their time at Piggly Wiggly.

"What I knew of Betty, she was a very kind lady," Kimen said. "She was all about her kids. That particular night Betty was telling me that her and Warrick were supposed to be going to Alabama that Saturday to look at things. Betty had a very warm smile, genuine. Friendly. She was a lady doing her job. And she was very helpful to me at the store, too. She would help bag groceries, bring me my keys. Betty never minded lending a helping hand."

One can just imagine Kimen's reaction when she showed up at the Baton Rouge Police Department in 2004 to fill out required paperwork for a background check when she applied for work at UPS. In the main hallway, Kimen noticed the plaques that honored Baton Rouge police officers slain in the line of duty. She saw Mom's and began to read.

"I can't remember exactly, but the plaque had the wrong date or the wrong year," Kimen said. "It's something I really don't talk about, but I went back up to the front desk and told them you have a plaque out here for Betty Smothers and you have the wrong date on it. She said what? I told her it was January 7, 1993, and she asked how I knew that. I told her I was with Betty. It was the wrong date and they needed to change it."

Much has changed, but life must continue for all of us.

"Everyone has had a different destiny," Kimen said. "Warrick made his own shadow, but he walked in his momma's, too. He was known for that, the son of a police officer, and that's all you heard. Warrick has made a name for himself. That name began with his mother, even if she was a Smothers. I have so much respect for Warrick. If other people with his power, that stature, the influence, could do just a portion of what he has done, that can make a difference. I always try to pay attention to what he has done, how he has played. As far as football, I am not a sports person. But I do know Warrick is a good person.

"He looks a lot like his mother. You look at that smile, you look at those eyes. . . ."

CHAPTER 9

PLAYING FOR BOBBY

SHOULD I STAY OR SHOULD I GO?

That's the question I faced following my junior season at Florida State: Should I return for my senior year at FSU or depart early for the National Football League and its millions of dollars? As I made my way to the podium that was set up in the bottom-floor atrium of our athletic center for a news conference to announce my decision, I saw the faces of family, friends, teammates, and coaches in the crowd of around two hundred people.

Our football season had ended two weeks earlier in the Orange Bowl, where I had 151 rushing yards on twenty-two carries in our 31–26 victory over Notre Dame. The win capped a memorable junior season for me. I rushed for a school-record 1,242 yards, including eight 100-yard games, to set the FSU single-season record. I was also within 991 yards of the Seminoles' career rushing record of 3,769 that was held by Greg Allen (1981–84). Those numbers were nice, but they didn't matter most to me.

As a team, we didn't accomplish our top priority, and that was to win our second national championship in three years. It was set up perfectly for us, too. We opened the 1995 season Number 1 in the country and won our first seven games over Duke, Clemson, North Carolina State, Central Florida, Miami, Wake Forest, and Georgia Tech by an average of nearly 39 points per game.

But then we tumbled at Virginia 33–28 on the game's final play—I don't care what anyone said, I know I scored on the 6-yard direct snap for the victory—and fell to Number 8 in the polls and out of the national-title race. That's how quickly your hopes of becoming a national champion can be snatched away.

While we rebounded and thumped North Carolina and Maryland, Florida beat us 35–24 in the regular-season finale in Gainesville. No matter how you slice it, it's always a bummer to lose to the Gators, and our fans let us know about it. The good news was that we rallied to beat Notre Dame in the Orange Bowl and finished with a 10–2 record and a Number 4 ranking in the Associated Press poll. That extended our NCAA record of top five finishes to nine overall and our NCAA record of consecutive bowl victories to fourteen.

After the Orange Bowl, I flew home to Baton Rouge to be with my family and discuss my future. Actually, it was to reinforce a decision I had already made prior to our bowl game. I understood the importance of education. It was a value that I had preached to my brothers and sisters following my mom's murder three years earlier. Plus, during my senior year at Catholic High, I promised Mom that I would attend college and graduate. I wasn't about to break that promise. Education was my top priority.

I informed Coach Bowden of my decision when we started to practice for the Orange Bowl in early December. I asked Coach to keep the secret, and he did. A month later I was set to announce it as I strolled up to that podium in our atrium that was located beyond the north end zone of Doak Campbell Stadium. I told the crowd that I had thought about things and taken in everyone's evaluation, as well as talking it over with family and friends: I am going to do what I want to do . . . and I want to stay!

The crowd erupted in applause.

For the next thirty minutes, I explained my decision to remain with the Seminoles in 1996. I was projected as a first- or second-round selection in the April NFL draft, the highest of any FSU tailback since Sammie Smith left FSU following his junior season in 1988. We had lost eleven underclassmen to the NFL since Smith had left, and that list included six players selected in the first round—Smith, linebacker Marvin Jones (1993/New York Jets), cornerback Terrell Buckley (1992/Green Bay Packers), fullback William Floyd (1994/San Francisco 49ers), defensive end Derrick Alexander (1995/Minnesota Vikings), and safety Devin Bush (1995/Atlanta Falcons).

I also saw what type of team we had coming back and I thought we had a better chance of winning a national championship. Plus, I had thirty-five credit hours left after the spring semester and was on course to get my degree in Information Technologies. I believed another year in school wouldn't hurt anything. The money? I hadn't had money for twenty-one years, so what was another year? When somebody says you can make a million dollars in the NFL, that's a lot of cash and it's tough to turn down. But I am a patient man and only God knows what's going to happen. I told the crowd that I was going to put it in His hands. My grandmother listened in the front row and smiled.

Of course, there were underclassmen running backs around the country who had different ideas and announced their decision to enter the NFL draft. Leeland McElroy of Texas A&M, Moe Williams of Kentucky, Lawrence Phillips of national champion Nebraska, and Tim Biakabutuka of Michigan all said they planned to leave school early for the NFL. I was happy for them, but I felt good about my decision to remain in Tallahassee for another year.

There wasn't any family or financial pressure to turn professional. I talked with several players, including Charlie Ward and Derrick Brooks. At that time, Charlie was a point guard with the New York Knicks after being selected in the first round of the NBA draft. When he graduated from FSU, Charlie made it clear that he would not consider playing in the NFL unless he was selected in the first round of the NFL draft. Charlie told me to follow my heart, as he did. Derrick also contemplated leaving FSU early for the NFL but returned for his senior season in 1994. I planned to take out an insurance policy against a career-ending injury, but I wasn't worried about that. If I got hurt, it would happen no matter where I was, be it at FSU or in the NFL.

I met with Billy Sexton, our running backs coach, during the season and we talked about the NFL. Coach told me to approach it as a business decision. He encouraged me to petition the NFL and ask the league to evaluate my draft status. Those people are honest and thorough. That's what I did, and the NFL informed Sexton that I was a potential second-round selection if I entered the draft following my junior season. Sexton believed another year of competition and weight lifting would improve my draft status. I agreed. When I announced my decision to return to FSU, Sexton joked with offensive coordinator Mark Richt that FSU had just signed its first prospect of the year. It was only a one-year deal, but at least I knew the plays.

FSU was my extended family, and it started with Bobby Bowden. We connected immediately when I arrived on campus in 1993. Coach often said during my FSU career that I was a great role model. Other players wanted to blame the system or blame society when they got into trouble or complained about the hand they were dealt in life. My mom was murdered and my father wasn't around. I was in Tallahassee, yet I had to raise my younger brothers and sisters in Baton Rouge. That was the hand I was dealt, but I didn't complain. I dealt with it. I spent a lot of time on the telephone during the week with my brothers and sisters. I listened to what was going on in their lives. I offered advice and I laid down the law if it was needed. Grandma always updated me, too. If I had free time, I jumped into my car and headed back home.

While coaches ordinarily kept an emotional distance between themselves and players, it wasn't like that between me and Coach Bowden. Sure, I talked football with Coach Bowden plenty of times, like my sophomore season when I asked Coach the last time FSU had a 1,000-yard rusher. When he asked why, I told him I would be the next player to eclipse that mark if I got enough carries.

But I usually stopped by Coach Bowden's office and asked questions or for advice concerning my brothers and sisters. We didn't talk father to son. We talked father to father. Coach told me how he handled his children back in his day, and I recycled it to today's way of doing things. It helped, too. We both agreed that discipline was important when it came to raising children. Coach was stern with his children; I knew I had to be stern with my brothers and sisters when it was needed. Even Rob Wilson, FSU's sports information director, admitted that the line between player and coach was blurred when it came to my relationship with Coach Bowden. Yes, it was special. If I told Coach I needed to go to Baton Rouge to deal with a family matter, I had his permission to leave at a moment's notice.

Most times, however, I dealt with issues on the telephone. Derrick, the second oldest, and I had our share of disagreements and arguments. In fact, it seemed like we argued more than agreed each time we talked. Derrick resented that I made decisions for him and the family because I was away at college. Derrick wanted to make his own decisions concerning himself and the family since he was at home on the front lines. Derrick was very, very strict with our brothers and sisters and he will be the first to tell you he was mean to their friends, too.

Derrick also had to deal with people who knocked on our door because they wanted something or had something to offer the family. He had to talk with the police, the lawyers, and the insurance agents following Mom's murder. Derrick was very protective in part because he never had the opportunity to show our mom he could be the man of the house. That role had always fallen on me as the oldest. But when I left for FSU, Derrick, who was a year older than Summer, made it his responsibility to take care of his siblings.

Even while Derrick was at Catholic High, he was the emergency contact for his brothers and sisters. When Samantha cut her hand on the playground one day, Derrick left school to make sure she was okay. He helped with their homework, their problems, and their questions. Many times he missed his own football practice at Catholic if he was needed at home. When Derrick and I talked, he quickly reminded me he was in Baton Rouge and I was in Tallahassee, too far away for me to raise the family and make immediate decisions. I would get mad, but I expected my siblings, Derrick included, to do the right thing.

The bottom line was, I was missing my family. And I was missing my mom.

It was especially tough before our home games. My grandmother, who always wore my number 28 jersey and was easy to spot, came with my brothers and sisters, and they were in the stands at Doak Campbell Stadium. They'd get on the road from Baton Rouge early Saturday morning and make a beeline to Tallahassee. Nothing would stop them—not even the time when one of the rear wheels on Grandma's van rattled loose at seventy miles per hour on Interstate 10. Summer slept on the floor of the van and never knew the wheel came off and rolled down the highway. Grandma slowed the van and veered it off the side of the highway, where she called Derrick and told him he needed to hurry with a new tire because they had wasted enough time.

They arrived late for the game, but they made it safe and sound. Grandma would not allow anything to keep them away. Each home game I looked up to make sure my family had arrived in Tallahassee. If for some reason I didn't see them, I asked Clint Purvis, our team chaplain, to check at the ticket office to make sure they had signed for their complimentary tickets and were at the game.

Also before each game, Clint and I said a quick prayer. We sat next to each other on stools in front of my locker and we prayed for my family. It was my sophomore season during Parents Weekend when memories of Mom overwhelmed me emotionally. I looked in the stands and saw my grandmother with my number 28 jersey on. I was so happy. But I also saw parents wearing their sons' jerseys, and I lost it. I started to cry and wondered what it would be like to see my mom in the stands with the other parents. I love my grandmother, but I told Clint that if I had one wish, it was for Mom to be in the stands. I cried on Clint's shoulder for twenty minutes before the game. Clint told me the one thing I could take pride and confidence in was that there is a God and He loves us. Clint said that my mom was at God's side and she could see me. Mom was not here in flesh, but she was here in spirit and she was watching me. The pain never goes away, but I think Mom would be proud of me.

I always tried to do the right thing at FSU, and that included dealing with the media. What a pain in the rear end that was at times. By my senior season, I was one of the most requested players by the media for interviews. It seemed like every day a television reporter, a radio personality, a magazine writer, or the newspaper guys, the "beat" writers, wanted to talk. Each day it was the same questions, over and over. It got so bad that FSU assistant sports information director Tina Thomas handled all of my media requests. Tina knew I hated doing interviews about my life story and about Mom's murder. It was the same questions, the same answers, and the same bad memories. I felt like the media wanted to sensationalize my life with every story.

It reached a point in my senior season when I became fed up. ABC Sports was in town for player interviews leading up to one of our games. I was in the elevator with Tina and I told her I wasn't going to do the interview with ABC Sports. I told Tina I was a person like everyone else with my own life and that I was burnt out. I was finished with interviews. Tina explained she had a job to do and she was very upset with me. I was upset, too. We called each other brats but quickly apologized to each other, but I also wanted her to understand my position. I had so many demands on my life and I tried my best to meet them.

The amount of fan mail I received was unbelievable. It filled boxes and boxes and boxes that were stacked in Tina's office. There were photographs, football jerseys, and footballs that fans, from grandparents to children, wanted me to sign. It reached the point where I didn't know what I was signing or for whom I was signing. I don't know how they got my address in Tallahassee, but fans also sent mail and paraphernalia to my one-bedroom townhouse off Ocala Road. I put it all in my closet—letters on the right side, clothing and other stuff on the left side. People also asked me to return the autographs, but I was a college student, and I didn't have the money to return everyone's request or letter.

Despite my quiet nature off the field, I wasn't afraid to stand up and address my teammates. After an unbeaten but slow start my senior year, we called a players-only meeting for offensive players following a victory over North Carolina. Several players, myself included, stood and talked. I told my teammates that I returned for my senior season to win. I didn't come back for the coaches. I didn't come back for myself. I didn't come back to position myself in the NFL draft so I could make more money. Ultimately, I came back to win and be with my teammates. It was time for me to step up and become a leader. I knew I wasn't going to win the Heisman Trophy because we simply didn't run the football enough. But that wasn't a concern of mine. I am not a player who is worried about accolades. I am far more concerned with the team.

Coach Sexton didn't cut me any slack, either. It was the Sunday prior to our game against Florida my senior season. I was at my townhouse getting ready to head to FSU for our scheduled running backs meeting. Well, the special teams meeting prior to our meeting had ended early, and Coach Sexton telephoned me and wanted to know where I was. I told Coach I was headed to FSU for our scheduled meeting. Our meeting started by the time I arrived, and Coach had written on the board: "10 minutes late, 10 stadium steps."

Needless to say, I was angry. I told Coach that I didn't need football and I didn't need him. Running those stadium steps hurt and I wasn't going to do it. I walked out, slammed the door behind me, and immediately bumped into offensive line coach Jimmy Heggins in the hallway. Coach Heggins asked what was wrong, so I told him. I ended up in the offensive line meeting, and I didn't see or talk with Coach Sexton again until our Monday practice the following day. Coach Sexton and I met and talked before practice and it was cool. Coach was right and I was wrong. I wasn't trying to disrespect Coach Sexton when I walked out of the running backs meeting. I had to be punished for my behavior, and Coach had me run ten 100-yard gassers instead of the stadium steps. We went back to work and we beat Florida 24–21 that Saturday.

Honestly, I never thought I was special or better than anyone else. When I attended our men's and women's basketball games, I blended in with the crowd as much as possible. I never walked around with an FSU hat or an FSU jacket on. I liked the little things. I enjoyed the chance to referee the managers-versus-trainers annual flag football game. Like many students, I ate at Denny's and at Fazoli's off campus because it was convenient and cheap. I just didn't want to draw attention to myself.

I attracted enough attention on the football field.

My collegiate career was blessed. I was a three-time first-team All-ACC performer and became the first running back in Florida State history to record three 1,000-yard rushing seasons. I finished as the program's career leader in rushing yards with 3,959 to surpass Greg Allen's mark of 3,769. I averaged 6.9 yards per carry as a collegian, an FSU record and the top mark by an NCAA Division I player in fifty years. My pass-catching abilities were also on display, and I finished with 132 career receptions for 1,314 yards. I scored 47 touchdowns to also set the school record and broke Allen's school mark for all-purpose yards (4,996) with a total of 5,321. I finished with twenty-one 100-yard rushing games, the most in school history, and, as a senior, earned second-team All-America honors from the Associated Press.

My decision to return for my senior season was the right choice. And it had nothing to do with a summer trip to Las Vegas, where I met Hugh Hefner and all these beautiful women at the Playboy mansion because I was named a *Playboy* preseason All-American! That was crazy. It was a crazy season, too. I rushed 189 times for 1,180 yards and 12 touchdowns and added 30 catches for 355 yards and a pair of touchdowns. I started all eleven games and averaged 6.2 yards per carry and 107.3 rushing yards per game. I was selected to the All-ACC first team for the third consecutive year and was presented the conference's Commissioner's Award, which was a story in itself.

Actually, it was two stories.

The ACC banquet was in Atlanta. Since Tina worked in the FSU sports information office, it was her responsibility to drive Peter Boulware, Reinard Wilson, and me to the Tallahassee Regional Airport for our morning flight. The three of us were being honored at the banquet later that day. Well, Reinard slept in, which made us late from the get-go. I told Tina I would drive her car because first, I'd make better time, and second, I had a better chance to beg our way out of a speeding ticket. We arrived at the airport with seconds to spare. But Peter—even though he stood at the departure gate and signed autographs—didn't have any identification on him, so he wasn't allowed to board. Reinard couldn't find his airline ticket, so he was left behind, too. I was the only one who somehow made the flight. And I say somehow because once in my seat, I discovered I had used Reinard's ticket to board. But it ended okay, as Peter and Reinard caught the next flight to Atlanta.

At the banquet, the league named Virginia tailback Tiki Barber its offensive player of the year. Minutes later, ACC commissioner Gene Corrigan created an award for one year only. He defended his decision by saying, "I can do whatever the hell I want," and then handed me the Commissioner's Award. I was stunned, but grateful. I thanked Mr. Corrigan, my coaches, the offensive linemen, and my teammates. I then looked up and thanked my mom, too. FSU athletic director Dave Hart said, "Anyone who saw that saw something they'll never forget. It's clear Warrick touched a lot of people around the conference in four years."

Really, the four years went quickly at times, but slowly at others. My brothers and sisters had grown up. Bricson, Travis, and Samantha still lived with their grandmother and two cousins in a five-bedroom house that I had purchased with my mother's life insurance policy a few months after her death. Summer was running track at Southern University not far from our house in Baton Rouge, and Derrick was at McNeese State in nearby Lake Charles, Louisiana. We all had to grow up fast, but it wasn't a secret that I dealt with my maturation better than I did with theirs. It was difficult being away for long stretches.

On the field, I guess it was only fitting that my college career ended with a pair of games against rival Florida. I rushed for 185 yards on twenty-four carries, and fullback Pooh Bear Williams scored his first two touchdowns of the season as we beat top-ranked Florida 24–21 on November 30, 1996, at Doak Campbell Stadium to secure a berth in the Sugar Bowl for the national championship. It was wild as our fans stormed the field and tore down the goalposts. I really didn't get a chance to join the celebration because I caught a whiff of pepper spray as police tried to unsuccessfully shoo fans from the field. The win didn't taste great, but it sure felt great.

A few minutes earlier we had possession at the 50-yard line with 1:14 to play. We needed one more first down to run out the clock and secure the victory. I spoke up in the huddle and told my teammates to give whatever they had left in their hearts. They gave me the ball and I went 14 yards around the right end. Game over. I had the chance to quickly talk with UF quarterback Danny Wuerffel at midfield before the place seemed to explode around us. I wished Danny good luck in the voting for the Heisman Trophy, and he whispered that I had his vote. Of course, we didn't have a vote, but it didn't matter. To beat Florida in my last game at Doak Campbell Stadium and earn the chance to return to my home state of Louisiana and play for the national title seemed like a fairy tale.

Our game with Florida was the first regular-season meeting between the Number 1 (Florida) and Number 2 (FSU) teams in the country in three years. We were involved in the previous game as the Number 1 team and lost at second-ranked Notre Dame 31–24 in November 1993 during my freshman season. But we went on to win the national championship that season by beating Nebraska in the Orange Bowl.

As I sat in the locker room, a trainer cut the tape from my wrists. "GOD" was written on the piece cut from my left wrist. "MOM" was written on the other. Just below "MOM" I also wrote "Mr. T," for Chuck Tanner, an elderly man who had befriended me during my time in Tallahassee and had died before the season. Travis and Bricson were in the locker room with me. I showered and dressed, and they wrapped their arms around my waist as we walked out into the crowd to hook up with Grandma, Summer, and Samantha. For me it was about family and friends.

While everyone figured we would play Nebraska in the Sugar Bowl, it didn't work out that way. Actually, it was crazy how it worked out. A week after we beat Florida, Texas upset third-ranked Nebraska in the Big 12 title game. That same night, Florida defeated Alabama 45–30 in Atlanta in the SEC Championship game behind a six-touchdown performance by Wuerffel, who was awarded the Heisman Trophy the following week in New York. Florida's win and Nebraska's defeat opened the door for the Gators to play us in the Sugar Bowl in a highly anticipated rematch. There was plenty of drama, too.

UF, which entered the bowl season ranked third behind top-ranked FSU and second-ranked Arizona State, watched Ohio State knock off Arizona State in the Rose Bowl in a dramatic last-second victory on New Year's Day. That result meant that the January 2 game in New Orleans against us was for the national title.

While playing my final college game so close to home meant that my career had come full circle, we knew that facing the Gators again wouldn't be easy. Most of the chatter that led up to the game came from UF coach Steve Spurrier, who complained the entire week about what he viewed were late hits on Wuerffel in the November meeting between the two teams. Our defense sacked Danny six times and intercepted him three times, and we were whistled for three late hits. Our defense was physical and aggressive and taught by defensive coordinator Mickey Andrews to hit until they heard the echo of the referee's whistle. The controversy grew heated during the week that led up to the game, and Coach Bowden warned Spurrier that his attacks had become personal.

Spurrier also said he expected a big game out of me against his Gators. In my five games against UF, I had 862 total yards, including a 79-yard scoring pass in 1993 and a 73-yard touchdown pass in the 1995 Sugar Bowl. I also caught a 37-yard swing pass in front of the UF sideline that helped set up our final touchdown in the "Choke at Doak" in 1994, when we rallied for 28 unanswered points in the fourth quarter to tie the Gators 31–31. Coach Spurrier, a former Heisman Trophy winner, even voted me Number 2 behind Danny on his 1996 Heisman Trophy ballot. We were excited about the re-match because of what was at stake—a national title. It was neat to be so close to home. A few days before the game, I took my offensive teammates to my house in Baton Rouge for dinner. My grandma did the cooking, and we had all of my favorites—crawfish, gumbo, étouffé, ribs, candied yams, and macaroni and cheese. The big eaters, like lineman Chad Bates, pushed themselves away from the table with full bellies and big grins.

We didn't have much fun against the Gators, though. It sucked, actually.

Wuerffel threw three touchdown passes to Ike Hilliard and ran for another as UF beat us 52–20 for the Gators' first national title. Danny connected on touchdown passes to Hilliard in each of the first three quarters, and UF erupted for 28 points to break open a tight game. Coach Bowden dreaded the idea of playing the Gators for the second time, and it was a bitter defeat for us. It was a frustrating game for me as well, since I battled cramps and dehydration for the first half and saw limited action in the second half.

I had a 12-yard touchdown run in the second quarter but finished with just 28 yards on nine carries. I argued with our training staff to let me back on the field in the second half. I cried as I laid on the training table, my entire body tight and cramped. My lower body was wrapped in ice and I was given fluids intravenously. Nothing helped. I couldn't believe it. I was in my home state in the biggest game of my life, and I was unable to help my teammates. I made it back to the sidelines in the fourth quarter, but it was without my helmet and pads. UF had ended our twelve-game winning streak and our eleven-game bowl winning streak—we were unbeaten in our previous fourteen bowls (13-0-1) since an 18–17 loss to Oklahoma in the 1981 Orange Bowl.

It didn't seem like I had changed much in my four years at Florida State. But then again, I had changed. It was a life process.

I've always been the same person, but I felt I had learned to open up more around people. My communication skills had gotten a little better. You change, you grow, you mature. Mom's murder was part of my life. I thought I had learned to cope with it better than when it first happened. Because of my time at FSU, I was able to better handle everything that went with it. I believed my life was getting back to normal. I was especially thankful for my opportunities at FSU and the chance to play for Coach Bowden. And Florida State sports information director Rob Wilson expressed his thoughts to me and my family in an open letter that appeared in *Tribe* magazine on November 26, 1996, the day we played Florida in my final home game at FSU.

Warrick Dunn
A letter to his family
November 30, 1996

Dear Derrick, Summer, Bricson, Travis and Samantha:

Just thought I would drop you a line. I know I haven't written in the past four years, but it's been unbelievably busy around here. After all, we've spent the better part of the last four years carving out our place as the most consistently successful college football program ever.

Back in 1993, we started the season number one and held onto it until we stumbled up at Notre Dame when the ghosts seemed to step in the way of our final drive. Funny thing, though, Notre Dame lasted only one week at number one before Boston College beat them and put us right back in the driver's seat.

We had to go down to Florida to play the Gators in what they called a swamp (nothing like what you've got back in Louisiana, though). A national championship match-up with Nebraska was on the line that day and Florida had not lost at home since Steve Spurrier took over as head coach.

Warrick had already done some remarkable things as a freshman. He contributed in every game, but it was Warrick and his roommate (Charlie Ward) who paired up to make the big play when FSU needed it. Warrick's catch and run for the fourth-quarter touchdown against Florida will be legend around here for years to come.

Oh yeah, he went on to defeat Nebraska for our first national championship.

Warrick ran awfully well as a sophomore and junior, gaining more than 1,000 yards in both seasons and becoming the first back in FSU history to do that. He was developing quite a fan base not only in Florida, but around the nation. Heck, even a lot of Gators will admit they like him.

Your brother was so good that agents started trying to convince him that he needed to enter the NFL draft after his junior year. Faced with taking the money and running, literally, Warrick did what he has done most of his life—he made a difficult decision.

Warrick came back to Florida State for his senior year and as you read this he is getting ready for the biggest game of his life. One of the biggest games in any college football player's life.

Think he's nervous?

Let me tell you some things about your brother that he probably has not told you.

Like most people, I had a soft spot for Warrick before he ever came to Florida State. I was there in the airport when former Washington Redskin Super Bowl MVP Doug Williams told Charlie about your family's circumstances.

I'll never forget thinking how small and sad he looked when he arrived on campus in August of his freshman year. I'm accustomed to seeing homesick freshman but not quite so heartsick and lonesome. When he stuck it out after those first few days away from home I suspected he might be special.

Your brother leaned on Charlie a lot as a freshman and when the Heisman Trophy winner left, I thought maybe Warrick would suffer without such a strong friend to help him. But Warrick is smarter and tougher than that. He had been preparing all along.

He prepared hard in school also, establishing himself as a good student and trying a major (information systems) that required more outside work than all but a few. But, just like when he didn't take the easy way and sign with backyard neighbor LSU, Warrick was just doing what he felt was right.

Your brother has progressed from timid freshman, to quiet leader, to the finest running back in Florida State history. And he's done it with an awful lot on his mind.

I know he has missed all of you.

Someone once asked him what he thought about during a football game. I think they were trying to get at the specifics of whether he sets up blockers or debates in his mind how to make an oncoming tackler look silly. That's not the answer they got.

"The games are fun," he said. "A chance to get rid of all the problems and worries of the week. A time to clear your mind of everything and just enjoy yourself. It's an escape in a way. The fans don't even have to be there. It's just 60 minutes of fun."

I hope the officials think about that the next time they reach in their pocket debating whether to flag Warrick when he dives into the end zone after tearing over 60 yards of gridline and 11 guys who tried to stop him.

His eyes tell a lot about this brother of yours. He carries a lot of sorrow in them. But when he smiles it is like a spring day when the clouds part and shafts of sunlight knife through that are so distinct they look like they could be climbed. When he smiles it is ear-to-ear and so joyous that I choose to believe they can see it in heaven.

He would trade it all for one thing though. He'd trade all the magnificent plays in his career. He'd trade the good friends he's made here and even the great education of which he's taken advantage. He would trade the fame, the potential wealth that teases on the horizon, the records, everything.

But he can't bring her back. "Every day," sighed Warrick when asked how often he thinks of your mom.

Your brother has taught us a lot in his four years. He has taught us about courage and dedication. He has taught us about determination, desire and pride. He has taught us about taking the right way and not necessarily the easy way. He has given us examples of patience and contentment.

He is the finest ball carrier in the storied history of Florida State University. There have been times when No. 28 was bounding through a defense and I thought it was the most remarkable thing I had ever seen.

Your brother has meant so much to this university and now we sit and wait for him to dazzle us for the last time on the Doak Campbell Stadium field that, I swear, he only touches a few times every run.

A mountain of records are coming Warrick's way. Among them a startling 49 career touchdowns. Most of which came at the end of runs so filled with highlights that you've got to watch the replay to appreciate it.

We will all miss your brother next year.

You know, he has always pointed to the sky after scoring a touchdown. At that moment of greatest joy, he points up as if to say, "did you see that Mom." I choose to believe she does.

Maybe it would be most appropriate today that if Warrick does get in the end zone, all the fans join him in pointing to heaven.

Betty, your son done good!

Sincerely,
Rob Wilson

P.S. I'll try and write again soon.

CHAPTER 10

TAMPA BAY YEARS

I **CAN SCORE TOUCHDOWNS. THAT'S WHAT I DO BEST.**

And that's exactly what I told Tampa Bay Buccaneers coach Tony Dungy leading up to the NFL draft in 1997. Although I was viewed by NFL brass more as a situational back rather than an every-down player because of my size—here we go again!—I knew what I was capable of accomplishing on Sundays if given the opportunity. I can get the football into the end zone from anywhere on the field. I had been scoring touchdowns all my life, from Baton Rouge to Tallahassee, and I didn't want to stop doing it now. I may not talk a big game publicly, but I've played, and played well, in big games. I was looking forward to taking the next step—better yet, clearing that next hurdle—in my football career.

After finishing last in the NFL in scoring in 1996, the Buccaneers, who had made their mark on defense, had little choice but to try to surround quarterback Trent Dilfer with the kind of players who could give him a better chance to succeed. Coach Dungy felt that I was one of those players. I thought so, too, and I told him as much.

I am a man of few words, but I was determined to make a lasting impression on the Buccaneers and Coach Dungy when we talked for the first time at length at the NFL Scouting Combine. The Combine, held each February in preparation for April's draft, is a week-long showcase at the RCA Dome, home of the Indianapolis Colts, in Indianapolis, Indiana. It's really quite the show. We performed physical and mental tests in front of NFL coaches, general managers, scouts, and personnel directors. It's a big deal, and your performance at the Combine can affect your draft stock. Tests and evaluations include the 40-yard dash, bench press, vertical jump, drug screening, interviews, and the infamous Wonderlic Test, a twelve-minute, fifty-question exam that assesses aptitude for learning a job and adapting to solve problems.

My only problem was convincing NFL types I could do the job in their league.

Let me say this. I was immediately impressed by Tony Dungy when we met for our interview. He's a devout Christian with an even-tempered personality. Tony, like Coach Bowden, has played a major role in my life. But don't be fooled by his easy, gracious manner. Tony wants to win and he says what's on his mind. I knew I had to make my best sales pitch to Tony, and, thankfully, it worked, that yes, I was big enough and strong enough and durable enough to play in the NFL.

Coach Dungy called me a "complete player," complimenting me on my run-blocking and pass-catching abilities in addition to my running ability. He also noticed another quality when he watched film of me at FSU. Many times I was the guy who made the tackle for us following an interception. I guess it was the old cornerback coming out in me, and Dungy said that really impressed him from an attitude standpoint.

General Manager Rich McKay was also a member of the Buccaneers brass who interviewed me at the Combine. McKay enters each draft with two primary concerns about players—their football character and their personal character. McKay said I scored A-pluses in both categories. McKay also said that many people may think that Combine meet-and-greets are a waste of time, but he believes players can make an impact in these sessions. And I made an impact on McKay. He felt the two best player interviews he had at the Combine were with quarterback Danny Wuerffel and myself.

McKay felt the Bucs' top priority in the '97 draft was to add some juice and firepower to the offense, something to make opponents sit up and take notice. And McKay said I fit the criteria. Anyway you sliced it, the Bucs kept going back to one number: forty-seven. That's how many touchdowns I had scored in four years at FSU. Tampa Bay's career record for touchdowns heading into 1997 was forty-six by James Wilder.

Following the NFL Combine, Coach Dungy saw me again at a workout called "Pro Day" at Florida State. It's far more low-key than the Combine, but it's still a great opportunity to show off. NFL management, coaches, and scouts were able to watch draft-eligible players at FSU participate in speed and agility drills on our practice field near Doak Campbell Stadium. We weren't in pads, but you still wanted to make a good impression. I went about my business like I always did, ignoring concerns and whispers about my size and if I was durable enough to survive in the NFL. I wondered if these folks knew I never missed a practice or a game in my four years at FSU.

The FSU coaching staff was definitely in my corner. Strength coach Dave Van Halanger told NFL scouts to look at the film of my games at FSU. The film didn't lie. Running backs coach Billy Sexton joked that I would be fine because if you looked close enough, I was actually bigger than the football. Sexton had been at FSU for more than twenty years and had sent running backs of all shapes and sizes into the NFL, such as Sammie Smith, Dexter Carter, Amp Lee, and Edgar Bennett. Sexton said I was the best of the group, pointing to my speed, vision, and ability to change direction at the snap of a finger.

FSU head coach Bobby Bowden gave me the highest compliment during his pre-draft conversations with Dungy. Although Coach said he couldn't talk about my size and how it would translate into the NFL, he told Tony that of all the great players he had at FSU, including Deion Sanders, I was the best all-around player he had coached up to that time. Can you believe that? I didn't know how to respond to a compliment like that other than to thank him.

But was the NFL listening?

I really didn't pay attention to the pre-draft lists, but many of the so-called "experts" had the University of Houston's Antowain Smith ranked ahead of me. Smith was a big, fast runner whom NFL teams loved. He looked great getting off the bus at six feet two and 224 pounds, while I was listed by the NFL at five feet seven and 180 pounds, give or take an inch and a few pounds! Everyone agreed that I could play in the NFL, but in their minds it was a question of how much I could play. I already knew that answer: every offensive down of every game.

I was apprehensive leading up to the draft because you just never knew what was going to happen. Coaches and GMs who winked and smiled could be the same ones who didn't want you. The Bucs, who had two selections in the first round, entered the draft wanting to take a receiver and running back with their first two picks. McKay said Florida's Ike Hilliard was their top choice at receiver and I was their top choice at running back in front of Virginia's Tiki Barber. When Hilliard went seventh overall to the New York Giants, however, the Bucs had to quickly regroup.

Their next choice at receiver was Hilliard's teammate at Florida, Reidel Anthony. While McKay and his staff decided they could live without Anthony in the first round, they agreed they wouldn't sleep well that night if they didn't draft me in that opening round. Adding to their concern were draft-day rumors that Green Bay wanted to trade up for me. The Bucs began the day in the number eight slot, moved up to number six in a trade with the New York Jets, and then dropped to twelfth in a deal with the Seattle Seahawks with the intention of selecting me. And that's what they did, making me the first running back selected in the draft. Antowain Smith, who had been rated higher than me entering the draft, went twenty-third overall to the Buffalo Bills. The Bucs also got their receiver in Anthony with the sixteenth selection overall in the first round.

While the Tampa Bay media called me a "surprise pick"—again, size does matter to some—Florida State's presence in that first round was hardly a surprise. Defensive end Peter Boulware was selected fourth overall by Baltimore, offensive lineman Walter Jones went sixth to Seattle, and linebacker Reinard Wilson went two picks behind me at number fourteen to Cincinnati. That made four Seminoles in the top fourteen picks. Our good friends at Miami (Yatil Green, Kennard Lang, Kenny Holmes) and Florida (Hilliard and Anthony, a new teammate of mine) couldn't keep pace with us in that opening round. And it was also a good day for Ohio State offensive lineman Orlando Pace, who was the first overall selection by the St. Louis Rams.

Honestly, I was thrilled to be selected by the Bucs. It was the perfect chance to continue my career in Florida. My fan base was in Florida. Sure, everyone, myself included, knew the Bucs' Sad Sack history. When the franchise entered the league in 1976, the Buccaneers lost their first twenty-six games. After a brief winning era in the late 1970s and early 1980s, the team suffered through fourteen consecutive losing seasons. But change—for the better—was in the air.

Improvements started in 1995, when businessman Malcolm Glazer purchased the Buccaneers for $192 million, the highest price for a professional sports franchise to that point, following the death of previous owner Hugh Culverhouse. Glazer surprisingly outbid interested parties that included New York Yankees owner and part-time Tampa resident George Steinbrenner and Baltimore Orioles owner Peter Angelos. Glazer, who placed his sons Bryan, Edward, and Joel in charge of the team's financial affairs, also purchased Tampa Stadium's naming rights from the Tampa Sports Authority. They renamed the stadium Houlihan Stadium after one of the family's business ventures, the Houlihan's restaurant chain.

A year later, in 1996, the Bucs hired Tony Dungy as head coach after Tony served as a successful defensive coordinator for the Minnesota Vikings. The Glazers scrapped the old uniform designs, replacing the red and orange pirate with a red pirate flag on a pewter helmet. They also convinced Hillsborough County voters to raise sales taxes to partially fund the construction of Raymond James Stadium, which would be located next to old Tampa Stadium on Dale Mabry Highway near Tampa International Airport, and would be ready for the 1998 season.

While the Bucs continued to struggle in the first half of Dungy's first season, opening 1–8, the second half was a different story. The Bucs went 5–2, primarily behind Tony's successful Cover 2 defense, led by linebacker Hardy Nickerson and the maturing of players such as my former FSU teammate Derrick Brooks, John Lynch, and former Miami standout Warren Sapp. I later learned that Brooks, who was a junior at FSU when I was a freshman in 1993, was as good a salesman as he was a linebacker. Brooks stopped by Dungy's office nearly every afternoon leading up to the draft and made sure I was on the Bucs' minds. Brooks stuck his head into Tony's office and said, "We need number twenty-eight! We need number twenty-eight!" Tony laughed and said Brooks drove him crazy and he had no other choice but to take me in the first round in 1997.

I also knew I had the chance to make a good first impression during training camp because returning tailback starter Errict Rhett, who played at the University of Florida, was unhappy with his contract situation. Rhett had held out for ninety-four days and missed seven games in 1996 in an unsuccessful attempt to renegotiate his contract after rushing for more than 1,000 yards in 1994 and 1995. While I would also learn in a few years that the NFL is a business first and a game second, I was ready to play and help make a difference.

Of course, everyone wanted to size me up, the Buccaneers included.

Many NFL executives felt I could be a great situational player but not a featured back in the NFL. I was the kind of player who could give defensive coordinators fits, but you'd better have other runners ready. Even though I was among the quickest players in the draft—I was clocked at 4.26 in the 40 in a pre-draft workout session—some questioned whether the Buccaneers' between-the-tackles running game would be the ideal fit for me. While Coach Dungy believed in me, he admittedly hedged, telling me I could still be special in a limited role. In addition to the powerfully built Rhett, the Bucs also had a bruising running back in Mike Alstott, who enjoyed a phenomenal rookie season in 1996 and was a first alternate selection for the Pro Bowl.

To determine my role, I had to get to training camp that opened in late July. But I also wanted to be treated fairly, and my agent at the time, Leigh Steinberg, was regarded as one of the country's leading sports attorneys. God had taught me patience and I relied on it during contract talks. Still, I missed only the first five days of camp as Steinberg negotiated with McKay. We agreed to a six-year, $8.6 million contract that included a $3.5 million signing bonus—more money than I ever knew existed. I was scheduled to earn base salaries of $550,000 in 1997, $687,500 in 1998, $825,000 in 1999, $962,500 in 2000, $1.1 million in 2001, and $1.2375 million in 2002.

The major sticking point in negotiations was our insistence on a contract that would be voided after the fourth season if I reached certain incentives. But the Bucs insisted on making it voidable after five years, when you become a free agent under NFL rules, as they had in negotiations with fellow first-round pick Anthony. The Bucs got their way, but that was fine. I just wanted to get into camp yesterday and help make a difference. I also wanted to make a difference in people's lives, and this is where and when my charity work began to take shape. Despite my ultraconservative approach with money, I was willing to share it—but not to spend it.

When I finally signed the contract's dotted line, everyone was happy, especially me. I had spent most of my time working out, so I was ready to join my teammates once I signed my contract. If I wanted to relax, I either drove around Tampa or rented movies. I rented so many movies that Steinberg actually called me the "Siskel and Ebert" of his client list, comparing me to those two Chicago film critics, Gene Siskel and Roger Ebert. All I knew was I couldn't wait to sign my contract and join the Buccaneer organization. I wasn't there to save it. I just wanted to help.

And as a rookie and the top pick, I helped in another big way—I had to make sure the veterans were fed breakfast every Saturday morning. We're not talking Wheaties and a banana, either. Hardy Nickerson, for example, liked a certain donut. He might be the only person who ate that donut, but you still had to buy enough donuts for everyone. Then there was the time I forgot to tell a fellow rookie that it was his turn to buy breakfast. Big mistake. That meant the veterans didn't have anything to eat that particular Saturday morning. That meant the veterans were very, very angry. And that meant us rookies were in deep, deep trouble. Unfortunately, there wasn't anywhere to hide. The veterans tied the rookies together in the middle of the locker room, doused us with powder, and tossed us into the cold showers. Needless to say, the veterans were fed breakfast and ate like royalty that next Saturday morning.

McKay joked that the worst day in a personnel director's life is the first day of mini-camp following the draft. That's when coaches experience amnesia when it comes to drafted players, especially if they play poorly. Thankfully, I made a good first impression, and McKay, despite my size, also liked my strength after contact on runs. I was jacked to get started. The exhibition season was used to find the right chemistry in the backfield between myself, Rhett, and Alstott. In our exhibition opener against the Redskins, I ripped off a 38-yard run on my fourth carry. By the end of training camp, I had established myself as an integral part of the offense. Offensive coordinator Mike Shula said he expected me to touch the football in three areas—rushing, receiving, and special teams. Dilfer also was excited to have me in his backfield, telling sportswriters, "You can do everything you want with him. There are only a couple of running backs in this league you can say that about. He will be a star because of that." I wasn't looking to be the star. I just wanted to help the Bucs win. The organization, players, and fans were tired of losing.

Rookies on the team also stuck together. Ronde Barber, a cornerback from Virginia who I played against while I was at FSU and knew from a few quick hellos on the field, and I hit it off immediately. Ronde's twin brother, Tiki, who also played at Virginia, was drafted in the second round by the New York Giants. Ronde and I respected each other and really didn't have to try hard to be friends. Ronde, with that great smile and personality, was more outgoing than me—imagine that!—but it seemed like we spent every minute together those first few months. We were roommates and stayed at an extended-stay hotel off the Veterans Expressway. While Ronde and I took advantage of an endorsement contract I signed with a local car dealer, we drove around the campuses of the University of Tampa and South Florida in a Jaguar with the top down so we could see the pretty women (and the pretty women could see us). Sure, my 1993 Mitsubishi Galant might not have been as sporty as a Jaguar, but it had only 60,000 miles on it and was as dependable as the day was long.

I wanted to show the Bucs I was dependable, too.

I started in our season opener at home against San Francisco and finished with 37 yards on eight carries. I also had a 67-yard kickoff return called back. If there was a game during my rookie year that proved I belonged in the NFL, it was the second game of the season against the Detroit Lions in Detroit. I rushed for 130 yards on twenty-four carries, scored my first professional touchdown on a 6--yard run, caught two passes, and returned a punt in a 24–17 victory. My ESPN highlight run went for 49 yards as I busted the arm tackle of linebacker Antonio London and outran safety Mark Carrier. I had 116 yards on fifteen carries by halftime, and it was the first time in a year that the Bucs had a 100-yard rushing game. On the airplane flight back to Tampa following the game, Coach Dungy kept stopping by my seat and looking at me. I asked him what he was doing, and Tony said he was checking on me to make sure I was okay. I laughed and told Tony I wasn't sore from the game, that I felt great and was ready to do it again next Sunday at Minnesota. Tony never had to worry about me after that Detroit game, though he also admitted he thought twenty-four carries in a game were too many for me.

It seemed like everything was coming together for the Buccaneers and me that first season. We started 5–0 with victories over San Francisco, Detroit, Minnesota, Miami, and Arizona. After dropping our next three games, we rebounded with victories over Indianapolis and New England to set the tone for the remainder of the year. We finished 10–6 and made the playoffs as a wild-card team, marking our first winning season and playoff appearance since 1982. In our final home game before moving next door to newly built Raymond James Stadium, we beat the Detroit Lions 20–10 in the opening round of the playoffs. But our ride ended the following week at

Lambeau Field against eventual NFL champion Green Bay, whom we had lost to twice in the regular season. We dropped our third game to the Packers, 21–7. I had 64 yards on eighteen carries, but our only score was Alstott's 6-yard run in the third quarter that made it 13–7.

Deep down, I knew I could be an impact player in my rookie season. And I was rewarded for my efforts when I was named the NFL Offensive Rookie of the Year by the Associated Press in 1997. What made that accomplishment even better was that my former Florida State teammate, Peter Boulware, who was drafted fourth overall by the Baltimore Ravens, was named the NFL Defensive Rookie of the Year, making it a Garnet & Gold sweep. The last time college teammates came into the NFL and won the rookie honors was in 1992, when Kansas City cornerback Dale Carter and Cincinnati wide receiver Carl Pickens did it out of Tennessee.

I was also the only rookie to make the Pro Bowl in 1997. I rushed for 978 yards and four touchdowns, caught a team-high thirty-nine passes for 462 yards and three scores, and from the beginning was the impact player that I had envisioned. I was even honored as the NFC offensive player of the week after my first two games in the league. Still, I wish I could have scored more touchdowns and gained more yards. Honestly, I didn't feel I was as consistent as I would have liked over the long haul. After a fast start, my production slowed, probably due to fatigue, before gaining 360 yards on seventy-five carries in the last four games. But as a rookie, I knew that over time I would get stronger mentally and physically and grow wiser to the game.

Mike Shula, the Bucs' offensive coordinator, described me as a player who could take it the distance just about any time I touched the football. Shula said my talents took pressure off Dilfer, Alstott, my receivers, and the offensive line. His comments made me feel good because I helped our offense improve from twenty-second to eleventh in rushing. I had five 100-yard games and ripped off a franchise-record 76-yard run against Chicago in the regular-season finale that showed why my style was being compared with that of four-time league rushing champion Barry Sanders. I had eight plays of more than 29 yards and my seven touchdowns averaged 33 yards. The Bucs had just fifteen plays longer than 29 yards and only one touchdown of at least 33 yards as a team a year earlier. "Anytime you get a guy who can put the ball in the end zone like that, you should be better," Shula said. I also knew I wanted to get better, too.

I was fortunate that FSU helped me prepare for the NFL. Guys like Boulware and me were able to experience things that other play-ers around the country weren't able to, like the hoopla surrounding the big games, the daily media demands, the expectations. It gave me a small taste of what to expect on Sundays. It was just a matter of making adjustments for a sixteen-game season. Of course, I had my share of critics who thought that because of my size, I couldn't make that adjustment from college to professional football. That's why I felt so gratified—but not satisfied—when my selection by a nation-wide panel of sportswriters and broadcasters helped give FSU a sweep of the AP's rookie awards. I was one of four running backs among the top five players who received votes in Rookie of the Year honors on offense. I received twenty-eight votes, while Corey Dillon of the Bengals had thirteen. Antowain Smith of the Bills and Tiki Barber of the Giants received one vote each. I was the first Bucca-neer to be selected top offensive rookie and was a key reason we had our best year since 1979 and made the playoffs for the first time in fifteen years. The January Pro Bowl in Honolulu was a great honor, too. My chair at the resort where we stayed was right next to one of my heroes, Barry Sanders.

I worried about my family in Baton Rouge, of course. Everyone says long-distance romances are tough. Try raising your younger brothers and sisters from three states away. I tried to get back to

Baton Rouge as much as possible, but it was nearly impossible during the season. My family traveled to Tampa to watch me play, but it was just as difficult for everyone to get away. While Derrick and I continued to butt heads and argue when we talked or saw each other, I knew he could fend for himself. Derrick was tough, and he was temperamental. But he was there for his brothers and sisters, too, and I appreciated it. Still, final decisions that concerned our family were my responsibility and at times he didn't understand that. Summer was adjusting well and was attending Louisiana Tech. But the three youngest, Bricson, Travis, and Samantha, were struggling. There were self-doubts, peer pressure, and temptations. I knew I had to make a decision. As I prepared for my second season in 1998 with the Bucs, I moved the three of them in with me in a four-bedroom home I purchased in Tampa.

Bricson was seventeen. Travis was sixteen. Samantha was fifteen. I was twenty-three.

It was like I had two jobs—playing for the Buccaneers and raising my family. Neither was easy. I knew the Bucs were concerned about the arrangement and felt I was distracted. They wanted me to hire a person to manage the household, but I just didn't feel comfortable with that suggestion. I wasn't going to pay a person to do something I felt I could handle. But it was tough. Other players headed out after practice for a meal or to socialize, but I headed home to help with homework and deal with the day's challenges. I was harsh. I yelled. I was mean. Bricson, Travis, and Samantha resisted the move because it wasn't home. It wasn't Baton Rouge. But I accepted it as my responsibility as their older brother and legal guardian to make sure they stayed on the right path. It was difficult for all of us, but I didn't complain. It was something I had to do. I had given up my time and life to make this work.

The main reason I had Briscon and Travis move to Tampa was because they weren't doing well at Redemptorist Senior High. They had each flunked a class and had to attend summer school. I was livid, and that was the last straw. I told them to pack their belongings, they were moving to Tampa. Derrick complained that I was the family dictator. He was right. My vote was the only one that counted. We nearly came to blows about my decision to move the three to Tampa, but I had no other choice. I enrolled them in Tampa Catholic High School and laid down the law. While Bricson and Samantha tried to make the best of their situation, Travis wasn't a happy camper. In fact, he turned into a camper.

Travis and I didn't talk for what seemed like six months. One night I was so angry at him that I told him if he didn't want to live by my rules, he could get out of my house. So he did—literally. With a blanket in hand, Travis slept outside on a patio chair by the pool for a couple of nights. Samantha opened the sliding glass door and let him in each morning so he could get dressed. Travis still didn't say a word to me. I know those Florida mosquitoes had to have been eating him alive because he eventually moved back into his room. We didn't speak to each other for the longest time.

Once they settled in, Bricson and Travis played football and ran track at TC, and both did well, too. Bricson ran the 100 meters, Travis was a state champion in the 200 meters his senior season, and their 4×100 relay team placed second in a photo finish. Coach Dungy's wife, Lauren, also was a big help. It reached a point where I admitted to myself that I couldn't do it alone, and Mrs. Dungy was there to add a mother's touch. Mrs. Dungy attended school meetings, helped with homework, and helped provide a soothing voice when I wanted to pull my hair out and just scream. I had to learn on the run. I mean, I had never even used an ATM card until I lived in Tampa.

Tampa Bay's identity during the Dungy era and my five years with the team was one of defense, fast and physical. Try as we might, we could never establish an offensive identity. There were games where we featured the power running of Alstott. I, the finesse guy, was the featured back in other games. And then there would be games where both Alstott and I would line up in the backfield—Mike at fullback and me at tailback. It sounded like a great plan on paper, since both of us were Pro Bowlers, but games are won on the field and not on paper. Many called it a mishmash of game-day agendas. But I worked hard, did what I was told, and was determined to make the most of any situation.

I led the Buccaneers in rushing in 1998, my second year, with 1,026 yards on 245 carries. I became just the fifth runner in team history to crack the 1,000-yard mark. I started fourteen of sixteen games and became the first primary rusher in team history to average more than 4.0 yards per carry for two consecutive seasons. I also played my first regular-season NFL game in New Orleans in '98. Naturally, since I was returning home to Louisiana, everyone wanted to talk about my mom's death, but I told the media I didn't want to talk about it anymore since it only brought up all the bad memories my family has had to endure. A three-game losing streak in mid-season slowed any momentum we built, and we won our last game of the regular season to finish a disappointing 8–8.

Our defense carried us for most of the 1999 season. The offense managed to score more than 20 points only once in the first seven games, which led to Shaun King's promotion to the team's starting quarterback. The move sparked us as we won six games in a row at one point and clinched the NFL Central crown with a franchise-best record of 11–5. We beat the Washington Redskins 14–13 in the opening round of the playoffs before a record crowd of 65,835 at Raymond James Stadium, but we lost in St. Louis to the Rams in the NFC championship game. That game hurt. We drove down the field in the final minutes for the win against the Rams, but a first-down pass reception from King to Bert Emanuel was overturned on an instant replay ruling.

The 1999 season was a difficult one for me. I started fifteen of sixteen regular-season games—I missed the Minnesota game with an ankle sprain and most of the preseason with a hamstring injury—but I only rushed for 616 yards on 195 carries. Alstott carried the running load, while my focus shifted more to receiving out of the backfield. I caught a team-leading sixty-four passes for 589 yards (9.2 average) and two touchdowns and returned kickoffs in the playoffs, averaging 19.5 yards on eight returns. The season taught me a lot, that I can't change my style and the way I run. When you are injured and put in a box, it's kind of hard to do anything. But I wasn't going to change. I was determined to go out and run and use my instincts. That's what got me into the league.

It was in 2000 when I dispelled the theory that I was too small to take a pounding or that I was best suited as only a third-down back. When Alstott went down with a sprained knee against Chicago in mid-November, I proved I could carry the Bucs' offense. Both Mike and I entered that Chicago game with 124 carries each in the first ten games. When Mike sprained a ligament in his left knee early in the game, I ended up carrying the football seventeen times against the Bears and averaged 21.4 carries and 112 yards over the next five games. The highlight came against a team and player I idolized while growing up in Louisiana—the Dallas Cowboys and Emmitt Smith—in early December. My running back teammate, Rabih Abdullah, laughed and said I looked like a kid in the sandbox because I was having so much fun. He was right. The first time I touched the football against the Cowboys, I ran 70 yards for a touchdown. It's a huge difference when you are the main ball carrier. I can stay patient, even if the holes don't immediately open up. I finished with a career-best 210 yards and three touchdowns. As I approached the bench toward the end of the game, the first player who rushed out to me with a congratulatory hug was Alstott. We were friends who pulled for each other and admired each other. When I had a big game at Florida State, I called my grandmother in Baton Rouge and asked her to package up some home cooking for my offensive linemen. I thought about doing that after the Cowboys game, calling her to say, "Hey, Grandma, get ready for the all-time takeout order!"

We expected more in 2000, though. We acquired receiver Keyshawn Johnson from the Jets in a trade prior to the season in an effort to give the offense an added dimension. At 10–5, we needed a win in our final game in Green Bay to win the NFC Central for the second consecutive season. But with temperatures in the low forties—we had never won a game before in those cooler conditions—we lost in overtime 17–14. Our kicker, Martin Gramatica, missed a 35-yard field goal for the victory at the end of regulation. We clinched a wild card for the playoffs, but lost in Philadelphia 20–3.

It was an extremely frustrating finish, one that made it hard to enjoy my personal accomplishments. I had a career-high and team-best 1,133 rushing yards on 248 attempts and eight touchdowns. I was also third on the team with forty-four receptions for 422 yards. My rushing total was the most since Errict Rhett had 1,207 yards in 1995, and I was the third Buccaneer besides James Wilder and Rhett to reach 1,000 rushing yards twice in a career. After I gained just 366 yards in the first half of the season, I more than doubled that over the last eight games (767) as I became the go-to guy on offense.

I was excited about the 2001 season because the Bucs wanted to be a perimeter running team that featured me in the backfield. I hadn't seen a commitment like that since I played at Florida State. The Bucs drafted tackle Kenyatta Walker out of Florida to help strengthen the offensive line, and offensive coordinator Clyde Christensen told the media he planned to utilize my talents. In my first fifty-eight games over four seasons, I had rushed the football twenty times in only six games—and never once back to back. When Alstott injured his knee late in 2000 and the team was reluctant to rely on

King's throwing arm, they handed me the ball. I had twenty-plus carries in four consecutive games, and we won them all to clinch a playoff berth. After relying on an offensive front that featured drive blockers, we now had players up front who could pull and trap and execute blocks in small spaces, where I thrived. We also signed free agent quarterback Brad Johnson, a Florida State alum, in hopes of revitalizing the offense.

Under my contract, I was also going to be an unrestricted free agent following the season. Tampa was now my home and I wanted to remain with the Bucs. While I wanted to get a new deal done, no substantive negotiations had taken place between the Bucs and myself. That was fine and I didn't consider it a snub. I planned to honor my contract. Still, I wanted the Bucs to believe in me and show they believed in me. I was also an empty nester at age twenty-six. My younger brothers and sisters were now on their own. Bricson, Travis, and Samantha each had graduated from Tampa Catholic High School and moved back to Baton Rouge. While I was no longer weighed down by the burdens of surrogate fatherhood, my family was still my primary responsibility. But I also knew I didn't have the pressures of home on me after practice and games. Even general manager Rich McKay thought I was burdened from the stresses and strains of outside pressures, but it gotten more manageable the past two years. All I knew was that I was hungry and I wanted the football more than ever.

Of course, there are days when things don't work out the way you would like. The 2001 season was, well, one of those days. A long, long day.

I was slowed for two months of the season with nagging foot and hamstring injuries. Alstott was recovered from his knee injury, so we again faced the dilemma of who should be carrying the rushing load when I returned. It wasn't our fight. Coach Dungy and Coach Christensen had to figure it out. They knew they had two running backs capable of doing pretty much anything they wanted to. They had to figure out a way to utilize us and let us get into a rhythm. I didn't want thirty carries a game and told Tony as much. Brad Johnson probably summed it up best when he told the media the Buccaneers needed both of us to make plays for the team. Still, it seemed like I was in the wrong place at the wrong time most of the season. I did not play in games against Green Bay, Minnesota, and our regular-season finale against Philadelphia. I played but did not start against Tennessee. The signature bursts at the line of scrimmage I was known for weren't there, and all everyone wanted to talk about were negative runs. I didn't make it to the line of scrimmage on twenty-four plays. I was frustrated and low, so low I could sit on a dime and swing my legs.

Of course, rumors swirled around Coach Dungy's future. We made the playoffs, but the season was considered a major disappointment, which led to speculation that Bill Parcells was in line to become our next head coach. The media and fans believed we needed to beat the Eagles in Philadelphia in the first round of the playoffs to help save Coach Dungy's job. But we lost in Philly 31–9, and Dungy was fired on January 14, 2002. Bucs management contended that Tony's conservative offense was too inconsistent for NFL teams. In three of our last four playoff defeats, the offense did not score a touchdown.

My season wasn't much to write home about. I rushed for just 447 yards on 158 carries—my top performance was 65 yards against Minnesota in the season's second week—and ranked second on the team with a career-high sixty-eight catches for 557 yards and three scores in 2001. While Coach Dungy was hired eight days later as the head coach for the Indianapolis Colts, Parcells had a last-minute change of heart and the Bucs were forced to scramble and find another coach. It would take more than two months for the Bucs to land Jon Gruden from Oakland in a deal that included Tampa Bay's

2002 and 2003 first- and second-round draft picks and $8 million in cash. The Bucs had expressed an earlier interest in Gruden, but Oakland owner Al Davis had originally refused to release Gruden from his contract.

When our season ended, I was unsure of my future in Tampa. I was an unrestricted free agent. The critics were back, the same ones who had questioned my size, my toughness, and my durability when I arrived in Tampa four years earlier. Jeez, here we go again.

Honestly, I didn't know if I would be back.

The nature of the business is such that we all could be gone tomorrow.

Look at that game face. From a very young age, when I stepped onto the football field it was all business . . .

. . . but I sure cleaned up nice for my school photos. Mom wouldn't have it any other way.

This is my mom's game face. She did her uniform proud . . .

. . . but she was always a mom first. I must've been going to something special because I haven't been decked out like that since.

My mom and me after my last high school football game.

The three oldest Dunn kids— Derrick, Summer, and me. Even three years after Mom's passing, Derrick had a tough time smiling.

Left: I am literally running for my life in Doak S. Campbell Stadium. COURTESY OF FLORIDA STATE SPORTS INFORMATION

Below: Just breaking another tackle on a Sunday afternoon. COURTESY OF TAMPA BAY BUCCANEERS

Above: A picture of my grandmother at her best celebrating her seventieth birthday.

Left: Choo Choo and me the night I hit 10,000 yards.

Below: At the Kentucky Derby with my sisters Summer and Samantha, both looking beautiful and showing me up!

Me kidding around with some soldiers at a military base in Kuwait. I'm a big supporter of our troops, especially when it's clear they like my jokes.

I loved helping this mother and daughter own their first home through my Homes for the Holidays organization in 2006. COURTESY OF THE WARRICK DUNN FOUNDATION

For a running back, there's no feeling like breaking loose and making a big play to help your team win. COURTESY OF JIMMY CRIBB

I'm receiving the Walter Payton Man of the Year Award at the Superbowl in Jacksonville. With me are two special people: Walter Payton's wife and NFL representative, Connie Payton, and Arthur Blank, the Falcons owner and the man who gave me a fresh start in Atlanta. COURTESY OF JIMMY CRIBB

The Dunn brothers and sisters today. From left to right in the back row: Derek, me, Travis, and Bricson. Summer and Samantha are sitting pretty in the front row. We're all smiles . . . well, at least Derek's trying.

CHAPTER 11

CHARITABLE APPROACH

ONE OF THE MOST IMPORTANT LESSONS I LEARNED FROM my mother's life was to never lose sight of where all blessings come from, and the responsibility we have as human beings to look after and serve one another. She lived that example every day, not just in the helping hand that she often gave to our neighbors or in her quiet thankfulness for what we had, but also in her choice of careers.

Police officers do not do what they do for the money, because it's just not there. Police do what they do because they love their fellow human beings and because they know that their work will serve the greater good of the community. My mother modeled giving her all for every moment of her time on earth, and it was one of the life lessons for which I am the most grateful.

I always knew that if I ever got a shot in the NFL, I would use the opportunity to change the lives of other people. But through high school and college, with everything that was going on in my life, the NFL always seemed a long way off. It was always on my mind, especially later in college, but it's hard to really formulate concrete plans when you're still just banking on a dream.

So when I was drafted by the Bucs, I knew that my chance had finally come, but now I was faced with the questions of *what* and *how?*

Thankfully, the Buccaneers had already anticipated this need for its players and had hired Stephanie Waller for its community relations department. Stephanie's job was to work with players who were interested in doing charity and community outreach and to help put their plans in action. This was something that Coach Dungy promoted heavily. He wanted to make sure that his players were personally invested in the lives of the fans who make our careers possible.

The first month with the Bucs organization was intense; there was training camp, of course, and new player orientation and meeting hundreds of new people and attending countless social events. In the midst of that, though, Stephanie made a presentation to the new players, telling us what her job was and what she did with the players to help coordinate giving. In closing, Coach Dungy told us, "If you are going to live here, you need to be part of the community." When he said that, it really encouraged me to do something different; it really challenged me to try to think of what I could do that would really have an impact.

Just a few weeks after Stephanie's presentation, we finally got to talk one on one. I was walking down a hallway in the Bucs building when Stephanie stepped out of her office to introduce herself. She laughs when I tell this story because, according to her, she just planned on saying hello to me and not taking any more time from "the popular new rookie," but I immediately launched into an indepth conversation about my desire to get involved with community work. I didn't even let her get back to her office; I just jumped right into it.

One of the things that the NFL stresses with its player outreach programs is that it shouldn't be about the budget or dollar amount, but about what is in the person's heart and their background. Their goal is to help players who want to give to really find their passion, to really identify what it is that moves them to give and motivates them to get involved.

My passion wasn't easy to identify at first. It just seemed like there were so many options and each one seemed important, but not quite right. I knew, for example, that I didn't want to provide a few families with a Thanksgiving turkey each year and consider my work done. A holiday meal is great and it meets a need, but it doesn't change a life. It's something temporary, something that is over and done with within a few hours. I wanted to change lives, I wanted to impact people for the long term, something that would help them on the path to better opportunities.

For me, the goal wasn't to do "charity." Charity is something consumable, something breakable, something that can wear out. The word "charity" actually means "love," but in today's society, it often carries the idea of pity, and that was definitely what I wanted to avoid. I thought about my mother and her humble soul but her proud spirit. She didn't want our family to be pitied; she wanted us to have a sense of accomplishment and of achievement. She believed in working for what you want and fostering personal responsibility because that is the surest way to respect. I wanted to help other families reach that goal.

Over the next few days and weeks, Stephanie threw out a variety of suggestions. When she mentioned a wonderful program called "Paint Your Heart Out, Tampa," I knew we were finally getting on the right track. The goal of Paint Your Heart Out is to identify the needs of disadvantaged home owners in the community and help them with repairs. For example, an elderly couple might need a new hot water heater, or a family with a disabled child might need help with yard work and maintenance. The organization steps in and meets that need.

Stephanie suggested that we look at putting air conditioners into homes; that's something that is an absolute necessity in Tampa. That started to hit closer to home for me because she kept asking me what I could relate to—what had happened in my life that I really understood in a first-hand way. I didn't know anyone with cancer or another serious disease, so that didn't seem like it was quite the right route for me. But wanting a place to live with the appliances working and a sense of permanence—I knew something about that.

That idea appealed to me and it was definitely getting closer to what I still couldn't quite articulate. Even so, it just wasn't what I felt called to do. I wanted to do something bigger because I had been so blessed.

I kept asking myself over and over, "What could I do that is something I relate to?" Home repair was definitely getting closer, but it still wasn't quite right. And one of the words I always used was *passionate*. I felt like I needed something that I've been through to eventually become a passion of mine. Stephanie and I had several conversations as we tried to find the right angle of helping to fix not only people's homes but their lives as well. I understood the magnitude of home ownership through home repair programs, but I couldn't figure out what my passion was in helping people to manage so large an undertaking.

She asked me what moved me and finally, one day I just blurted out that when I drive down the street and see a woman at a bus station with a child on her hip and another holding her hand, I just think, *What a tough life. She's got to wait on the bus to take the children to day school and then she's got to get back on the bus to go to work in order to provide for them.* I knew I wanted to do something to help those women out, but I just didn't know how to help them, how to fix it for them.

I told Stephanie that my mom always wanted to own a home but she couldn't afford the down payment. Then Stephanie mentioned working with an organization that provides housing to struggling families; I immediately knew that was the way for me to go. One of the most daunting challenges for single-parent families is saving enough for a down payment on a home in a better neighborhood. It's almost impossible, when you're living from paycheck to paycheck, to scrape together enough money to make that first deposit on a place that will enable you to get your family into a better situation. I wanted to help deserving families take that first step.

But even the down payment wasn't quite enough. I still wanted to do something else, something bigger. I wanted to make sure that these families had no excuse to fail because if you have struggled your whole life and finally take that big risk and it doesn't work out, most people will be too discouraged to ever try again. The children need a model of success to help break the cycle of poverty.

The next day, Stephanie approached me with the idea that we fill the homes with everything the family would need—all of those little expenses of not just owning but maintaining a home—so that they would be able to make it work. "That's it!" I said. "*That's* what I want to do."

What I had been through was watching my mom struggle just to pay rent, watching her want to buy a home but never quite reaching the point where she could achieve it. That was one of her dreams and her goals. One of the reasons we felt that we should furnish the whole house was because the people I wanted to help could afford the down payment but they couldn't afford to furnish the house. We wanted to eliminate every possibility for them to fail, and to set them up for success.

As a child growing up in a variety of apartments, I craved continuity. I wanted to have the growth marks in the doorway where Mom measured our height each year. I wanted to have memories—memories of breaking the window or having a family birthday; memories in the dining room, or of playing inside, playing basketball, wrestling on the floor, playing carpet football. We broke a lot of stuff and we bumped a lot of stuff. Sometimes you want to know where you bumped your head, or where, when you were six years old, you ran around the corner and hit the wall. Those are the type of memories I felt like I didn't have because they were so spread out over so many different places. I wanted to know the story of each bump in the wall or smudge on the paint. I wanted to feel like the rooms knew us and knew our stories and were a part of our lives, rather than just where we slept at night for a few months or a few years.

I know my mother wanted that, too. She had always wanted to buy a house for our family, so the six of us kids could really have a place to call home and have a sense of ownership of something tangible. She wanted a center for the family—a place where we could return with our spouses and our children. She spent years working toward that goal, and never got to see it realized.

From a child's point of view, having a room of my own in our own home would have been the greatest luxury I could imagine, and I couldn't quite understand why it was so difficult to achieve.

But from an adult point of view, there is so much more to buying a house than just finding the money to make a down payment, not to mention finding a bank that is willing to give a mortgage to a single mother with six children, no matter how hard she is working. There are the cleaning supplies and the lawn mower to think about. There is the fact that if the heater goes, you can't just call the maintenance man to fix it—you have to pay for the repairs yourself.

And, of course, there are the long-term goals to consider. You know how you are always so careful about avoiding that first scuff on a new pair of shoes, but you'll tramp through the mud in an old pair? The pride of not only ownership but also the desire to maintain something as nice and new was what I wanted to make sure would be instilled in each recipient.

I wanted the family to have a sense of personal responsibility—a demonstrated willingness to commit to a new lifestyle. I wanted them to have taken classes on financial management, on building or rebuilding their credit history, on understanding the intricacies of home ownership. Courses like these are usually offered as part of Habitat for Humanity or a city's first-time home buyers' program, and I wanted the families I helped to have been involved in those classes.

What does it say about a family if, after they take possession of their new home, the yard is full of weeds and trash in six months? Or if they fail to make their mortgage payments after a year because they couldn't hold a job? That doesn't help lift people out of poverty; it only moves the mind-set of poverty to a new place.

My goal, by stocking each house with all of the necessary supplies to keep it up, was to help with that sense of newness and pride. I wanted new furniture, new linens, new pots and pans—everything that a family could hope for as they truly started over with their lives.

Once Stephanie and I determined what my mission was and identified what kind of family I was looking for, our next step was to figure out where to find these families. Stephanie knew a member of the Tampa city council named Bob Clark, so she called him and he pointed us in the direction of the mayor's First-Time Home Ownership Program. It was an organization sponsored by a combination of the City of Tampa and private grants that helped families purchase their first homes. The participants had to go through a variety of courses like the ones I had envisioned, and then they were able to get assistance to make that first down payment.

I asked the program to send me a profile sheet on each of its eligible single-parent families that told me about their lives, their children, their jobs, their goals, and basically just helped me to get to know them on paper. Stephanie went out to each house that the families were trying to buy and took photographs of the home itself as well as the neighborhood, and put it together in a packet for me, so I really had a complete picture when I sat down to make my decision.

It was exciting, but it was also challenging. We didn't have much corporate sponsorship that first year, and many of the companies we contacted didn't seem to quite grasp what we were doing. They didn't seem to understand how complete we wanted each house to be when the families moved in, and to be fair, I wasn't even exactly sure how many families I could take on that first year.

I had been looking for a way to express the essence of what I was envisioning, but somehow I just couldn't seem to boil it down. Finally, one day Stephanie was in a meeting with someone who said dismissively, "You can't expect to fill a house to the point that all they do is walk in with their clothes and their toothbrushes."

She said, "Yes! That's it exactly! That's what he wants. Thank you for putting it into words."

The idea still seemed a bit radical to most people—a house that is more than move-in ready, but also life ready? A home that is completely put together, from a stocked pantry to a full linen closet to an operational toolshed? Not too many corporations were willing to bite at that, so we were absolutely thrilled when we received word that a furniture company had agreed to step forward and donate everything we would need. I couldn't believe it—this was the kind of corporate/community cooperation I had only dreamed of.

The first year, I selected four families. Each of the mothers was very different from the others, and I wanted each home to reflect their uniqueness. We found everything we could about the color and style preferences of each woman and tried to adapt our purchases accordingly. We also tried to make the bedrooms special for each child, so that they could see a part of themselves reflected in their new home.

All of our work was done in secret. The families had no idea that they had been chosen for this surprise. Our goal was to have them moved in by Christmas, and we moved forward with our plans, getting ready to stock the houses just a few days before the papers were signed. Things were really coming together when we received some terrible news: two weeks before the big day the furniture company backed out. They decided that they would not be able to make the donations after all.

It was a severe blow, but it was short-lived. A small family operation in the Tampa area, connected with Badcock Furniture, told us that even though they couldn't afford to donate everything outright, they could give it to us at cost. It was a gesture that helped us out of a pinch and made a huge difference in helping to launch the program. We were able to get the sofas, tables, beds, and mattresses moved in on time, and everything looked absolutely beautiful.

I also purchased appliances and made sure the fridge was full and that each family had at least six months 'worth of laundry detergent waiting for them. And after one of Stephanie's shopping trips for the homes' provisions, she remarked on how cheap toothbrushes were, so we amended our unofficial motto. The families only needed to show up with their clothes. Of course, we'd supplied the toothbrushes, too!

I have to admit that I did feel bad about what we did to get the families to come to the houses for the grand reveal because it involved a lot of lying on everyone's part. We told the mothers that they needed to come to their new house in order to sign the closing papers, and that they needed to bring the kids along, too. Some of them would ask why they needed to take the kids out of school and Stephanie would have to tell them, "Oh, it's the one hundredth house in the First-Time Home Ownership Program and we're going to have balloons and a few photos" or something like that.

They still didn't have any idea what was coming.

The reception from each family was as unique as they were. The first woman was very quiet. She had a small baby whom she held very close as she walked from room to room, just taking it all in. She was very excited, but also a little overwhelmed and just thanked us with smiles and tears.

Another recipient didn't speak much English, so her children had to translate for her. This made it a little more difficult to convey what we were doing, but once she finally understood, she just cried and cried.

Maybe the most memorable experience that first year was the woman who scooped me up into a giant bear hug and said, "I think I'm going to squeeze him to death!" and she did hug me so enthusiastically that I actually came up off the floor. I've never been hugged so hard in my life—and this was all before she had even gone inside the house. At that point, she just knew that we'd made the down payment. Once we went inside and she saw everything that was waiting for her, she was laughing and crying and shouting and clapping and hugging. It was wonderful to watch. With each room she went into, she'd come running back out and say, "Where is that little man? I want to hug him!"

For many of the children, it was the first time they had ever had anything new in their lives, and it was wonderful to see them looking around with huge eyes, like they were in a palace. We made sure to have fresh flowers in vases so that everything looked welcoming, and all of the women were just so happy with how beautiful everything was.

It was just the most amazing feeling to watch those four families receive their homes with such excitement and gratitude. I had done it for the families, of course, but I had also, in a small way, done it for myself. I could see myself and my siblings in each of those children as they raced around, checking out their rooms and their yard, and I could see my mother in each of the women as they unlocked the front door with a smile that came from the very depths of their souls.

It had taken a while, but I'd realized my dream. I was finally able to translate my talent on the football field into something truly meaningful for hard-working, determined people who didn't want handouts, but just needed a boost. I knew that was what my mother would have been the most proud of: not my records, not my awards, but the way I used my worldly success to give something back.

When it was all over and we'd handed over the last set of keys to the last family, Stephanie asked me, "What do you think?"

I said, "I want to do it again. I want to do it next year and I want to do it in Baton Rouge, too."

And that's how Homes for the Holidays got its start.

As it grew in scope and scale, it started to take on a life of its own. When I moved from Tampa to Atlanta, I didn't want the project to stop just because I was no longer in town, so I took the necessary steps to set up my foundation that would keep this work going in Tampa, even if I was no longer part of the Bucs organization. It also gave me a head start for getting the work going when I joined the Falcons.

To date, Homes for the Holidays has helped 77 families with 201 children in total. The Warrick Dunn Foundation now has the capacity to sponsor ten homes annually. We aim to do three in Tampa, three in Baton Rouge, three in Atlanta, and one in Tallahassee each year. I am happy that I am able to give something back to each of the cities that has contributed to my development as an athlete and that helped me get to where I am professionally.

We now have a number of established partnerships with corporations such as Aaron's Sales and Lease, which has donated all of the furniture for several years. We also have a great partnership with Prudential Tropical Realty, which challenges its employees to contribute toward the company's annual $100,000 pledge to the foundation. It can cost up to $30,000 to furnish each home from beds and sofas to a television and drapes to Q-Tips and Band-Aids, window cleaner and dish soap.

We spend an additional $500 on groceries to get the pantry stocked with cereal, peanut butter, and spaghetti. And since most of the homes are ready between Thanksgiving and Christmas, we make sure that there is a holiday turkey in each refrigerator when the family arrives. I know I said that I didn't want to just be a turkey-at-the-holidays kind of guy, so even though it's a nice gesture for the family, it's also a reminder to me that I need to remember to stay focused on both the long-term and short-term goals of each home.

The families I help are always really great about keeping up the spirit of giving. They will often give their old furniture and dishes to family or neighbors who need it. They want to make sure that their loved ones are taken care of.

Many of them are so eager to start their new lives that they are ready to get going right away. More than one family told me that once they saw their new home, they returned to their old apartment, packed up their clothes, and just propped the front door open as they left, calling out to the neighbors, "Take what you want—we're not coming back!"

Other families have returned only to pack overnight bags and then rush back to their new homes. They figure that there will be time later to figure out what they want to move, but right now they just want to sleep in their new home.

I've even had a few families early on who, after the tour of their new home, said, "The house looks very nice. Now, when is someone coming to pick up all this stuff?" I had to explain to them that it was all theirs to keep; we didn't just rent the furniture to show them decorating tips. Many of them started crying all over again at that point. I try to make a point of it now to make sure that they understand right from the start that everything inside will stay after we leave.

We try to think of everything we can to make the homes as welcoming as possible. On the day that the family takes possession of the house, in addition to the fresh flowers in all of the vases there is an apple pie on each counter. A number of people have even commented on the fact that we fold the ends of the rolls of toilet paper to look fancy. It may seem silly to go to that degree of detail, but we truly want to make each family feel special—we want them to know that the home is something they have earned through all of their hard work and dedication to a better life.

I always wear my football jersey when we do the home presentations, because it often helps the families to recognize who I am if they don't already know. That way, things make a little more sense to them than just some strange man approaching them with keys and smiling. Stephanie, who became a close friend and stayed with the foundation for almost ten years until 2007, teases me that it's kind of like a superhero—you don't recognize him without his cape. I think that's stretching things a bit, but she always tells me that my jersey is my cape.

I just feel that these women should not have to live in fear—not just fear in the immediate sense, like for their family's welfare and safety, but also fear for the future. I don't want them to have to wonder where they are going to get the next rent payment, or how they are going to be able to afford the car repairs or if they will be able to buy a new pair of shoes for each child for back-to-school. I don't want fear to mark their lives, because the children sense that and they learn to live in fear, too.

We hear all the time how the family is the building block of our society. It's true, and we need to make sure that we are taking care of those people who are working to keep their families together—the people who refuse to walk out on their responsibilities.

I can't even begin to explain the rush that I get each time I hand over another set of keys and watch the look of surprise and joy on each person's face. The only charge that I give them as we tour their new home is, "Please don't break anything." I'm joking with them, of course, but they really take it to heart. They recognize that they have been entrusted with something and they are all committed to stepping up to the challenge. In fact, only one family in almost ten years has ever lost their house.

The success rate is just phenomenal, and that's what thrills me the most—these are amazing women, and I am not giving them anything except a chance.

I am also taking steps to ensure that the foundation is well enough endowed to continue after my retirement from professional football. It can sometimes be a challenge to first start with fund-raising and building partnerships, because it takes a while to build people's trust. Understandably, people want to make sure that you really stand behind your message and that there are positive results from your work before they are willing to pledge their support. Now that we've made those relationships and have gathered momentum for our efforts, we want to make sure that the foundation is able to continue changing lives.

NANCY'S STORY

Nancy Bevilacqua and her son Carl faced a series of challenges when they moved to Florida to start their lives over. They lived with Nancy's older son for a few months, but the solution was not a permanent one. Then they shared a home with another single mother until that family moved to Tennessee.

Meanwhile, Nancy was struggling with employment. She graduated from college with a degree in music and was working as the choir director and organist for a local church, but the work was only part-time. So she took a night-shift job that would work with her teaching schedule, as she also offered piano lessons out of their home.

Ninety days after her employment began and just as her health benefits were set to begin, the company laid off its entire night staff because of a downsizing order from corporate headquarters. She then got another job, working as the front desk receptionist for an automotive company, and once again, at ninety days her position was terminated and the shop closed down a month later. She eventually found work with a senior citizen community choir and playing as an accompanist for concerts at local schools, but there was hardly enough money to live on, let alone to save for a house.

The employment setbacks were frustrating for Nancy because not only was she a very hard worker who just had unfortunate timing, but she was beginning to develop crippling arthritis in her hands and wrists, which was threatening her employment as a music teacher and director as well.

Nancy and Carl eventually found a trailer in a park run by a man who accepted tenants only by recommendation, so they felt that they had found a good solution: a bit of privacy in a safe neighborhood. "We thought we had really gotten something great because we were finally in our own place," she said. "But it left a lot to be desired. The trailer was one of those old, old tagalongs that didn't even have square corners—just rounded walls and ceiling where it sloped down. It had a tiny kitchen and an even tinier eating area, and then someone had built a cinderblock living room, bedroom, bathroom, and closet."

The bedroom was Carl's, so he would have a place to do his homework while Nancy continued to teach piano lessons with a small electric keyboard in the front of the house. She slept on the sofa.

"It was in such bad shape—one day we found a hole in the floor that led directly to the outside underneath a fake drawer front. It was a constant battle to keep the bugs out. We're lucky we didn't have snakes and raccoons coming in with that hole there," Nancy recalled. "At one point, we even thought we had mice until we learned that termites eat soap, and the bars of soap under our sink were just getting gnawed away."

For three years, Nancy and Carl did their best to make the trailer a home and to keep their spirits up, though it was difficult, given the circumstances. As Nancy described it, "It was so poorly constructed—the whole thing sagged. The plumbing, the electricity—everything was just terrible. There was a hole in the wall repaired with tape and cardboard. It was sad. It was really sad. And it cost so much to heat and cool the place. And half the windows in the place didn't work, so when the weather was decent, you couldn't open them to try to get a breeze or fresh air."

Finally, in August 2004, in the midst of the series of hurricanes that tore across Florida that year, the family came up for their interview with Habitat for Humanity. The timing couldn't have been better—they had been evacuated with each storm that blew through the area. After Hurricane Charlie, their trailer was really on its last legs.

Throughout the past year, both Nancy and Carl had been putting in the roughly 500 required construction hours needed to secure a house of their own—an effort that was made more difficult because of Nancy's advancing arthritis. Carl, who was twelve at the time, stepped up and put in extra hours. When the Habitat for Humanity people came over to their trailer for the evaluation, Carl laughed because the inspectors already had two pages of notes on the condition of their current living space before they even went inside the trailer. "The first thing they saw was that the carport had been blown into a tree from the storm," he said. "We knew they'd notice that."

About that same time, Nancy and Carl started to develop some serious respiratory issues, and it was discovered that their trailer was filled with black mold. They had to leave, but they had nowhere else to go. Another family took them in from September until Thanksgiving when, due to Nancy's determination, Carl's hard work, and the dedicated staff at Habitat, their home was completed.

On November 29, 2005, Nancy and Carl were ready to move into their cozy two-bedroom, one-bath home north of Tampa. They had been told that there would be some special attention given to their closing owing to the fact that it was the tenth house completed during Habitat's tenth year in the Tampa area. What they did not expect was the scene that greeted them when they pulled up to their new home.

There was a large tent set up out front, a number of cameras set up, a small podium near the front door, and television trucks parked up and down the street, and the yard was filled with people. Nancy noticed that there was some decoration: "There was a park bench out front, a table next to it, a little potted palm, a wreath on the door—but I honestly thought that they were just put there for the day. I didn't know they were gifts at first."

Still unsure of what was occurring, Nancy's confusion quickly grew. "Someone introduced me to Warrick, and he knew immediately that there was no recognition when we made eye contact," she said. "But I think he was tickled by it because he knew that we were truly going to be surprised. Some people see him and know what's coming as soon as they see him. I was excited because I was going to gain ownership of the house and that was it."

A small ceremony took place with various Habitat for Humanity workers speaking, as well as the ministers from the church where Nancy worked. Then Nancy had to pause while a camera crew went around the house to the back door to film her reaction when she went inside.

As she was waiting, one reporter asked if she had anything to say to Warrick. Nancy shook her head, recalling the moment. "I thought that Warrick was just someone who had something to do with Habitat. So I was already nervous—I was shaking and Warrick could see that I didn't know what to say. I didn't know who Warrick was. So he whispered something in my ear, but I couldn't tell what it was because I was practically deaf from the nerves, so finally I turned to him and I asked, 'What did you say?' He said, 'Don't forget to tell everyone how cute I am.'"

The laughter helped to ease her nerves, but when she finally walked through the door, she was dumbstruck. "The first thing I saw was the piano and I almost passed out," she said. "My knees nearly gave out from under me."

In an earlier meeting between Habitat and the Warrick Dunn Foundation, someone had mentioned that Nancy needed a piano for her career and asked if the foundation would consider giving the family less in the line of furnishings and buying a piano instead. The response was "'You go find a piano and tell us how much it is'—they didn't hold back on anything," Nancy said.

There in the front room of her new home, Nancy sank onto the piano bench and played "Solfeggietto" by Bach, which was the first song that came to her mind. She just couldn't stop looking at the shiny brown wood of her Remington upright, even as she was encouraged to explore the rest of the house.

And while the piano took her breath away, the rest of the house put on a pretty good show, too.

All of the cabinet doors stood open so that they could see what was inside. "Cereal and cookies and crackers and anything you could possibly eat," Nancy remembered. "There was flour, sugar, laundry baskets, brooms, a vacuum, dustpan and brushes, a scrub brush, a bucket, toothpaste and mouthwash, toothbrushes, a case of toilet paper, a case of paper towels, laundry soap, Woolite, fabric softener, dryer sheets—and it was all displayed. In the freezer was a big ham and all kinds of frozen vegetables and pizzas and pocket things and eggs and milk, butter and bread, and they had an apple pie and a cookie jar filled with cookies, and flatware, dishes, glasses, pots and pans, roasting pans, baking pans, a can opener, a toaster, a blender, a hand mixer, the drapes were hung, and our beds were made up. I felt like I had walked onto the set of *The Price Is Right*."

And because the closing was scheduled for eight in the morning, there was even a breakfast tray with a rose in a vase set up on Nancy's bed. No detail was overlooked.

Even Carl's dog, Frank, had been remembered. He had a new collar and leash, a huge jar of dog biscuits, and a new bed that matched the rugs in the living room. "I was amazed at how much they made Frank feel like one of the family," Nancy said.

Nancy's arthritis is still painful, but she has been able to continue teaching and directing. Carl is a huge help for his mother around the house—he has painted walls and built new shelving. He also continues to volunteer with Habitat for Humanity on other homes. He thinks that he might want to use his experience with construction to one day pursue a career as an architect.

They both consider Warrick one of their heroes. "I knew in my heart that it would get better," Nancy said. "I didn't know how, but I always knew in my heart that it was temporary." She added, "Warrick was an answer to so many prayers."

CHAPTER 12

ATLANTA BOUND

A FTER FLYING CROSS-COUNTRY, FROM DETROIT TO PHILadelphia to Los Angles to Atlanta, I found myself in a booth at Copeland's restaurant in Tampa near the Veterans Expressway with one of my agents, Jeff Moorad. As we sat and talked about my professional future, my cell phone buzzed.

It was the Atlanta Falcons.

The past week had been crazy. I was an unrestricted free agent, which meant I could negotiate with interested teams for my services, including the Buccaneers. Still, I never thought I would leave Tampa. Buccaneers general manager Rich McKay, who calls everyone "Big Dog," told me when I started the free agency process not to worry. "Don't worry, Big Dog. You are going to be here. Don't worry," he said. While I had to think about my financial future, I tried not to worry. Sure, the Buccaneers slow-played their negotiations with me as other teams maneuvered to determine my market value. But Rich repeatedly told my agents that I was his top priority and the Buccaneers would pay me more than any other team in the end. So I finally took Rich's advice. This "Big Dog" wasn't worried.

The Atlanta Falcons, who were coached by Dan Reeves and had a new owner in Arthur Blank, the cofounder of Home Depot, had called and left numerous messages on my cell phone during my visits to Detroit and Philadelphia. When I landed in California and met with Jeff, who was part of Leigh Steinberg's sports agency, at his office in Orange County, we finally telephoned the Falcons for the first time.

Atlanta wanted to meet.

Since I was scheduled to fly back to Tampa through Atlanta the next day—and Jeff was headed to Florida to meet with some of his professional baseball clients because spring training had started—we agreed to meet with the Falcons. Word around the league was that tailback Garrison Hearst was set to sign with Atlanta, but at the last minute he decided to remain in San Francisco. I didn't know it at the time, but Hearst's decision shot an emergency flare over Tampa Bay. That's when Rich McKay, who was at the Competition Committee Meetings in Naples when he first heard the news involving Hearst, and the Buccaneers began to worry. A lot.

McKay knew that Blank, as a new owner, wanted to make a signing splash. Plus, the Buccaneers had a formula for winning games and building a championship, and the team's salary cap reflected that approach by the large amount of money it spent on defensive players. How highly regarded was our defense? Bucs Warren Sapp, Derrick Brooks, John Lynch, and Ronde Barber started on defense for the NFC in the 2001 Pro Bowl. Extra money was further squeezed when the Buccaneers signed quarterback Brad Johnson from the Minnesota Vikings prior to the 2001 season. From a salary cap standpoint, McKay had to keep my contract number at a manageable figure.

When I landed in Atlanta, we hit the ground in full sprint. I toured the team's corporate headquarters and training facility in Flowery Branch, just northwest of Atlanta. I underwent a physical and met briefly with some of the coaches, including Reeves. I believe Coach Reeves respected me as a player and a person, but I wasn't sure that I was the kind of running back he wanted. He favored bigger, physical running backs.

Most of my time was spent with Mr. Blank, however, and he was determined to finalize a deal with me. We thought it would happen, too. But it did not. Everyone was frustrated and upset, and we jumped on an airplane to Tampa not sure of our next step. But at least Tampa was my home, so there was no need to worry, right?

The 2001 season in Tampa had been difficult for me. I spent most of the season trying to get over a case of turf toe that was especially cruel for someone with a running style like mine—built around sharp cuts, quick moves, and bursts of speed. In five seasons as a pro, it was by far the least productive season of my career. Even so, I had managed to go over 1,000 yards again in rushing and receiving yards combined. I expected to come back strong and have an outstanding year with the Buccaneers and Coach Gruden in 2002. Coach Gruden liked the Dunn–Alstott combo in the backfield, and by all accounts he was motivated to keep me.

You hear all the time how professional sports are a business first and a game second. It seems players change teams the way runway models change outfits. It was easy for fans to question loyalties. From the outside looking in, you might assume that players don't really care about the teams they play for or the cities they represent.

Trust me, that wasn't the case for this "Big Dog."

My heart was in Tampa, and not just because I had a girlfriend and a home there, along with relationships built around my work in the community. As players, we felt like we were getting close to a breakthrough season in which we could compete for a Super Bowl championship, and I fully expected to be a part of it. Two consecutive years of losing to Philadelphia in the first round of the playoffs had forged a team unity in Tampa, and we had grown together in pursuit of a singular goal—not just to beat Philadelphia but to bring Tampa its first Super Bowl trophy.

As I sat in Copeland's restaurant, the Atlanta Falcons were on the phone and wanted to discuss business. Bottom line, Mr. Blank wanted me in Atlanta, and he took it upon himself to make it happen. Following my visit, Mr. Blank spent most of the night working on my contract and said he hoped I liked it. Liked it? I loved it—it was a six-year, $28.5 million deal that included a $6.5 million signing bonus. That was $3 million more *per year* than the Buccaneers had offered. We immediately called Rich McKay and asked Rich if the Buccaneers could match the Falcons' offer. It was a relatively quick conversation. Rich told Jeff Moorad he could not, and then wished me luck. Click. End of conversation. Rich and I never talked. Just like that, in the back of a local restaurant, my playing days in Tampa were over. I sat there happy but stunned. I knew my life at twenty-seven years old was going to change in a big way.

And change it did.

Honestly, Atlanta wasn't a team that looked all that attractive from a distance. Even though it had played in the Super Bowl in 1999, it seemed to always be 7–9 in the years that followed. There simply wasn't a whole lot of excitement around the franchise. But change was in the air. Quarterback Michael Vick, the first overall selection in the 2001 draft, had started only two games but displayed flashes of brilliance. The Falcons had a new owner, and Mr. Blank was fired up about changing the team's fortunes and making them into winners, sooner rather than later.

I had a great impression of Mr. Blank. He was different from what you would expect from the owner of an NFL franchise—his whole feel, his approach, I liked that a lot. We connected on a personal level. We didn't talk much about football when we first met. I mean, I actually rode in his car with him and went to his house—that was crazy. When I was in Tampa, I talked with the Glazer family a little here and there. Here I was in Atlanta hanging with the team owner. Mr. Blank loved the work I did in the community with my Homes for the Holidays and he definitely wanted to bring me in for that aspect. But he also knew I could play. It's funny: Mr. Blank made his fortune with Home Depot, and something extremely important to me was my project to help build homes for single moms. Maybe it was a partnership that was meant to be. I mean, not only did Mr. Blank personally rework my contract and increase his original offer, but he also made it clear how much it meant to him for me to play for the Falcons.

In contrast, the Buccaneers acted like I wasn't important. In fact, Tampa lowered its original offer to $2 million a year. It basically wanted me for nothing compared to the going rate of other running backs with my record, and I had been to two Pro Bowls at that point. Plus something odd began to happen as the free agency period opened, and I wasn't sure what to make of it. I began to receive similar contract offers from several teams, including Detroit and Philadelphia. They were all around $2 million per year. Not only was I frustrated because I felt I was worth more than $2 million per year, but it was also weird that all the offers were so close in value. The NFL has rules against collusion, which is basically an attempt by team owners to keep salaries down. I wanted to stay in Tampa, but I couldn't leave $16.5 million on the table over six years. If the difference was, say, a half-million per year, I might have stayed in Tampa because of my love for the community and because of Florida's tax laws. In the end, though, $16.5 million was just too much money to pass on.

The Falcons deal was great for me. I admit I was bitter and upset with how the Buccaneers handled my negotiations during the free agency process, but things happen for a reason. I think Mr. Blank fell in love with me, and that's what usually happens—somebody falls in love with you and they do what they can to sign you. And on March 15, 2002, I signed with Atlanta.

Of course, there were fans up in arms about my deal with the Falcons. The consensus around the National Football League was that the Falcons overpaid me. They pointed to my size (surprise) and my production (surprise). While I averaged only 17.4 rushes and receptions per game in my five seasons with the Buccaneers, in my mind I had proven I was more than a situational back. My gifts as a running back were different from most. I was a small back who wanted a big back's workload. Plus, the Falcons agreed to pay me a lot of money to help carry their offense over the course of a full season.

But Coach Reeves had other ideas.

As I started the second chapter of my NFL career, I needed more than ever to prove myself, despite the fact that I had averaged more than 1,300 rushing and receiving yards combined over my first five seasons in the league. The irony was that Coach Reeves didn't consider me his type of running back. The Falcons had new ownership, but they had the same coach who won an NFC title five years earlier when he let Jamal Anderson pound the line and carry the football an NFL single-season record 410 times.

And imagine my surprise when I showed up at the Georgia Dome for the team's annual Fan Fest, a meet-and-greet for fans and players. The 2002 NFL draft was also being held that day, and I scooted into a back room with my new teammates to watch the first round of the draft on television. Everyone talked about how badly we needed a receiver, and the media projected we'd take Ashley Lelie of Hawaii with our first-round selection.

When it was our turn to select at number eighteen, it blared across the TV, "With the eighteenth selection in the first round, the Atlanta Falcons pick . . . running back T.J. Duckett of Michigan State." *T.J. Duckett of Michigan State?* Every player in that room turned around and stared at me. I was surprised and puzzled to say the least, but what could I say?

I telephoned my agent, Jeff Moorad, for his reaction. I didn't scream and shout, "Why?" I just quietly left the Georgia Dome and walked to the mall. What could I do? I split time and carries with Mike Alstott in Tampa, and it was like déjà vu. T.J. was just like Mike, a big, strong, physical runner at 254 pounds. Although Reeves was undecided exactly where I fit into his offensive scheme once we started practice, I knew I wouldn't be with the Falcons if they simply saw me as a third-down back. I expected around twenty carries per game. Plus T.J. was a good young player, and I wanted to do anything I could to help make him better.

The move to Atlanta from Tampa was an adjustment for me personally as well. Tampa is more of a family city with palm trees and beaches. Atlanta has plenty of families, too, but there's a different vibe and tempo. Atlanta is Georgia's state capital, with over 100,000 more people than Tampa. It's also closer to the Great Smoky Mountains in Tennessee than to the Gulf of Mexico in Florida. I quickly discovered that life barreled at you at a much quicker pace, and if you didn't keep pace, you'd be run over, especially on the roads. Bumper-to-bumper traffic is also the norm, and it seemed like I spent half of my day in the car. While the Falcons' training facility is in a fairly rural area in Flowery Branch, I knew I wanted to live in the city. I found a townhouse in northeast Atlanta and immediately felt right at home.

Feeling at home on the football field took a bit longer.

Overall, though, my first season with the Falcons went well. Coach Reeves and I got used to each other, and he figured out how my style could be used effectively in his offense. I was part of the "DVD" rushing offense that featured Dunn, Vick, and Duckett and combined for 2,211 yards. I carried the football 230 times for 927 yards and seven touchdowns, and I also caught fifty passes for 377 yards. T.J. added 507 rushing yards. Michael rushed for 771 yards and threw for 2,936. We finished second in the NFC South and beat Green Bay in the opening round of the playoffs before we lost to—guess who?—Philadelphia 20–6 in the second round. Man, I was so tired of losing to the Eagles in the playoffs.

I also faced my old team, the Buccaneers, in 2002, as the NFL's sweeping realignment sent the Bucs to the NFC South Division with us, the Carolina Panthers, and the New Orleans Saints. I have to admit that it was a weird experience to see my friends on the opposite sideline. As I jogged around the field before our first meeting in October in Atlanta, I made eye contact with Rich McKay. He knew I was still upset with how my career in Tampa ended. The Buccaneers, of course, were a great team and they beat us twice, 20–6 and 34–10. I had only 14 rushing yards on nine carries in that first game and missed the second game due to an injury.

Worse yet, I also missed out on a Super Bowl championship with the Buccaneers in 2002. They finished with the team's best ever record at 12–4 and went on to rout Jon Gruden's former team, the Oakland Raiders, by a score of 48–21 in Super Bowl XXXVII. Talk about being conflicted emotionally. I was in San Diego for the Super Bowl festivities, but as the game approached, I couldn't escape the hurt knowing that I wouldn't be in uniform with the Bucs on Super Sunday. I had to bolt. On game day, I caught a flight to Los Angeles and then back home to Baton Rouge. It was like I was in a daze. I was so out of it that whole day that I honestly can't remember where I was when the game started. I watched as much of it as I could, but it was too painful for me.

Naturally, I was thrilled for the guys I played with because we had been through the battles together. But I couldn't escape the feeling of, "That could have been me." A Super Bowl title is what we played for, and it was tough to see it happen without me. Even Rich McKay admitted that the hardest part for him as he stood on that podium to accept the Lombardi Trophy was to know that people like me, Hardy Nickerson, Tony Dungy, and Jerry Angelo who helped the franchise achieve this goal were no longer around. It was tough, but it's part of life. You try not to be upset, but it's a struggle. When I ran into guys like Sapp, Brooks, and Ronde over the next few months I congratulated them. But it wasn't like I had my telephone on speed-dial after that game. I missed out and wanted to let them enjoy it. I truly was both happy and sad when the Buccaneers won the Super Bowl.

I didn't enjoy the entire 2003 football season, though. I started six of eleven games and rushed for 672 yards on 125 carries (5.4 average). I was named the NFL Offensive Player of the Week for my performance in our 27–7 victory over the New York Giants when I gained 178 yards on 25 carries. I followed it with 162 rushing yards against New Orleans on November 16, pushing my two-game total to a new club mark of 340 yards and surpassing Jamal Anderson's 310 yards in 1998. But I went on the injured reserve two weeks later for the remainder of the season with a mid-foot sprain that required surgery. Coach Reeves also didn't survive the season. He was fired by Mr. Blank and replaced by interim coach Wade Phillips as we limped to a 5–11 finish.

The year took another surprise turn a month later in December, when Rich McKay left the Buccaneers and joined the Falcons as president and general manager. As general manager for the Buccaneers from 1993 to 2003, Rich directed six teams that reached the NFC playoffs and, of course—don't remind me—the team that won the Super Bowl in 2002. He also hired Tony Dungy as head coach, and drafted players like John Lynch (1993), Trent Dilfer (1994), Warren Sapp (1995), Mike Alstott (1996), and myself (1997). Plus, our forty-one Pro Bowl selections between 1997 and 2002 were the most in the NFL. Although Rich and I hadn't talked since I left Tampa, I was excited for him and left him a congratulatory voice mail on his office phone in Atlanta.

My early relationship with Rich was hard to explain. When I was in Tampa, I know players like Sapp and Brooks would call Rich and grill him with questions about the team. "What's going on? Why are we doing this? Why are we doing that?" I was young and I followed the chain of command. I was the player, Tony was the head coach, and Rich was the general manager. I respected it and never crossed that line. Everyone had told me that Rich loved me and I was one of his guys. Jeez, I was even his youngest son's favorite player. That's why it was difficult to describe my feelings when I left Tampa. I was hurt. When Rich and I saw each other for the first time in Atlanta, he wanted to sit down and talk because he knew I was still steamed with him. It was a great idea because we were open and honest with each other, and over time any hard feelings went away. I was comfortable in Atlanta. The move actually forced me to mature as a person and a player. I learned more about the business side of football. That's how it was, but Rich and I could still have a great relationship.

The 2004 season couldn't have gone any better, either. Mr. Blank hired Jim Mora as our head coach. Mora was a somewhat surprising choice because Mr. Blank passed over more prominent assistants such as Lovie Smith, who landed in Chicago. But Mr. Blank looked like a genius. A former defensive coordinator in San Francisco, Mora was a first-time head coach when he led us to the NFC South title in his rookie season. We finished 11–5, beat St. Louis 47–17 in the opening round but lost to—not again!—Philadelphia 27-10 in the NFC championship game. I started all sixteen games for the first time in my career and rushed for 1,106 yards—the third 1,000-yard season of my career—and had a career-high nine rushing touchdowns. I established a Falcons postseason record and career-high 142 rushing yards on seventeen carries with two touchdowns in the NFC divisional playoff win over St. Louis. My 62-yard touchdown run was the longest rush and longest touchdown run in Falcons postseason history. I also received the prestigious Walter Payton NFL Man of the Year Award, which honors players for their volunteer and charity work as well as their excellence on the field. And because of counseling, I also felt better about myself as a person. I was more inquisitive, more curious, more interested in life. I was in a good place.

Better yet, we opened the 2005 season with a bang, too.

A 6–2 start gave us a share of the NFC South lead. Our two defeats were by three points each to the Seahawks (21–18) and the Patriots (31–28). I also had four 100-yard rushing games, including a 155-yard performance against the Giants, during that span. My offensive line, which relied on zone blocking, created creases and daylight. I was part of the NFL's best rushing backfield with Vick and Duckett. It seemed that everyone knew the moniker "DVD."

Then the bottom fell out.

We dropped consecutive games to Green Bay (33–25) and Tampa Bay (30–27), and we couldn't regain our footing. We dropped six of our last eight games, including our final three to Chicago, Tampa Bay in overtime, and Carolina. While I was frustrated with our collapse—it's a team game—I couldn't have been more pleased with my individual performance. I earned my third Pro Bowl appearance and started all sixteen games for the second consecutive season.

I established career highs with 1,416 rushing yards on 280 carries (5.1 average) and helped the Falcons lead the NFL in rushing (159.1 yards per game) for the second straight season. One of my best performances came against the Jets, when I rushed for a season-high 155 yards on twenty-four carries on *Monday Night Football*. My 1,416 rushing yards ranked fifth all-time in team history behind Jamal Anderson (1,846 in 1998), Gerald Riggs (1,719 in 1985), William Andrews (1,567 in 1983), and Riggs again (1,486 in 1984).

And to think only three years earlier the franchise was ridiculed for signing me to a six-year $28.5 million contract because I was viewed as a situational back. You are aware of what's being said on the radio and in the newspapers. I knew fans always looked at my size, but their concerns and questions motivated me to prove them wrong. Over time, though, I believe those same fans really started to respect my game. They understood the way that I played. They recognized that I played the game as hard as I could, and that they could count on me to give it everything I had, no matter what.

OUR START TO THE 2006 season was similar to 2005. We opened 5–2, with one of the defeats to the Saints in what was the first game in the Louisiana Superdome since Hurricane Katrina struck a little more than a year earlier. But we quickly hit the skids, dropping four consecutive games at one point to the Lions, Browns, Ravens, and Saints again, and finished 7–9. We actually had a slim chance to make the playoffs with a .500 record in the regular season's final weekend. But that ended when the Giants won at Washington and we lost 24–17 at Philadelphia, even though the Eagles rested most of their key playmakers. It was easy to pinpoint our struggles. We went a combined 4–13 during the final two months of 2005 and 2006 and were an astonishing 0–17 when we entered the fourth quarter of games with a deficit.

While we led the NFL rushing under Coach Mora, Michael Vick and offensive coordinator Greg Knapp never seemed to mesh. And the media pointed out that Mora's tenure was marked by an odd series of off-field distractions that included the embarrassment he caused himself during a Seattle radio station interview before a December game against Dallas. Coach Mora said his "dream job" was to coach at his alma mater, the University of Washington, and that he'd jump at the chance to take it—even if we were in the middle of the playoffs. Coach Mora claimed he was joking with the radio host, former college teammate and former backup Atlanta quarterback Hugh Millen. Even so, the comments upset Atlanta fans and

Mr. Blank. And Mora's father, Jim, a former head coach, created another awkward situation for Coach Mora when he agreed with a radio co-host that Michael Vick was a "coach killer." Michael was upset by the comment and wondered if the father's opinion was influenced by private comments from Coach Mora.

In the end, Mr. Blank decided a change was necessary at season's end and he fired Coach Mora, who went 26–22 in his three years and joined Leeman Bennett as the only coaches in Atlanta history to leave with winning records. Despite the distractions and our poor finish, I felt good about my accomplishments in 2006. I started all sixteen games for the third consecutive season and rushed for 1,140 yards—my third consecutive 1,000-yard rushing season and the second-highest rushing total of my career. I also added twenty-two receptions for 170 yards and one touchdown. Michael Vick (1,039 yards) and I became the first quarterback/running back duo to each surpass 1,000 rushing yards in a single season and were one of only four teammate duos to accomplish the feat in NFL history, with the last being Cleveland Browns running backs Kevin Mack and Earnest Byner in 1985. To top it off, my 90-yard touchdown run against the Giants marked the longest in franchise history.

It's really tough to break off a long run in the NFL—defensive players are just so quick. On my 90-yard run, I took the handoff on a play that looked pretty routine, up the middle against the Giants defense. I picked up a great block from my fullback, Justin Griffth, at the line and then spun off a couple of tacklers, including cornerback Sam Madison. Once I headed free down the sideline, it was a foot race that I won.

The play broke Jerious Norwood's two-week-old team record, a 78-yard touchdown run in our last game against Arizona. It was also the longest run of my career—the previous long one was 76 yards against Chicago in 1997, my rookie year.

While the Falcons may have struggled on the field, I will say this: the move to Atlanta changed my life.

SONJA'S STORY

Sonja Pania has worked all of her adult life to help her family into better circumstances. She worked as a crime analyst with the Baton Rouge Police Department during the day and had a second job doing janitorial work at night—and everything was focused on her two major goals: to buy a home and to send her children to college.

Sonja was living with her four teenage children in Plaquemine, Louisiana, a town about twenty miles southwest of Baton Rouge, in the home of Sonja's deceased grandparents. But the neighborhood was going downhill, with a sharp increase in drugs and crime, and they knew they wanted out. Finances were already tight, and the family was also facing college tuition costs for the oldest child, who was looking to begin nursing school a few hours away in Natchitoches at Northwestern State University.

They found their solution in Habitat for Humanity, which was beginning construction on several homes in Sonja's neighborhood. She walked over to talk with some of the building crews one day, to ask about how to enroll in the program and what work she could do to help the organization. They told her that she would need to apply once they opened up for a new series of applicants, so she paid attention to television and radio ads, and about a year later, she was able to begin the application process, which involved a great deal of paperwork, credit checks, financial documents, and classes on home ownership.

After her approval, Sonja's family began their 350 hours of sweat equity on homes in and around Plaquemine, which was where they assumed their own home would be located. But as the time to begin work on their own home grew nearer, they received a call from the Habitat director, asking if the family would be willing to move to Baton Rouge instead due to land title complications in their own town. Because Sonja was already working for the Baton Rouge Police Department, the change of location might be an advantage and would cut her commuting time in half.

The family agreed, and construction began on their home. Working alongside the other volunteers, the Panias got to know a number of high school students who were helping to construct the house. In fact, there were close to 100 students from four area high schools who donated time to the Pania home. Students from Episocopal High, St. Joseph Academy, University, and Warrick's own alma mater, Catholic High, banded together to get the home built. "We had a great time," Sonja recalled. "They took shifts: some would come out in the morning, some would come out in the afternoon, some would stay all day. I really had a great time working with the kids. There were lots of kids, and probably never under fifty kids working at one time."

With such a large and energetic work crew, the home was completed very quickly, and the Panias were looking forward to moving in during the Thanksgiving holidays in 2004. As they prepared for their new home, Sonja recalled a surprise she received as she was doing follow-up work on their construction.

"After the house was completed, they had little things to do, and every day my mom would ask, 'Did you go out to the house today to check on it?' and I'd say, 'No I didn't go out to the house today.' I think she was maybe even more excited than me," she recalled, laughing. "So one day I decided, 'Well, I'll go out to the house to see what they are doing with hanging blinds and such, so that I can tell her and she can stop asking me every day!"

What she discovered at the house, though, left her with a lot of questions. "I went out to the house and there was a crew of people out in front of my house. I didn't know who they were," she said. "I had a key, because I had been going in to do a little work myself, and this lady stopped me at the door and said, 'Can I help you?'

"I said, 'Yes—I'm going into my house.'

"She said, 'I'm sorry, but you can't go in there. You might want to call the Habitat office to find out when you can come back.' I was kind of baffled and puzzled. I wanted to know why I couldn't go into my own house."

A few days later, Sonja received her answer . . . or so she thought.

"I received a call from Habitat," she said. "They wanted to set up a meeting with me and a few other families that were receiving homes at the same time. So we went in and the woman I had seen was at the meeting and she said she was from CNN in Atlanta and they were doing a feature on model homes for Habitat. They were using our homes and they were going to fix them up and they wanted us to come out because they were going to interview us and if we had children, we should bring them out, too. They warned us, 'You're going to be on TV, but we don't want you to be nervous or anything. I know you were probably wondering why we were out at your house so that's the reason.'"

The move-in day arrived, and the Pania family was prepared for the cameras and reporters who were all over their new front yard as they pulled up. "I knew we were supposed to be on TV," Sonja said, "but I looked around at the people there and I saw Warrick and just said, 'Oh no.' And I knew what was going on. I'd seen him on the news here in BR with the families he's helped, so when I saw him in my yard, I was just blown away. I could not believe it."

Her joy was mingled with shock and disbelief as Warrick handed her the keys to her new home and began to show her around. "I was blown away," she remembered. "All I could do was laugh. Warrick asked if I was okay and I told him, 'I have to laugh to keep from crying.' I just could not believe it."

The home had been decorated in the deep burgundies and greens that Sonja loved. She remembered a few of the women from Habitat asking how she was planning on decorating her home and had told them her dream plans of rich colors and transitional furniture. She guessed that they must have passed the information along, because the home was everything she had ever imagined. "It was beautiful. I could not have done a better job if I had done it myself," she said. "Warrick even asked my son, Arthur, if he thought I liked it, and Arthur told him, 'Oh, this is just like her. This is exactly how she would have done it.'"

And the extra touches were every bit as meaningful. Sonja said, "There were fresh flowers everywhere, food in the kitchen— everything was just so beautiful."

The children's rooms were special as well. Her two daughters who were still at home were sharing a room done in beautiful pinks and greens, while her son had a room painted navy and white and equipped with his own computer, which was perfect for his dreams of pursuing a degree in computer science. Though there wasn't anything with the Atlanta Falcons logo on it at the time, he has since added a number of items, including a Falcons screen saver, in honor of Warrick.

"We even had a lawn mower," Sonja said. "Warrick opened the door to the garage and told my son, 'I have something just for you!' He told us we had no excuse not to keep our yard looking nice, and my son knew right away that it was his job."

The entire day was an emotional experience for Sonja's whole family. "I was laughing the whole time. I just couldn't believe it. My daughters were crying. My son was smiling the whole time," she said. And she knew right away what she would be doing with her old furniture. In the spirit of Homes for the Holidays, "I gave it away. I knew a family that was in need and I gave all of our stuff to them." She was determined to share the blessings.

Her family continues to be surprised by Warrick's generosity. Sonja remarked, "Warrick also blessed my children and me last year with tickets to the opening game of the New Orleans Saints against the Falcons. I'd been trying to get tickets to that game because I wanted to go see Warrick play, and it was very hard to get tickets because it was the first game back in the Superdome since Katrina, so tickets were very hard to get." Sonja had all but given up on her efforts until the morning of October 21, 2006. "The day of the game," she said, "Stephanie Waller called me and said, 'We have tickets for you—they are at Will Call.' So I took off the rest of the day from work and made my way to New Orleans. It was really exciting to have a chance to see Warrick play other than just on TV.

"I have no idea what made my application stand out, but I am just so happy that he picked me," said Sonja. But anyone who has met this quiet mother who works hard for her large family with the Baton Rouge Police Department can see the reason her story and her spirit stood out right away.

CHAPTER 13

NEW TREND

IF A HOLE OPENS ALONG THE LINE OF SCRIMMAGE, I AM going to find it. That's what running backs, of all shapes and sizes, are supposed to do. We are supposed to turn small gainers into big gainers, routine plays into touchdowns.

I am also more than willing to drop my head and run between the tackles and pick up bigger, blitzing linebackers in pass protection. I like to hit, too. Let's remember that I played defense in high school, and I don't mind returning the favor because I know those guys on defense want to knock me out every chance they get. And because of my size and quickness, I am looked at as a serious threat as a receiver out of the backfield.

It all sounds easy enough, right? Wrong.

I will be perfectly honest. I never thought I was good enough or big enough to play professional football. It wasn't until after my junior season at Florida State when I thought, *Damn, I may actually play pro football.* That's when all the chatter started about me possibly leaving FSU early for the NFL. I had no idea. Seriously, I had no idea that I might play pro ball one day. I figured I would be a nine-to-five employee in a desk job somewhere in Baton Rouge after I graduated from FSU.

When you look around, the NFL has had its share—and will continue to develop its share—of great running backs. When fans talk about some of best running backs of all time, they mention players such as Jim Brown, Walter Payton, Emmitt Smith, and Barry Sanders.

Brown was one of the NFL's big backs. He never missed a game. But he also surprised fans with his balance and quickness. Payton was small and compact, but he ran with incredible energy. Emmitt was a cutback runner with an explosive burst. And Barry, of course, had incredible balance and was a human pinball on the field.

My favorite of all time, however, is "TD," Tony Dorsett. I idolized TD as I grew up. If I played pro ball, I always wanted to be like Tony. Tony played for "America's Team," my favorite team, the Dallas Cowboys. Tony was taller than me at five feet eleven, but he only weighed 183 pounds and still played twelve years in the NFL. And here's a guy who has said he thought he might play five years in the league, tops, because of his size. TD was larger than life to me at one time. His career is proof—Tony was enshrined in the NFL Hall of Fame in 1994, when I was in my sophomore season at FSU. I wanted to be just like Tony.

I had watched what happened to David Palmer, a guy I identified with because of his size and abilities, and I wasn't sure what to make of it. Palmer was listed as five feet eight and 180 pounds when he played at Alabama. The things he did in college were crazy. I watched him play, and he did everything at Alabama—quarterback, running back, flanker, return punts. He was the school's first 1,000-yard rusher. Palmer would have had more yards, but he subbed for an injured Jay Barker at quarterback. Palmer was unbelievable.

Palmer left school a year early, maybe because in 1993 he was an All-American and a finalist for the Heisman Trophy, and I guess people told him to take advantage of the opportunity and jump into the draft. Palmer was picked in the second round by Minnesota in 1994. And even though he ended up playing seven years in the NFL, what happened to him those first two seasons, 1994 and 1995, sort of made me wonder.

Here was a guy who could do it all in college, but in the NFL he only started one game during his first two years, and had a total of eight rushes for 16 yards and no touchdowns. And he was my size. That's not the reason I went back to school for my senior year, but you definitely notice when a guy you can compare yourself to in ability and size goes from dominating in college to barely playing in the pros.

Of course, many good things happened to me and to Florida State during my senior season, and all things considered, it turned out to be a blessing that I returned for my final year of college. The highlight was when we beat Number 1–ranked Florida in Tallahassee in the final regular-season game. While it was a cruel twist of fate that we ended up having to play them again in the Sugar Bowl for the national championship, that game in Tallahassee was one of the most exciting games I've ever been a part of. I was fortunate to rush for 185 yards, the most I gained in a game all season.

I take pride in knowing I had my best games against the toughest opponents, but I also got more opportunities with the football against Florida and Miami than I did in most other games. Being able to show that I could make more plays with more touches was important when it came time for the NFL scouts to evaluate me. But something else happened around that time that, I think, worked in my favor to help the Bucs see me as worthy of the twelfth overall pick of the draft.

There had been a long period in the NFL when running backs like Earl Campbell, Herschel Walker, Bo Jackson, and Christian Okoye—all extremely large and powerful, but also blessed with good speed—were seen as the prototype of what an NFL back should be. It's hard to find guys that big and fast, but fortunately a new trend had begun to emerge in the years leading up to my entry into the league.

Guys like Emmitt Smith; Barry Sanders; Thurman Thomas, who was inducted into the Hall of Fame in 2007; and Curtis Martin were having sensational seasons in the years just before I was ready to join the NFL. They were giving NFL coaches a chance to see that quickness and vision can be just as important as strength when judging how well a back will play in this league. There was another guy, too, who probably helped open the Bucs' eyes to what someone with my size and skills was capable of doing.

In 1996, while I did my thing at Florida State, Dave Meggett had the best season of his ten-year NFL career. He had nearly 2,000 yards in all-purpose yardage that year and helped lead the New England Patriots to the Super Bowl. Here was a guy my size—they listed him as five feet seven, 180—and he was going to his second Pro Bowl. He had led the NFL in punt returns during his rookie season, when he helped take the New York Giants to Super Bowl XXV in Tampa, and now he was doing it again with New England

The big difference, though, was that he was mostly a return specialist who also got chances on third down. That definitely wasn't my mind-set when I headed to Tampa following draft day. A big part of being able to play the role I envisioned for myself was staying healthy and being able to stand up to the physical demands of the NFL. But for that, I felt as if I was ready.

One of the things I have prided myself on throughout my career—high school, college, pro—is staying healthy. People constantly worry that someone my size can't take the punishment a position like running back involves, but the reality is that I have not only survived, I have also in many ways fared better than backs much bigger than me. For that, I credit both my running style, which makes it difficult for defenders to get a solid shot at me, and my dedication to working out.

As for my running style, it's something that comes naturally to me, though I have developed it over many years. I have a low center of gravity and an explosive quickness that allows me to change directions in a blink. I have a muscular lower body that I train very hard. Even when there's not much left in a play, I can still make moves that prevent defenders from teeing off on me toward the end of a run.

People ask me all the time what's the hardest I've been hit, and my answer is "by the ground." Yes, I've taken some licks, but I don't want to give credit to anybody for a hard hit. You never want to give them that credit. I don't ever want to let somebody feel like they got to me. I mean, hits are hard sometimes, but I take them in a way that I'm good with it. I just bounce up, tap the defender on the helmet as a sign of respect, and go on to the next play.

Coach Billy Sexton, my backfield coach at Florida State, used to joke around about running backs who couldn't dodge a telephone pole and avoid those kinds of hits. He'd say, "You better go to All-state or State Farm and get some collision insurance." He also used to tell us that when the journey is over, get down, because that's when you fumble or get hurt. Live for another down.

Even though I'm a competitor, I have learned to protect myself when I run, and that has helped me stay healthy, too. I already ran with a style that made it hard for defenders to get a piece of me, and Coach Sexton and others reinforced that thinking. I remember during my rookie year with the Bucs, being in the middle of a pile and getting stripped of the football. I was like, Man, I knew I should have gotten down. I was pissed. I was trying to move the pile forward, but that's not going to work very often against the size and strength of the defensive players in this league. You are exposed to bad things when you are stopped.

I've learned to take what I can get out of a run and then get on the ground—gain positive yards and don't let them strip you at the end of a play.

Of course, Coach Sexton and others at Florida State used to frustrate me, too, when it came to their ideas of preserving my health. There were many times when I'd be fired up for practice or a scrimmage and they'd come tell me to take off my pads because they weren't going to let me play. Coach Bowden would walk over to Randy Oravetz, our trainer at Florida State, and I knew what was going on. I couldn't hide even if I tried. The next thing you know, Randy wants me to yank off my pads.

I would get upset at Coach Bowden for doing that. I mean, we had a great defense at Florida State and I loved the challenge of going out there and competing against those guys. I hated to miss practice and I rarely did. But then the coaches stepped in and I couldn't scrimmage, with the exception of the drills and stuff. It's funny; when I practice now I never want to get hit. But at Florida State I always wanted to prove myself. I never shied away from wanting to compete, and when guys would come up and hit me, I'd be prepared to fight back.

Now I'm in a different position and I understand how important it is to preserve my body. I think I've done a pretty good job with that. I was on injured reserve just one time in my first ten seasons in the NFL, when I tore a ligament in my foot and missed the final five games of the 2003 season with the Falcons. Right now, the NFL is making a big push to help players avoid concussions. Here I am, playing one of the most punishing positions, at my size, and I have never had a concussion.

Concussions among NFL players have made plenty of news. A study of more than 2,500 retired NFL players found that those who had at least three concussions during their careers had triple the risk of clinical depression as those who had no concussions. The study was performed by the University of North Carolina's Center for the Study of Retired Athletes and the story was published in the summer of 2007 in *Medicine & Science in Sports & Exercise,* the journal of the American College of Sports Medicine. It was also noted that many of the retired players were on the field before the NFL began a concussion management program in the mid-1990s and before studies sponsored by the NFL and NCAA promoted new helmet designs.

A forensic pathologist who studied Andre Waters's brain after he killed himself in November 2006 said it had been damaged by concussions. The *Boston Globe* and the *New York Times* reported in February 2007 that Ted Johnson, a Patriots linebacker for ten years, showed early signs of Alzheimer's disease. Johnson said his mental problems began in 2002, when he had two concussions in four days. In 2007, the NFL said it was spending $2 million on a study of concussions of retired NFL players.

I feel lucky and blessed. Every morning I get out of bed with no soreness, and I'm not hurting the way other people in my position are. I don't have to walk gingerly, I just get up and go. In my first ten years in the league—that's a total of 170 games, including playoffs—I missed only ten games because of injury. Even when I had surgery to repair a bulging disc in my back before the 2007 season, I returned to practice twenty-three days later.

I saw a special on ESPN about Jerome Bettis, who played all those years with the Pittsburgh Steelers. Of course, he's a much bigger guy than me. Bettis talked about how long it takes him to get going in the morning. When I heard that, I realized how much my running style and my fitness routine have helped me stay healthy. What's crazy is that I've had younger backs tell me they were sore the day after a game. I'd say, "I carried the ball twenty times and you carried the ball ten, and you're sore and I'm not?"

Because of my size, I run for my life on the field. I've done it for so long and I am so used to it that it comes naturally to me to protect myself. I've learned to live for another down, live for another play. I don't need to get every yard on every play. I can get the extra yard and get hurt and never play again, or I can get up and go back to the huddle and make something happen on the next play.

Maelen "Choo Choo" Brooks taught me that as a youngster in Baton Rouge. Pops (as I called him) told me to protect myself when I run and to keep defenders from getting a chance to take a shot at me. I could make them miss with my quickness and vision, and now I've learned not to give defenders an extra opportunity when somebody has a hold on me and is preventing me from being able to squirt away from another incoming defender. Luckily, Pops also gave me the plan and was always there pushing me to be the best. He helped me to get the most out of myself physically.

Pops was my Pee Wee coach in Baton Rouge. Our team, the Rams, never, ever lost a game. Pops worked and pushed me and I accepted it because I knew how much he cared about me. I believe a lot of what he says to this day. And even though I'm my own man and make my own decisions, I listen to what he says.

My trust in Pops has led me to do all kinds of crazy workouts with him: sprinting up hills, one-legged jumps, leaping boxes. In high school, I also started working out with Gayle Hatch, a U.S. Olympic weight lifting coach in Baton Rouge. A lot of what Gayle does is Olympic lifts—sprint jerks, cleans, step-ups. It's a full-body workout to increase your speed, your strength, and your quickness. Gayle also stresses plyometrics, which uses explosive movements to develop muscular power. That's what my game is all about, so it works with me. I return to Baton Rouge, where I still have a home, each offseason to work with Gayle, who also served as the head coach for the men's 2004 U.S. Olympic Weightlifting Team that competed in Athens, Greece. Gayle is a 1957 graduate of Catholic High School, too. In fact, the school's new weight room is called the Gayle Hatch Strength Training Center.

But if you want to know why I've remained healthy after ten years in the league, you have to look beyond my running style. I train like the devil. My daily routine in Louisiana is to run in the mornings and work out in the evenings. I run hills and mix in sprints. You have to do some quick stuff, but I also spend a lot of time conditioning my lower body and legs to be able to break tackles.

Even though I feel like I get the most out of myself with my work-out routine and my running style, I still can't help sometimes thinking about what it would be like to have those things and also have a little more size. I mean, I already think I can see things other guys can't see. I can hit holes other guys can't hit. I think over the years I became much more patient and a better runner. Sure, I've wondered what type of runner I would be if I was bigger, say five feet eleven and 210, 215 pounds. Then I realize, if I was 215 pounds, I probably wouldn't have the skills I have now. I wouldn't have the same quickness and burst in my step. I have to be thankful, and I've been blessed with skills that have brought me a long way. Hopefully there's a long way still to go.

If I can stay healthy and maintain my conditioning, I have a chance to become one of the top all-time rushers in the NFL. In the 2007 season I became a 10,000-yard guy. Can you believe it? Sometimes I can't even believe it, considering it wasn't that long ago, early in my career at Florida State, when I didn't even think I'd be an NFL player.

Derrick Brooks said I remind him of Barry Sanders, and that's a great compliment. Another former FSU teammate, Greg Spires, is a ten-year NFL veteran, too. Greg, a defensive lineman, and I have faced off over the years, and he has talked about my vision, that if a hole opens up, I will find it. If you are on defense and you don't cover your gaps, I can find the seam. But I think the greatest compliment when I was in Tampa came from the way Coach Dungy treated me after he realized I was right about being able to be more than a role player.

Now I'm in position, if I stay healthy, to do something special. I've been consistent enough over the years to where I might have a chance to move past guys like my idol TD, Tony Dorsett, in career rushing yards. Finishing as one of the top five rushers of all time is a possibility. When I look back at the uncertainty about whether I could play a big role in the NFL, I realize how far I have come, and it motivates me to keep going. It makes me want to push myself that much harder so that I know when I'm finished playing I'll be able to say that I got the most out of myself.

I have been recognized as the NFL Man of the Year for my work with single parents, and many people have applauded the things I do off the field. I'm appreciative of that, but I don't put forth the humanitarian efforts to bring recognition to myself. I do it because I know firsthand what people go through and how much a helping hand can mean in a person's life.

As a football player, first and foremost I am a competitor. I have spent a career proving myself. While it's nice to be recognized for what you do as a person off the field, I hope people don't forget I am a football player and that I am working to be the best at what I do. Like anybody else, I would love to be acknowledged as one of the best to play the game.

I know if I can continue to work hard and make plays, I have a chance to put my name up there where I have earned a place as one of the best. Then when I am done playing they won't say, "He was a good situational player." They will just see my name up there with the great running backs who have played in the NFL.

Trust me, when you've spent so much time trying to prove yourself, a goal like that is very motivational.

CHERYL'S STORY

Cheryl Caro grew up in Tampa and decided to move back to the city to start over again with her two young daughters, Ashley and Trinity.

Her parents and brother still live there, so Cheryl felt that the support structure would make for a solid environment in which her daughters could grow up.

She was determined to provide a strong example for her children, stressing to them the importance of personal responsibility and self-sufficiency. She worked two jobs, never taking a day off. "I hated that I had to spend so much time at work," she said, "but I had to take responsibility of my life and my family. I told my parents that I was not going to be one of those mothers that their children are embarrassed of."

Cheryl was first hired by the public school system in a substitute role, but was quickly tapped as the cafeteria manager in a local middle school. This job blended perfectly with Cheryl's interests in diet and health. She started taking online college courses to become a registered dietician, specializing in children's issues.

She also refused to accept public assistance to make things easier. "I am able-bodied—I need to work," she insisted. "There are people who need help more than me. I need to be able to take care of my own family."

Her determination is even more remarkable in light of her two-year struggle with intestinal cancer.

"People kept telling me to take disability, or to take some time off, but I wouldn't do it," she said. "I could still lift and manage, and I just brought my toothbrush to work with me so in case I got sick after the chemo treatments, I could just brush my teeth and get back to work. I mean, what kind of example would I be to my girls if I stopped working because it just got too hard?"

And in the midst of all of this, Cheryl decided to go forward with purchasing her first home. She wanted something permanent—a place where her daughters could grow up feeling a sense of ownership and security, and a place that she could feel was truly her sanctuary from the stresses of life.

She started looking around Tampa and eventually found a shut-tered stucco house with a nice-size yard and hardwood trees just a few blocks away from her parents' house. She fell in love with it and began the process of making the purchase, which went much more smoothly than Cheryl had anticipated.

"I had a wonderful relationship with my mortgage broker," she said. "She helped me with whatever I needed. She was the one who told me about the various programs for first-time buyers; I didn't know any of that existed!" Meanwhile, Cheryl's broker sent a letter to the Warrick Dunn Foundation telling them about the remarkable woman who was looking to buy. Cheryl, of course, had no idea this had happened.

In early December 2006, Cheryl prepared to sign the papers for her house. Her supervisor was driving her over to the site, but Cheryl couldn't understand the big deal that everyone was making. She asked why so many people from her family and work wanted to show up; she was told that the mayor would be present at the closing, and that the City of Tampa First-Time Homebuyer's Program had asked that she pick up Trinity from day care and bring Ashley along, too—a move that Ashley did not welcome.

"She's always concerned about having perfect attendance at school," Cheryl said. "She was so upset that something might mess that up for her, but I guess someone from the foundation called her principal and explained the situation, because we were assured that everything would be okay for her."

At the last minute, Cheryl was told the mayor had gotten sick but to come on over with the girls anyway so that they could take care of everything. They headed over to the new house, but despite her countless previous trips by the house, Cheryl was confused. "I kept thinking I must have the wrong street, just like you forget where you park at the store," she said. "I know they had to think I was crazy, but when I saw all the media vans and the people standing around, I knew that couldn't be the right place, so I said, 'Maybe it's the next street over.'"

When she finally arrived, someone from the media asked how she felt, which confused Cheryl even more. "I thought, 'I'm taking possession of my house, so that is exciting, but I'm also having to hand over a load of money, and that's never fun—I don't know. How am I supposed to be feeling?'"

As she climbed out of the car, she caught a glimpse of a decorated Christmas tree through the living room window and thought her mother had set it up to make her move-in feel a bit cheerier. She still didn't know what was waiting for her inside.

As Warrick approached her family in the driveway, someone— whether Cheryl or her mother is still debated in the family—said out loud, "Oh—he's cute!" Cheryl was still unsure, though, of not only why he was there but who he was in the first place.

"I'm so embarrassed about my reaction," Cheryl said. "I didn't know who Warrick Dunn was. I mean, I've got little girls and I'm not really into sports myself. I'd heard my friends talking in the past, so I knew his name, but that was about it. As he was walking toward us, my dad asked me if I knew who he was. I asked, 'He's a football player, right? Um . . . does he play for the Bucs?' My dad whispered, 'Not anymore, so don't say that.'"

When Warrick handed Cheryl the keys and escorted her into the home, she finally began to comprehend everything that was happening. "There was a sofa and a computer and a TV. They had personalized the girls' rooms: Ashley likes fashion and glamour and Trinity loves Hello Kitty, and they did up each one's bedroom that way," she said. "Their faces when they saw them just lit up and they just said, 'It's mine!' Ashley was on ABC News saying, 'I never want to move again! I'm so happy.' And little Trinity finally had her own room because she'd always slept with me."

Cheryl's room was personalized as well. "They had even done mine in my favorite colors," she recalled. Her room, furnished with dark wood and a smoky purple bedspread, was accented with sage green pillows and curtains. Even her bathroom was coordinated with her colors, and the fresh flowers in every vase incorporated them, too.

"I love Asian style," she explained, pointing to the Chippendale-style table and chairs and the artwork on the walls. "They just took all of my favorite things and pulled them together to make a gorgeous home!"

But as excited as she was about the new furniture and decorations, she was most thrilled about something else. "I put away so much money for the down payment for the house that there was no refrigerator, no stove. I was planning to keep my food in a cooler and cook it in a microwave until we could afford to purchase the appliances," she said. "But when I walked in, there was a new refrigerator and a new stove—I just couldn't believe it. I thought we were going to have to wait a while before we could afford any of that. You would think that with all of the furniture and everything else, I would have been most excited about that, but as soon as I saw the refrigerator, I just lost it."

The day still wasn't over for her, though. Cheryl shook her head, and said, "And just when I thought, 'This man can't do anything else for me,' he hands me a check for five thousand dollars and told me to go give it to the mortgage broker, because it was my down payment. I have never, ever met a man who was generous like that. Stuff like that just doesn't happen to me.

"We are so grateful to Warrick—so grateful," she said. "I still can't believe that he did all of this for us—and not only that he gave us everything but that he actually personally cares about us. Every time we see him at one of the foundation gatherings, he always asks me how my health is doing."

There was a handmade card hanging on her fridge from her daughter, letting Cheryl know that her health is in her daughter's prayers. "I can't wait to tell him that I got a clean diagnosis two days ago," she said, grinning. "It's finally gone. I can't wait to tell him because what he did changed our lives and helped to give me the hope to keep fighting."

CHAPTER 14

ROLE MODEL

HOMES FOR THE HOLIDAYS IS NOT MY ONLY PROJECT, though. I've found myself with a variety of opportunities for service in a variety of circumstances. In fact, it feels as if the projects find me sometimes, and this is one of my greatest joys.

For example, the first house that I bought—even before any of the foundation homes—was for my grandmother. I didn't even have to think about that; it was automatic. Grandma stepped in to raise my five brothers and sisters after my mother died so that I could go to Tallahassee for college, and I knew that she would do an amazing job. After all, this was the woman who had raised my mom. My grandmother and my youngest sister, Samantha, now live in The Highlands of Santa Maria in East Baton Rouge. It's an elegant brick home on a golf course with plenty of space for family and friends.

I also wanted to take care of some of the men who had stepped up and given me a chance when I was younger. Malen "Choo-Choo" Brooks was such a role model for me while he was my coach that I still call him Pops. I got him a car as soon as I was able, even though I knew that I could never fully pay him back for all that he has done for me.

Sid Edwards was another one of my coaches who needed some help. He has two autistic children who needed medical attention, so I stepped in and took care of the hospital bills. Some people act as if that was a big deal, but I feel that it's the least I can do for the man who kept me from flunking out of high school.

I'll admit that the reality of becoming a role model did not sit well with me at first. During my first season or two, I was very reluctant to sign autographs. I was uncomfortable with the idea of it—why should anyone hold me up as a role model? Whenever fans would ask or we needed to sign jerseys or balls for charity events, I would always cringe. Someone would have to talk me into doing it because it wasn't an aspect of professional sports that I was willing to embrace.

I remember one time when a member of the Bucs organization asked me to sign something for his father and I turned him down. I felt so terrible about that later because that individual had never been anything but nice to me, but I couldn't bring myself to accept the fact that athletes are role models, whether or not they choose to be. But turning down people who want to take pictures with you and want you to sign things only furthers the idea that it's okay for sports figures to be egotistical or even rude toward the very people whose fandom makes us wealthy. Once I got used to my new "hero" status, I became more comfortable with fan interaction, and started taking a look at some true heroes, as well as challenging other athletes to step up and live in a way that makes us a little more deserving of the role model label. And the main way that I try to show my gratitude to those people who shaped my life is by passing that love along or, as the expression is now, "paying it forward."

One cause to which I am dedicated is my visits with the men and women of the United States armed forces. In May 2004, I got the opportunity to travel with Falcons teammate Keith Brooking and Todd Heap of the Baltimore Ravens to Germany and visit with the soldiers from the 1st Armored Division and the 64th Replacement Company, many of whom were getting ready to mobilize to Iraq over the next few days.

It was so great to get to talk about football with these soldiers; there were a bunch of Bucs and Falcons fans, and even some die-hard Seminoles there. As we were talking and joking around, I felt that if I could take their minds off the worries about where they were headed and about their families back at home—even for a minute or two—then my trip was completely worth it.

I also had a chance to visit a hospital for the soldiers wounded in Iraq and Afghanistan. I thanked them and told them how much America appreciates their willingness to serve, and they just blew me away with their spirit. They all wanted to know how the rest of their unit was doing—if anyone else had been wounded or killed. And the main concern each one of them had was if they would be able to go back and rejoin their buddies in the field.

We have teamwork in sports, and a special camaraderie of athletes, but that was a dedication that I had never seen before. It was truly amazing. They have a bond where if one of them goes down, everyone feels it; everyone is affected. There are some truly great men and women serving in our military, and I was really privileged to get to spend time with them.

In late March and early April 2005, I got to spend even more time with the troops, though this time I was actually headed over to the Middle East. Patriots linebacker Larry Izzo and I headed to Afghanistan to help the USO dedicate its new building, the Pat Tillman Center. The soldiers all had such respect for Pat because of the fact that he walked away from millions of dollars and a flashy professional football career in order to join the army, and then tragically lost his life in the line of duty.

It was humbling to be a part of a ceremony honoring the fallen NFL-player-turned-solider, and it was surreal to travel through not only Afghanistan but also Iraq and Kuwait and to get to talk to military personnel there.

In Iraq, for example, you see the barricades and the checkpoints everywhere, and then you see the people who have been living there—all I could think of was that it was like they were free but living in prison at the same time.

We could actually hear car bombs go off and live rounds being fired in Baghdad, and a few of the camps that we visited were still cleaning up from being hit the night before. The whole experience was very eye-opening—not only because of the war raging around us, but because in the midst of all that, we would meet guys who were still following our teams and could rattle off our stats. It was such a strong reminder that visits like ours really do make a huge difference for those soldiers and Marines.

Later in 2005, another opportunity came about that would challenge not only my own community efforts but those of all Americans. The unprecedented devastation of Hurricane Katrina shocked our nation and left many of us feeling helpless as we watched the suffering of our neighbors on the news.

I felt helpless, too. The need was so massive and the problem was so widespread. It felt as if nothing we could do could even make the smallest amount of difference. Finally, I decided to write the following open letter to my colleagues in the NFL. I knew that we all wanted to help, and if we banded together, the impact we would be able to have could be dramatic. After all, these people who were hurting had given so much to my family years before. It was the least I could do to step up and try to help them in their time of need.

To my fellow NFL players:
Last week the football community was devastated by a hurricane that tore apart an area where so many of us have grown up, competed, made a good living and won championship rings. A lot of

guys in the NFL were born near the coast in Texas, Louisiana, Mississippi, Alabama or Florida. This could have happened to any of them. Brett Favre is from Kiln, Miss, and his family lost its house. Marshall Faulk is from New Orleans, and as of Monday he was still waiting to hear from four of his brothers.

But you don't have to have family on the Gulf Coast to feel the connection. Maybe you played in the SEC, in the Sugar Bowl or against the Saints at the Superdome. Maybe you partied at Mardi Gras or at one of the Super Bowls the city has hosted. How many of you got scouted at the Senior Bowl in Mobile?

My point is this: Football is embedded in the culture that Hurricane Katrina disrupted, and if you play the game, this is in some way your community and your tragedy. As professional athletes, and as Americans, we know we have a responsibility to take care of those who cannot take care of themselves. That's why I am challenging each one of you—except for the players on the New Orleans Saints—to donate $5,000 to relief efforts.

Full disclosure: I'm one of those people for whom Katrina hit especially close to home. I was born in New Orleans in 1975 and raised in Baton Rouge. So many of my memories—some beautiful, some sad—are from Louisiana. I played youth football for the South Baton Rouge Rams and went on to play for Catholic High School. In my sophomore year we played the state championship game at the Superdome—a place that has lately become the site of so much misery. When I was 18, my mother, Betty Smothers, a single mom supporting me and my five brothers and sisters as a Baton Rouge police officer, was shot and killed in the line of duty while working overtime. The community banded together and established a trust fund for me and my siblings. Without the kindness of the people of my hometown, I probably wouldn't be playing in the NFL today.

If you've been to the area where so many people are suffering right now, and so many have died, you know that even as a visiting

*player, you are treated with Southern hospitality. People are po-
lite in those parts. It's "yes, sir" or "no, ma'am." People care. Now
we have to return that hospitality.*

*When I was home last week in Atlanta watching the story
unfold on TV, I kept thinking, What can I do? Can I rent a plane
and bring supplies? Can I get a truck down there with food and
water? I just couldn't sit there and do nothing. Many of the people
I saw had little to begin with, and now they've lost even that.
Where are they going to live? Where are they going to work? I
decided the best thing I can do is to mobilize the players of this
league. This crisis needs money, and lots of it.*

*You and I—the players of the NFL—can afford this kind of
contribution. The average guy in our league makes $1.33 million
a year; he can certainly give less than 1% of that to help people
who have lost everything but the shirts on their backs. If we all
give $5,000 we'll have raised $8.5 million. That is a neighborhood
of rebuilt homes. That is a new school. That is real. That is help.
That is changing lives. And that is why I am working with the
NFL Players Association to get every one of you to contribute.
This open letter isn't the last time you'll be hearing from me.*

*But I get the feeling I'm not going to have to beg you. I've al-
ready spoken to some of you, and I sense a strong desire to help.
Tom Brady, for one, says he's all for it. I've spoken to players on
several teams—Travis Minor in Miami, Aaron Stecker with the
Saints, and Allen Rossum, Michael Vick, Patrick Kerney and Todd
Peterson on our team—and they're all receptive to it. But this is
only a start. It is my hope that 31 teams will take the same initia-
tive. Troy Vincent, the president of the Players Association, wants
us to mobilize and get the job done.*

*Even though our minds are understandably on the season that
begins this week, we cannot put this matter aside and we must
move fast. Towns in three states have been leveled. A city that has*

given our league and our sport some of its best moments is in ru-
ins. An entire region is in pain, a region filled with people who
have paid to see us play, a region filled with people who have
bought our jerseys, who now have nothing. What will it say about
us—not as football players but as human beings—if we don't give
back?

We managed to raise $381,000 just from the players on the Fal-
cons. The NFL also stepped up and challenged owners, players, and
fans alike to give. The total from those donations topped $22 mil-
lion. Those numbers were great, but when you consider the destruc-
tion spread from Florida to Alabama to Mississippi to Louisiana and
even farther north into places like Arkansas as the storm moved in-
land, even that much money really made only a small dent. Americans are such generous people, and I really hope that people will
remember their material blessings and be willing to share them the
next time a natural disaster strikes.

Thankfully, my family was blessed in that they did not sustain
any damage to their home, but we did have some relatives from along
the Gulf Coast who stayed with my grandmother during the storm
out of precaution. It was a terrible time for everyone—those who
suffered loss and those who had to help their neighbors through it.

I know that you sometimes hear about "giving until it hurts," but
philanthropy doesn't have to be painful. In fact, one of the best
fund-raisers we have for the Warrick Dunn Foundation is the annual
Foundation Gala, which is really a great time for everyone involved.

We started this as a small event back in 2003 at Maggiano's Little
Italy, a fantastic restaurant in the Buckhead neighborhood of Atlanta, but the seating was limited and the fashion show soon became
such a big hit that we had to move it. Now we host it at the King
Plow Arts Center or another large venue in downtown Atlanta in
order to facilitate the crowd that shows up each year.

In 2006 alone, the show raised about $30,000 for the Homes for the Holidays program. It's amazing the enthusiasm that people have for watching Falcons players like Brian Finneran, Allen Rossum, DeAngelo Hall, and others strut their stuff down the catwalk. It's also funny to see those big, tough guys next to the real models we also feature in the show, who are so thin and delicate and glamorous.

We try to bring families along who have benefited from our Homes program, too. It is really a positive thing for the donors to hear from the real people for whom their contributions are making such a difference. One of the women told the crowd, "From the bottom of my heart, I love you all." It was really an incredible moment.

I am also very grateful that my efforts have helped other people to give as well. Several of my NFL colleagues have started their own Homes for the Holidays organizations. We partnered with Kurt Warner to get similar programs up and running both in his hometown of Des Moines, Iowa, and in St. Louis, home of the Rams. Shelton Quarles established a program in Tampa. It's so exciting to see athletes across the country stepping up across the nation to build their cities and help set the future course of countless lives.

I met Gary Pajcic at Florida State's annual Garnet and Gold Game in April 2006. There he presented me with a check for $100,000 on behalf of the university and his law firm, Pajcic and Pajcic. Gary had played quarterback for the Seminoles in the late 1960s and later attended the FSU law school. As he handed me the check made out to my foundation, he announced to the crowd that the gift was "a token of both my own and Florida State's appreciation for his life's work on the field and, more importantly, off the field." My life's work—I like the sound of that.

In the spring of 2007, I was approached by a new outreach program called Athletes for Hope. It sounded like a wonderful effort, but I just didn't feel that I could contribute. I am contacted by many philanthropic and charitable organizations, and as much as I would love to help them all, it's just not possible. Regretfully, I declined the offer, but wished them the best of luck.

They wouldn't give up, though, and talked to Stephanie about trying to get me on board, and she talked to me about it a bit, too, but to be honest, I didn't quite understand what their mission was. It just sounded a little strange that all these athletes were banding together for philanthropy—like Super Friends or something. I was content to continue my work; I didn't want to lose the focus of my own goals. It had taken me a while to discover the niche for my philanthropic passion, and now I really didn't want to give it up to pursue someone else's cause.

I was surprised a few days later when I received yet another phone call. "Warrick?" said the voice on the other line. "This is Andre Agassi, and I'd really like to talk to you about reconsidering your decision and teaming up with Athletes for Hope after all." I just stared at the phone for several seconds and couldn't even answer. Andre Agassi— calling *me*? He had been one of my sports heroes while I was a teenager with his long hair, earring, crazy shirts, and reported love for cheeseburgers. He was talented and quick and different—the epitome of everything I thought was cool. And here I was, being anything but cool, as I tried to squeak out just one word to him over the phone.

Thankfully, I was able to recover and we chatted a bit about the Athletes for Hope organization. It came about when Andre, along with Lance Armstrong and Mia Hamm, decided to band their efforts together and launch a new foundation that could have exponentially more impact because of its breadth—"And we'd love for you to come on board," he told me. Sponsored by Genworth Financial, Lance, Andre, and Mia combined the power of their own foundations and invited nine other athletes to join their ranks as they began work on an organization intended to help rookies and lesser-known athletes find an outlet for their own philanthropic interests.

Once Andre explained it to me, I was completely sold. It was a wonderful concept and an effort I absolutely wanted to be a part of. I couldn't wait to see who else would be joining up—but once I found out, I was starstruck all over again.

Looking around the room at that first meeting at Muhammad Ali, Jackie Joyner-Kersee, Andrea Jaeger, Jeff Gordon, and Tony Hawk, I couldn't help but wonder if there had been a mistake. What on earth could these sports legends want with me? Was there really anything that I could bring to the table? I definitely felt like the small man in the room, but for once, it wasn't because of my height.

We discussed the aims of Athletes for Hope, which, as Andre pointed out, is intended to help change the goals of aspiring sports figures. We want tomorrow's star to enter the realm of professional athletics with the desire to give back. It is often very difficult for new players to figure out how to navigate various charitable opportunities and to figure out tax laws and tax-exempt status when beginning a foundation. In many ways, Athletes for Hope can serve as a mentorship.

We also want to help athletes who don't carry as much name power but who also desire to give. By banding together with more widely recognized figures, they can increase the impact of their gifts and time. Together, the twelve of us have raised more than *half a billion dollars* for our own community work. Our goal was to see what we could do if we joined forces.

Many times, an athlete has a desire to get involved but doesn't necessarily know where to turn or doesn't have a specific cause. They can come to our foundation and Athletes for Hope will help match them with a program that appeals to their interests. Mia Hamm, for instance, has a passion for individuals going through bone marrow treatment because her brother lost his own battle to a blood disease. Muhammad Ali has established centers for the study

of Parkinson's disease and other neurological conditions in both Louisville and Phoenix.

Other times, players are connected to a cause because of geo-
graphical loyalties. A player with the Cardinals or someone who
grew up in Missouri might want to pitch in with Jackie Joyner-Kersee's
work in underprivileged neighborhoods in East St. Louis.

It's about finding what inspires a person; even if he or she doesn't
have a direct connection to either of those causes, it is our hope that
the vision of the work may move them to action, and the fact that we
already have the groundwork in place will help to expedite their own
resources without tying up extra time and money in the administra-
tive side of things.

The response we received to Athletes for Hope was incredible. In
the first forty-eight hours following our website launch, we received
more than 124,000 hits. The program generated so much interest in
both the sporting world and among fans. After all, there are opportunities for nonathletes to participate as well. We welcome all volunteers and interested parties. The goal is to reach out and connect
people who are looking for a way to serve.

The generosity I have seen in people my entire life has always
impressed me, and it continues to do so now. There are so many
people who want to give, want to share, and want to use their resources or their influence for something other than just looking out
for themselves.

I had a really good time in 2006 when I got to participate in the
NFL's "Take a Player to School" day. It is a nationwide program in
which thirty-two students are selected on the basis of their entry
videos and essays to be joined by a professional football player as a
show-and-tell surprise for their classmates.

I spent the day at an elementary school in the Atlanta area with a
fourth-grader named Josiah Pearson. We visited his class and then

went to the gym for a school assembly. I talked to the students about reading and studying and being true to themselves while chasing their dreams. We talked about education and sports, and then got to play a bit of football, too.

I am so glad that the NFL has a program like Take a Player to School day. It reminds the children that the athletes they see on TV are real live people, and it reminds us players that there are young, impressionable children looking up to us

After my letter to the NFL following Hurricane Katrina in 2005, the *Evening Standard*, a London-based newspaper, announced, "In Warrick Dunn, American sport may have found its conscience." That is certainly an overstatement; there have been many selfless players before me, and doubtless there will be many more to follow. However, I appreciated the use of the word "conscience" because that is something that I do try to live by and encourage others to follow as well. Personal values are so essential in steering a life in the right direction.

One of the things that really saddens me when I look at young people is the mentality that "as soon as I get a lot of money, I'm going to buy myself an expensive car." There is nothing wrong with having nice things, and I think it is great if you are able to buy yourself a fancy car. However, in today's society we are all too often conditioned to look past the necessities and go straight to the desires.

Especially if you're coming from the 'hood or the streets, you get some money and the first thing so many young athletes want to do is what they see on TV—they think, "Let me get the ice and the fancy cars and the expensive toys." Like I said, there is nothing wrong with living well, but people need to learn to take care of the necessities first and then, once you get everything in order, you will be able to do all of that stuff. I'm not coming down on having nice things; I have three nice cars myself—but I didn't buy my first new car until my eighth season in the NFL. My Mitsubishi Galant was fine; it ran well and it got me where I needed to go. I didn't need anything fancier, so I prioritized. I probably had the oldest car in the entire league!

I think it is essential that we teach children early on that there is a responsible way to handle money, and that is to take care of paying bills, making ends meet, and saving for the future rather than spending every check as soon as it comes—or even going into debt—for luxury items.

The idea of reaching children when they are young really resonates with me, and I believe that is why I am drawn to helping families. I feel that if we are able to influence children while they are still developing, we have a better chance of breaking cycles of behavior and mind-sets that damage the culture.

I want young people to understand that there is a certain way to dress if you are going on a job interview, or the workplace, or a nice restaurant. There is a certain way to eat, a way to speak, a way to carry yourself. I'm not saying that you shouldn't be yourself, but there is a pattern of behavior that leads to success, and a pattern that makes success a lot more difficult. I really want to urge kids to get on the right path early, so that they can learn about good decision-making and life choices that will affect them in the long term.

In the end, though, the real role models are the parents. Parents have to control their children and be invested in them. They have to be involved in their lives to make sure they are following and doing all the right things. They have to try to shape their children's minds and teach them to think in certain ways. Parents have that authority, and they need to exercise it. My siblings and I knew we had to mind our mother because she represented authority not only in our house but also in our community. She did what she had to in order to keep us out of trouble, and I've always been grateful for that.

There is a lot of talk about professional athletes branding themselves and creating a new image. My feeling is that there needs to be substance behind that brand. It's also so encouraging when other people start to notice a difference resulting from our hard work and investments in others' lives. It means that we are doing something right and that the people we are helping are truly being served. I've received a lot of recognition for my work from the National Center for Black Philanthropy to the Giants Steps Award in Civic Leadership to the Henry P. Iba Citizen Athlete Award. I was also honored by the National Alliance to End Homelessness with the John H. Macy Award for Individual Leadership, and Oprah Winfrey named me one of her "Angels" in 2001. In 2003, *Sports Illustrated* magazine added me to their list of the 101 Most Influential Minorities in Sports.

Actually, it's all been a little overwhelming.

One of the greatest honors of my life came when I was named the 2004 Walter Payton Man of the Year by the NFL. This is an annual award that is given to one player who has demonstrated a dedication to philanthropy and personal giving. I was the first member of the Falcons organization ever to receive it. I was so overwhelmed when I learned that I had been selected. To be selected from such a huge pool full of generous, selfless individuals was absolutely incredible.

The *Sporting News* named me to their Top 75 Good Guys in Professional Sports several times, and in 2005, they put me at the number-one spot. They considered more than 500 athletes from all sports and compiled a list of finalists. According to editorial director John Rawlings, *TSN* based their decision both on "dollars [donated] and commitment of the heart."

The thing is, though, that all of this attention to my community work is a little bit embarrassing. I don't do these things to get noticed, and it's even a little uncomfortable writing about them here, but the fact is that those of us who have been given the opportunity to live the life of a professional athlete become role models for America's youth whether we want to be or not.

If I am going to receive recognition, I'd rather have it be for my playing than for my giving, because I am supposed to be noticed when I'm on the field. I'm not trying to get attention when I do work in the community.

The fact of the matter, though, is that we live in a culture that values athletic ability. Kids are going to look up to professional athletes because it is a glamorous profession. As a rule, kids aren't really going to look up to philanthropists as much, even though the impact on people's lives may be much greater through the philanthropy efforts than the athletic victories. I know that I am a role model for many young people, and it's not because of my community work. It's because I work hard on the field and play with discipline and dedication. I don't want people ever to lose sight of that, because that is what makes my playing style work, and my playing style is what makes possible everything else that I do.

In the end, though, I just feel incredibly thankful that I have the opportunity to live the life that I've been given. I am so humbled and grateful that I am able to take the gifts that I've been given on the field and convert them into something that impacts lives off of it. I really take to heart the words of one of the great leaders in African American history, Frederick Douglass, when he said, "It is easier to build strong children than to repair broken men."

Because I have been able to build a reputation as a talented player, I have been able to build futures. Because I am able to play, I am able to make a difference. Because I have been blessed with a talent, I also have been given a responsibility.

VERALL'S STORY

Verall Robinson grew up in Baton Rouge in a close-knit family with nine siblings, but she was closest to her sister Angela, who was two years older than her.

As a young woman, Angela was diagnosed with breast cancer but succeeded in fighting it off. At the age of thirty-seven, when she was pregnant with her first child and thrilled about this new start to her life, the cancer returned. This time, it was discovered, it had spread to her lungs and her hip and was continuing to grow aggressively. "Verall, I want you to be there with me every day," Angela told her sister.

"So I made a vow to her as well as to the Lord to be there for her no matter what," Verall said. She gave up her hairstyling business and joined her mother and aunts at Angela's bedside to support her through the struggle. There, they prayed and encouraged one another, relying heavily on the faith that is such an integral part of the family's life. "My focus was just to take care of her and believe in God that He would just turn this thing around and give her another chance. But God had other plans."

When Angela reached her seventh month of the pregnancy, the doctors determined that they could successfully remove her baby, a boy she'd named Kyle, without any harm. Angela could begin intense chemo treatments and her baby would be protected from the strong chemicals about to enter her body. Kyle survived. Angela did not. She managed to keep up her fight for a while, but when Kyle was nine months old, Angela finally succumbed to the disease.

Verall was heartbroken in those final days, watching her sister lay in the hospital bed, unable to speak and barely able to move. "She was responding by shaking or nodding head," Verall said. "She couldn't open her eyes. I asked her, did she want me to raise Kyle and she just nodded her head yes, so I promised her that I would."

Looking back at the ordeal, Verall is still able to see the hand of God through the tragedy. "I just thank God that I did take that time out because even though our plans were just to believe that she would live, He had other plans for her. But then, also, he had to do something within me, as well," she insisted. "Because I was a person who just didn't have any goals in life. Who are we to question what God's plans are?"

And so suddenly, at the age of thirty-five, Verall found herself a mother but, by her own admission, still in need of some growing up. She had given up her business to stay with her sister, had accumulated debt in the meantime, was living in a one-bedroom apartment in a dangerous neighborhood, and had never been faced with real responsibility for anyone but herself.

"Everything for me was starting over again then," she said. "A reality check came in. I was in a place where I knew that I could not raise a child. So I'd been living my life for me, me, me, then the Lord said, 'Okay—I'm giving you this child. You now have authority over this child and you are accountable for him'—I had to grow up, literally."

She had always been very involved with her church, and it was here that she found the comfort, support, and motivation that she sought. A hairdressing client had told Verall about Habitat for Humanity and how to apply, but Verall had yet to act. She was struggling with her own mourning over her sister's death, the adjustments to taking care of Kyle and working toward his adoption, and the stresses of rebuilding her life. It was at this point that Turmelovea Smith, an older woman at Verall's church, stepped in and started the fire that pushed her to take action.

"I call her my 'spiritual mother,'" Verall said. "She told me, 'You are going to get up; you're going to get out of this apartment; you are going to apply for your house. If you have a lot of issues in life and you never try to resolve them, then those issues take over you.'"

Turmelovea's tough love motivated Verall, and she remains grateful for the challenge. "Some people tell you it's okay when it's really not okay," she said. "But to have someone who took authority and said, 'No—we are not going to have any pity party. We are going to do something about it'—that made the difference."

Six months after Angela's death, Verall finally submitted her application with Habitat and the next week, she began the orientation classes. There, they worked on credit-building and responsible credit usage, they discussed money management, and they studied home-ownership skills. Two and a half months later, Verall and Kyle received their home visit and were on the road to receiving a house of their own.

There were still more challenges to overcome, however. It was difficult for Verall to accrue the required 350 sweat equity hours between trying to rebuild her business and look after Kyle. One night, she prayed over the matter with Turmelovea and the next day, a letter arrived for her from Habitat informing her that they needed some help with office work and asking if she'd be interested in fulfilling her hours that way.

"I called them right away and they said, 'We could use some help right now.' So I said, 'I'm on my way' and jumped in my car," she recalled. Within a year, she had her hours and she and Kyle were ready to move into their new home.

Verall laughed, remembering move-in day: "That was a day to remember!"

She had been extremely busy for several weeks and was exhausted; and she admitted, too, that she was feeling slightly annoyed with all of the questions from her friends at Habitat about her plans to decorate the house. "I kept thinking, 'What do you need to know that for?'"

Like several other recipients of Baton Rouge Habitat houses in late November 2004, she was told that CNN would be interviewing her about the new home for a piece they were doing on the organization. She didn't feel like going to the interview that day. "I was dragging that morning," she admitted. And not helping her stress level was the fact that her mother and siblings were calling her, telling her to hurry up and head over to the house. "I just thank God for Habitat. They were a blessing," she said, shaking her head. "That's why

I was able to make myself get over there—because they'd asked me to be there. But I really didn't want to go."

When she pulled up, the Habitat director was waiting and told Verall to leave her car running in the middle of the street. "She was smiling and yelled, 'Don't worry about it—somebody will park it. Just get on up there! Hurry up—run!'" Verall remembered. She got Kyle from the backseat and dashed up to their new yard.

There she noticed that their house had ribbons on it, and there were a number of men in black shirts standing on the lawn. Someone asked her, "Do you see that man in the black shirt?"

"I didn't know who she was talking about because there were so many men in black," Verall said. "Finally a neighbor said, 'It's Warrick Dunn!' and I asked 'Where? Where?' Because, of course, I knew him—he grew up in the same neighborhood as my aunt, so I had known who he was as a kid, and there was the situation with his mom, too. That was devastating to the city. So I definitely knew who he was."

And then she began to put the pieces together. Warrick Dunn was standing in front of her new home where she, as a single mom, stood ready to make the down payment. "I just couldn't believe it. I'd heard about the work he'd done, but I never knew to what extent. I'll be honest with you—it was mind-blowing."

There were several homes furnished by the foundation that day, and when Verall's turn came, she was shaking. "Warrick blessed the home and handed the key to me and that was such a blessing to me," she said, getting choked up. "I was honored just to be in his presence. He is a real sweet, real genuine person. I just thank God for his lovingkindness and his spirit—his sweet, sweet spirit."

She cut the ribbon as best she could with her shaking hands, and then walked inside. "I can't even talk about it now, I'm so overwhelmed," she said. "They did over what I could ever have done, over what I could ever have hoped for. I hadn't hoped for anyone to do anything, of course, but this was beyond my imagination."

The home was decorated in Verall's favorite colors of green, brown, and burgundy, and the furniture was all a rich, deep cherrywood. "Have you seen *Extreme Makeover*?" she asked. "That's how it was to me. It was just awesome. It was just so, so pretty."

She was thrilled, too, by everything in the kitchen and pantry, but she was found herself most overcome when she came to Kyle's room. It was done in a SpongeBob SquarePants theme and was furnished with everything she would have liked to have bought him on her own, but had never been able to provide. "I was okay up until then," she said. "I just broke out crying, and crying in front of Kyle made him start crying. I said, 'Don't cry, too. I'm sorry. I'm okay, baby. I'm just happy.'"

Despite the pain she still feels over the loss of her sister, Verall considers herself to be truly blessed by both Habitat for the house and Warrick for everything inside it and the down payment. "I thank God for him, I truly do," she said. "He was—he is—such a blessing."

CHAPTER 15

TALKING ABOUT IT

IT WAS AFTER PRACTICE ONE DAY IN THE SUMMER OF 2003 when Shawn Jefferson and I were sitting in the Falcons' locker room. Shawn looked at me and said something that would change my life. "Warrick," he asked, "for all the things you've accomplished in your life, why don't you seem more happy? You can't look people in the eye very well. I just don't get it."

For the first time, it was like someone had caught me, someone had just cut right to the heart of what I was feeling. I was shocked. I couldn't really say anything because for some reason, Shawn's words at that time just resonated with me. And as he went on, I just became more confused. He told me he'd had some similar problems and challenges, and he really thought that talking to a counselor might help me. "Let me give you her number," he said. "Just give it a try. I really think it might help you out."

I did not share Shawn's optimism.

First of all, I know that I am a little guy competing in a big guy's league. The last thing that I want when I'm at the bottom of a pile of six-feet-five, 300-pound guys is for them to be thinking, "This little dude may be fast, but he's also *crazy*!" Beyond that, though, there is a broader cultural taboo about going to therapy. Maybe it doesn't seem like that much of a big deal, but the fact of the matter is that counselors, psychologists, therapists, shrinks—that whole realm is really looked down on in the African American community, especially among the males. It's viewed as a sign of weakness to admit that you need help and to think that you can get it just by sitting in some office talking to someone. There is also just the stigma of airing your dirty laundry. You aren't supposed to talk about what's going on in your family—especially not to someone outside your circle. And here I was supposed to open my guts, talk about my mom's murder, and spill my emotions to a sweet-natured little old white lady and expect her to understand me? It just didn't seem like this could possibly work.

I couldn't shake Shawn's words, though. Over the next few days, I kept thinking about what he had said. Was my pain really that obvious to other people? I had always thought that by not ever showing much emotion, I was concealing it well. People would just think that was what I was like, how my personality was—and yet, apparently, other people *could* tell that something was wrong.

I finally agreed to take the number from Shawn, but I didn't want to be the one to call. I convinced a friend to make the appointment instead, and I wanted to make sure that it was listed under another name. I was very, very worried about people finding out that I was going to counseling—would they think I was crazy, or weird, or weak? I talked to Dr. Pauline Clance on the phone and let her know who I was, but I insisted that I wanted everything to be kept quiet about my identity. I asked if I would be able to park in the back of the clinic and use a side entrance. I just wasn't ready for people to know what I was doing. In a way, I don't think I was ready to admit it to myself, either.

Dr. Clance really respected my desire for privacy. Professional athletes don't get a lot of privacy, on the field or off. In a lot of ways, we deal with as much stress as the CEOs of major companies. I know it's just a game, but it's also a billion-dollar business. My job is performed in front of millions of people week after week, and every move I make, every slight misstep or turn or hesitation, is magnified. Every decision is going to be questioned and debated, played and replayed by a million commentators, dedicated fans, armchair quarterbacks, and critics. The anxiety that creates is just unbelievable, and the last thing I wanted was for people to start to scrutinize my moves off the field and to pass judgment on me for them—especially for something as private as this.

The clinic made the arrangements for me to park and enter in a discreet manner behind the building. Dr. Clance even went to extra pains to make sure that my identity was kept a secret from the rest of the staff. It's a large clinic: ten psychologists and their supporting staff. She made sure that the only people who knew who I was and what I was doing there were herself and the office manager, since she had to be aware for the sake of billing and also my privacy arrangements. I met them both so that I could establish a feeling of confidence in their commitment to helping me keep a low profile, and I started to feel a bit more at ease about the entire process.

Until I actually sat down for the first session, that is.

I couldn't look Dr. Clance in the eye. I couldn't bring myself to look at her or even really speak with her directly. I kept fiddling with my cell phone—which I'm sure drove her crazy—but it was all I could do to release some of the nervous energy. I was looking down; I was looking away; I was just very disengaged. We didn't really cover any ground during that first session, but I came back because I have always felt that if you try something once and give up, you aren't giving it a fair shot. I just felt like I had to give it another chance and I had to be real with myself and be more engaged this time.

It took several more sessions before I was able to start looking up at her and make eye contact, even briefly. I even started to smile occasionally. One of the techniques she employed just to get me talking was to discuss subjects that I was proud of—my football career, my community work—and eventually we got around to my family.

One of the motivating factors for me to really start to open up was when I injured my foot in 2003 and ended up missing the last five games of the season with the Falcons. When I play football, I have an outlet for whatever is bothering me at the time. I guess it's almost cathartic for me. Suddenly, though, I didn't have that outlet. I couldn't just play through the frustration. I had to deal with it in another way, so I finally started to talk about it. Even if the relief was just a temporary one, at least I had a chance to put the burden down briefly when I was on the field. But without some kind of physical exertion, I still had the burden of everything on my shoulders. I think when I got hurt it taught me a lot about myself. I had to battle back, but I also had to face what it was that was weighing me down. What was it about my mother's murder that had stayed with me so long that I couldn't seem to shake the depression? What was making me feel so heavy-hearted? Why was I always worried?

By talking things through with Dr. Clance, I finally realized that I wanted to let my family go. I needed to relieve myself of that burden of always being responsible for them. My brothers and sisters were all old enough to take care of themselves, so they needed to do it. I needed to let them go. They needed to be free. I needed to live my own life—to live for Warrick, for once.

And when I finally realized that—and said it out loud—I started relaxing more. I started having more fun. I just think I became a better person. It wasn't that I stopped loving my family, of course, but I stopped letting my worry for them control my world. In everything I did, in every decision I made, I was looking at them first, and how it would impact their lives. Dr. Clance finally made me admit that I was worth worrying about, too—that I had to make sure Warrick was okay first before I could make sure anybody else was okay. If I didn't do that, I could very likely end up worrying myself to death, literally, and my family would be left alone again.

Despite the progress we were making with regard to my family, I still wasn't ready to talk about my mother. It wasn't until 2005—two years later—that I felt ready to discuss my feelings about her murder and its impact on my life.

We didn't just jump into talking about Mom right away. Instead, Dr. Clance tried to get me to discuss what happened by doing it in pieces. Apparently, that is something that is considered very necessary, so as not to make the person relive the event by retelling it in detail all at once. She said that can retraumatize people sometimes, because they can end up reexperiencing the event in a way that leads back to how they were when it happened in real life. It had to be a gradual release of emotion and memory of the event, and not so much that it became overwhelming.

We talked about how my worldview fell apart after my mother's death. Sometimes she'd ask me to discuss how I had envisioned that my mother would always be there, and how I wished that she could see me do various things, because she was my biggest fan. Other times, we'd discuss how my mom held the family together. We finally reached the point of discussing how my world blew apart with Mom's murder and that my sense of innocence, of childhood, of safety were all destroyed, too. Dr. Clance made me realize that I had become aware of something that she called "human vulnerability" at an earlier age than most. People like me suffer in a different way because we become aware not just of the adult world but also of human mortality long before many other people. No one wants to be aware of death. It's an unpleasant reality of being human, but it's not something that any of us wants to think about, or have at the forefront of our mind. Sooner or later, though, we all have to face death in some form or another, and when something happens suddenly and to someone very close to us—the way my mom's murder happened—it immediately wipes out any sense of order that we have in life. If we are young when this happens, it can be especially damaging because we are faced with these life issues before we are really old enough to understand or appreciate what life is about.

Dr. Clance and I also talked about my time in college, and how I never went out to a club or a party once—*not once* in four years. She asked me why I lived by myself and I admitted that it was easier to cry if I was alone. The important thing to me wasn't to not appear sad on the outside, but just to appear as if I had no emotions at all. It was a lie, of course, pretending that I didn't carry those emotions with me—but it was just easier that way. I wanted to experience joy and connections with people and I wanted to laugh and enjoy life, but I needed to get over my pain. I didn't want to get over my mom, though. I think I equated the two and felt like it was a betrayal. But I had to deal with it—just in a different way than I knew how.

Dr. Clance kept working with whatever I was experiencing at the time. That's how she first got me to open up and talk, and that was how she was able to pull out more of my feelings about my mom. Sometimes we'd discuss books or music—anything to get me to open up and talk to her. Then things got more personal; as we'd be discussing something going on in my life, like girlfriends and relationships and football, it would spark a memory, and I'd suddenly launch off in a new direction. The point was to get me to begin to say these things out loud—to give a voice to the emotions I had refused to let another human being see for so long.

Sometimes we would talk about things that were bothering me in a different way. I used to really struggle when well-meaning people would ask me, "What do you think you mother would think about that?" It made me mad sometimes because I just wanted to say, "I don't know—and I'll never know. Please don't remind me that she isn't here to see me, to talk to me, or to tell me how she feels or what she thinks. I already do that to myself enough."

One of the things that I really needed to learn to concentrate on was the ability to see myself succeed with a healthy mind-set. One of the trends of my behavior that Dr. Clance made me see was that I was relying almost superstitiously on succeeding through my lack of emotion. Because I had been playing so well for so many years without dealing with my fears and worries, it was almost as if I was afraid to let them go because my mind subconsciously connected the two things: as long as I kept my emotions buried, I would continue to play well; but the moment I let them rise to the surface, or even let someone else become aware of them, then my game would start to suffer. I know it doesn't seem to make any sense, but because the trauma of Mom's death had coincided so closely with the start of my serious collegiate football career, my mind was equating success with emotional turmoil.

What made things a lot easier for me in my therapy, though, was that Dr. Clance pointed out to me that I do think through complex issues. All this time, I just thought that I wasn't thinking through the issues at all, but as she explained to me how my mind was sorting and making connections subconsciously, it showed me that my head was already doing what I had agonized over doing for years, which was to deal with everything. My community work and foundation were evidence of this as well, because they were an attempt to work through the pain and reconcile with my past, even though I didn't really realize it at first.

I had "homework" to do between sessions, too. I had to practice certain patterns of positive thought and challenge myself to try to put a hold on certain damaging thoughts and feelings. Apparently, this is a pretty common route that a lot of counselors will take, but a lot of patients don't follow through with it. Dr. Clance told me later that she was pretty certain that I would follow through, though, because I struck her as the sort of person who would totally beat himself up over messing up. And she was right. I felt that if I wasn't committed to doing the work, then I was wasting everyone's time and was undoing any progress we'd made. I might feel like an emotional failure, but I would not allow myself to fail while I was trying to reach beyond that.

The main thing that helped me to emerge on the other side was the fact that I had such a solid foundation. We discussed in my sessions the groundwork that Mom had laid for our lives and the sense of love and concern and care and togetherness that she had made sure to instill in all of us early on. Mom had good standards, and high standards that she expected us to meet. It was never like she was pushing us to try to reach unrealistic goals, but she did expect us to live up to our potential and refused to allow us to be lazy. She wanted us to understand the benefit of hard work, and when we did succeed, it was so validating because Mom would be the one who was the most excited for us. If we failed, she wouldn't let us wallow in self-pity. She made sure that we were okay and that we knew that she loved us no matter what, but then we had to get back up and try again. It was always about pressing on and refusing to be held back by any kind of circumstances.

I think I felt that I had to stay unhappy because I knew that she couldn't be there with us, celebrating our victories and our achievements anymore. It was almost like that was my sentence, and I would carry it out for her, so she wouldn't be alone. But the fact of the matter is, she didn't believe in hanging back or giving up. She always wanted us to be moving forward and being confident and sure of her presence. Once Dr. Clance got me to really realize and accept that, then I felt that it was okay for me to feel again and to be happy in my life and in the world around me.

The change was gradual. I didn't have one great big "ah-ha!" moment. Instead, it was the small pieces that started falling into place. I started feeling more comfortable talking to people; I was more willing to open up if I felt I needed to. I even got to the point where I could talk about my mom without falling apart, and that was huge when I realized that I'd crossed that line. And then I started noticing that I was drawing joy—real joy—from things beyond football. I was able to put the burden of worry down long enough to start noticing good things around me.

My coaches were probably some of the first people to start noticing the changes in me. I think my family was aware that something was happening, but because I was able to be myself in a different way around them, I don't think they had any idea how unemotional I had become toward everyone else. Coach Boudreaux used to call me for my birthday every year and we'd talk on the phone to catch up. It was great to still feel connected to that part of my life, but it was a reminder, too, of everything that was weighing on me back in Louisiana. So I'm pretty sure that I wasn't very open or talkative with him when he'd call. He'd always told me that I needed to find someone to talk to, and so I think he was really tuned into any changes that might indicate to him that I'd finally taken his advice.

Coach Weiner seemed to notice a change, too. He told me that I seemed more loose, more happy-go-lucky. I guess I had always seemed tense after Mom's death and now I finally seemed like I was a bit more relaxed and open. I was more willing to talk in interviews and really carry on a conversation with folks from back home. He said he could really tell that I was finally dealing with so much of the pain they all knew I'd kept buried for so long.

I think my playing was affected positively, too. My stats didn't really change, but it was how I felt about the game, how I felt when I was playing. When my mom was alive, I played differently. I had more of a swagger, more passion in my plays. That doesn't necessarily mean I was any better, but I played with a different kind of heart. At Florida State, though, I just wasn't very emotional. I made a play, got up, went to the sideline, went to the huddle. I ran another play, and did it again and again and again. Even as I was leaving my emotion on the field, I still wasn't allowing it space for expression; I was just playing through it. After I started opening up and admitting my feelings, though, I found that it felt like I was starting to breathe again. I wasn't some kind of machine—I could feel the excitement of each play, I could experience the thrill and the charge. And I could become a better player for it.

Probably the first time that I felt comfortable about mentioning my counseling in public was in April 2006, when I had an interview with Andrea Kremer for ESPN. I actually admitted that I'd been to see a counselor. We discussed this a bit, and she asked me how it felt to talk about everything so openly. I thought for a second and then I told her that it meant I was free. I didn't have the burden anymore, and I'm not ashamed of who I am or the things I've struggled with or the questions I've carried and thought about and agonized over. Just a few weeks before the interview, I had been sitting in the running backs' room at the Falcons complex and somehow a question came up about my past and I told them all about it. I explained in depth about the night my mom lost her life, what happened, where I saw her on the table in the hospital. It was the first time I ever sat down and told my story to people I play with. It was the first time I was able to talk about it to my colleagues. That was huge. Huge. It was something I had been terrified of doing for so long, but once I realized not only that I could do it but that I *was* doing it, it was incredibly freeing.

I think I shocked a lot of people that I was suddenly willing to speak openly about my counseling—I know my family was surprised, and Dr. Clance said she was shocked that I'd gone from wanting to use the back door and registering under a pseudonym to talking about it on national television. I know that Shawn Jefferson was surprised, too. After all, it had taken a lot of encouragement and persistence to make me finally give it a try. But now, all I could think of was that if counseling had helped me deal with so much, I had to encourage other people in the same way to be open to the idea. I had to let other men know that it's not a sign of weakness to want to work through your issues in this way.

Shawn gave me my life back, and I am truly thankful to him for that. He opened a door for me in a way that no one else had been able to. My focus had always been on my brothers and sisters, and on my suffering and what I'd been through. I'd never been able to make the commitment to helping myself that I'd needed to make.

I've always made a name for myself with my running. From the first time that I was "discovered" at age nine by Coach Williams for the K-Y Track Club, to my mad sprints down the field at Catholic and Florida State, then for the NFL, it's always been about the ground I've been able to cover. This time, it proved to be that first step that was the hardest, but one of the most important that I've ever taken.

CHAPTER 16

FAMILY BOND

I **FEEL BLESSED TO COME FROM A LARGE FAMILY WITH** five brothers and sisters. We joke that between the six of us, we've got a basketball starting lineup plus a sixth man. On a more serious note, though, it means we've had the opportunity to develop close relationships with five other people, and each one of us has a unique bond with the others.

In spite or maybe because of this, it has been hard for me to let my family go—to watch my brothers and sisters grow up. After my mother was killed, I felt such a serious responsibility to them that it has really taken some getting used to the fact that they are all adults now.

For example, Samantha was only nine when Mom died, so it's sometimes difficult to not look at her as a baby anymore because I've had to be a father figure even longer than I was just her brother. I feel that way for all of my siblings because I have had to take on a double role in their lives for so long, and it's not always been an easy role for any of us to accept.

As I mentioned before, I brought Bricson, Travis, and Samantha down to live in Tampa with me after I signed with the Bucs. I thought it would be easier on everyone that way; our grandmother had been working so hard to bring them up and I knew she needed a break. The three kids would have one another in a new town, and they could start over in a place where people maybe didn't know quite so much about their lives—they could find their own identities.

Derrick was playing football at McNeese State University and Summer was already at Louisiana Tech, so they were okay, but I felt that it would be best if I kept our younger siblings until they finished high school. I enrolled them at Tampa Catholic and learned to balance my practice and game schedules with their homework time.

I would be lying if I didn't say that we butted heads sometimes. The hardest part of moving the three younger kids down with me, though, was the discipline. I hated having to be the authority figure, but someone had to do it; as soon as our mother died, in fact, disciplinarian was another role I had to take on. I quickly learned how to be stern when necessary and how to actually spank my younger brothers when they acted out. It wasn't fun for anyone, but we made it work because we had to.

I am very proud of the adults that all of my siblings have become. They have all found themselves, in one way or another, and are all stories of success in the way that they have overcome the challenges of our past.

Summer, for example, is really an amazing woman; she transferred to Louisiana Tech from Southern University and took a gamble by walking onto the Tech track team. The next year she received a full scholarship and had a strong record as a sprinter during her college career.

Now she lives in Atlanta and works as a counselor at an alternative school for troubled teenage girls, and she draws upon her experiences from growing up to relate to these young women. Summer relates to them in a special way because our past is similar to many of theirs, growing up poor and in a single-parent household.

She says that if they happen to find out that I'm her brother, they always make comments about her being rich. She said she always responds by telling them that the only way I made it to the NFL was by staying in school and maintaining my eligibility to play. Then she reminds them, "It's not my money; it's my brother's. There's a reason I'm working for a living—so that I can make some money for myself, and that's what you've got to do. You've got to rely on yourself."

The main point she emphasizes, though, is that it's not where you start but where you end up that really matters. She really stresses the fact that circumstances don't make the person as much as choices do, and that's a message that really hits home for me.

We've butted heads in the past like any brother and sister will, but it's been such a blessing to see her mature into a responsible and reliable woman. And if I'm the dad, Summer has really taken on the mom role in the family. I had to be tough and a disciplinarian, but Summer has grown to be a very nurturing and gentle person, so as the years have gone by, we've all started turning more and more to her in that capacity—and I think it's an arrangement that suits her well.

We get to see each other quite a bit with both of us living in Atlanta—Summer would probably tell you it's too often. But I really feel like she's one of my best friends beyond just being my sister, and I am so proud of the path she has taken with her life and the work that she does with at-risk teens, as well as her important place in our unique family relationship.

Bricson kept up the family tradition of being a competitive sprinter. He arrived in Tampa as a junior and I know that starting over was really tough for him; he managed to make the best of the situation, though. At Tampa Catholic, Bricson set or tied several school track records. He even placed in the top ten for the state in several events at the Florida finals in Gainesville during his junior and senior years. Bricson continued to run track in college, going first to Hinds

Community College in Jackson, Mississippi, and later transferring to the University of Louisiana at Lafayette.

He currently lives in Atlanta, too, and works for AirTran. I like to tease him that with the travel benefits, he has no excuse to miss any of my games now—at home or on the road. He recently told me something that really meant a lot to me. "There's no telling where I would be, how my head would be—it's on straight—but it could be loose or I could have strayed," he said. He said that my being there and staying on him and the others really helped tremendously. It was really great to hear that and to know that the effort and the worry really did make a difference.

I feel very blessed that both Summer and Bricson live in Atlanta now because we can meet up for dinner or help one another out if need be but still have our own lives. I've really enjoyed having some family so close, but in a city that is large enough to give them privacy despite my career.

Most of us kids take after our mother—we tend to be pretty reserved and not very talkative; Travis, however, is the complete opposite. He is the clown of the family and is always the center of attention when we all get together. Travis really is one of the funniest people I have ever met, and it's great to have him around to get the conversation moving, since the rest of us just aren't that outgoing. He'll always bring up a story about something crazy that we did as kids, or he'll start in with teasing one of us and then everyone else will jump in and pretty soon we are all just laughing hysterically.

He excels in things other than comedy, as well. When he was a senior in high school, he won the Class 2A state championship title in the 200-meter dash, and set a Tampa Catholic High School record for the event with 21.56 seconds. In college, Travis started out at Hinds, like Bricson, and then the Ragin' Cajuns of the University of Louisiana at Lafayette got another Smothers brother when Travis transferred there to play running back.

He's now married with three great kids, and is an executive with Target. He tries to make as many of my games as he is able to, which is usually about five or six a season. I love knowing that he's in the stands at my games, and I really enjoy watching him with his family. Now that he is a parent, I think he understands the struggles that I went through in trying to take on that role. Being a dad is about sacrifice and discipline, and I think he really has a different perspective on the dynamics of our relationship from when he was younger because of the fact that he has now become a dad himself.

Samantha moved back to Baton Rouge after I left Tampa so that she could be close to our grandmother. She is pretty quiet, but can still get feisty if we start picking on her for being the baby. If I ever tell her she's being pigheaded, she'll put her hands on her hips and say, "Oh really, Peanut?" You have to be careful with those quiet ones.

She complains, too, that it is hard for her to shop for birthday gifts for me. She always says that I'm just a T-shirt, jeans, and tennis shoes kind of guy. I don't have any jewelry and I'm not into anything too exciting. I've told her before that it's her responsibility to keep me up with the latest fashion, but I think I probably drive her crazy. We'll go shopping and she'll pick out all kinds of clothes for me to try on, but I hardly ever end up buying them—and if I do buy them, I'll rarely ever wear them.

Last year she finally gave up trying to make me hip and bought me a normal outfit for Christmas: a simple shirt and some jeans. I thought it was great, but I know she thinks I'm a boring dresser—and she's probably right.

Samantha is a lot of fun, but she is also someone I know I can call on to do some legwork if I need anything done in Baton Rouge. It's nice to have her close to home so that when I go back to visit our grandmother or friends in Louisiana, she's there, too. It helps to keep Baton Rouge feeling like home, even though I've been living somewhere else for so long now.

My grandmother is doing well, too. She used to cook us amazing meals after the games when she'd come to Tallahassee to watch me play, and she is still going strong in the kitchen. She even does some cooking for the Homes for the Holidays families when we are first getting them moved in.

Despite her amazing kitchen skills, we tease her because she isn't a stereotypical grandmother. She doesn't sit and knit when she isn't baking; she heads down to the creek and fishes. She likes to brag that she fishes every single day, and I know that I've never seen her miss an opportunity to cast a line. She strings her own poles, baits her own hook, cleans her own fish, and is more than happy to give pointers to anyone brave enough to join her.

We also tease my grandmother about her newspaper clippings. She has saved all the articles she could get her hands on about each of us kids, and laminates them so she can pull them out and read them again and again. She has kept them all in a white plastic box in her bedroom for years and can still probably talk you through every single article and photograph.

She is a tough, no-nonsense lady who will speak her mind if she feels it's necessary. However, she is also a warm, loving woman with an unshakable belief in God. Her faith was so important to me when I was growing up, and now, as an adult, she continues to be a source of strength for me. She raised her children to have a strong faith and she encouraged that in her grandchildren, too. Her trust in God's plan was part of what was able to pull our family through some of the most difficult times, and I am so grateful for the example that she gave us because even now, I rely on my faith to keep me grounded and humble and focused on the right things.

Not all relationships were perfect in my family, though. My brother Derrick and I were on rocky terms for a number of years and we have only recently been able to repair things between us.

We had some sibling rivalry as kids because we are only two years apart and were both athletic and competitive. I think he had some resentment, too, toward the special relationship that I had with our mother and always said that I was a mama's boy.

I also know that Derrick was upset with me when I chose to go to Florida State rather than staying closer to home at LSU. It meant that he had to step up as the man of the house—a role that I had always filled. I don't think that he was angry with me, but I know that the responsibility had to be pretty daunting for him.

He ended up going to college just two and a half hours west of Baton Rouge, which was a mixed blessing. He was close enough to get home easily when he needed to, but it also meant that he ended up making that trip fairly often. I know that was exhausting and I think the stress of his campus life and his home life really wore him down. Eventually, he was even elected the president of the NAACP chapter at McNeese State, so he felt even more pressure to balance his life as a leader on campus and a leader at home.

Meanwhile, I was still trying to manage my obligation to the family from Tallahassee and later from Tampa, so I returned home as often as I was needed to help sort things out, but I know it bothered Derrick that I was still trying to be involved even though I wasn't as close geographically. When I called a family meeting to discuss the option of moving the three youngest kids down to Tampa with me, Derrick became very angry and said that I could not continue to make decisions for the family if I was going to live so far away. He told me that I was acting like the president and governing from a distance, but that he was the boots on the ground, actually dealing with the situation firsthand.

We were both extremely upset. I know that Derrick has his pride, but I knew that I had the means to take care of our other siblings now and that as the oldest, it would always be my responsibility to step up and take action when I saw a need arise. I still believe that.

There was a period, too, where he also started to blame me for our mother's death. I was the oldest and I really did have a different relationship with her than did the other kids. She depended on me in a different way and I had a different position as the man of the house. In Derrick's mind, I think that really cut him deeply. Because I was planning to leave for FSU in the fall, Derrick was finally going to have his time as the oldest and as Mom's go-to guy. But before that transition could happen, she was killed and his time as her man of the house was taken away. His grief took the form of jealousy, and our relationship really deteriorated after the funeral. He seemed to feel that I had stolen all of her time and attention, and that everything she had done—like working the second job where she ultimately died—was for me.

I think we both carried the stress and the shock of our abrupt life change with us for a long time. Whereas I coped with the pain by retreating into myself and becoming even more reserved, Derrick coped with it by becoming, in his own words, "meaner." We both dealt with the situation facing our family in the best way that we saw fit: I felt a need for action and order; Derrick felt a need for toughness.

Derrick has also had his share of health problems. A few years ago, he was diagnosed with a slow-growing and inoperable brain tumor. He'd suffered from severe headaches since high school, but the discovery of his condition came as a shock. Even so, he is able to keep the tumor in check with a regimen of medication, and has been able to keep up with a very full schedule and active life. He runs his own electronics business in Baton Rouge and is also the assistant coach of the Catholic High freshman football team and coaches the K-Y Track Club, both organizations that meant a lot to us when we were younger.

Now that we are older and have seen the rest of our family grow to adulthood and steer their own lives, it's been easier for Derrick and me to resolve our issues. Both of us were thrust into adulthood so suddenly that I don't think we had a chance to really evaluate what being a grown-up meant before we had to take over the role. We were each feeling our way through the process and now that we are fully on the other side of it, with everyone grown up and responsible for themselves, Derrick and I can finally reevaluate our relationship with each other.

Most of our conflicts ultimately arose from both of us wanting the same thing: what was best for our family. I know that we both acted in the way that we each felt was necessary, and all things considered, I think we did a pretty good job.

I really can't stress enough how proud I am of the way in which my family has grown and how my siblings have turned out. There are so many things in our past that any of us could have fallen back on as a justification for failure: poverty, race, a single-parent household, moving around a lot, the loss of our mother—any one of these could have become a source of excuses to quit or to get in trouble or to let rage consume us and dictate our lives.

We've all gone through difficult periods, of course, but it makes me so happy to see how all of my brothers and sisters have worked past their issues and refused to let anything hold them back. To me, that is one of the most important lessons that I can offer people: it is our decisions and not our circumstances that determine who we will become.

My siblings have all decided to become well-adjusted, law-abiding, productive members of society, with careers and relationships and families and joy in their lives. We've looked out for one another, encouraged one another, challenged one another, and held one another accountable—and we still do. I couldn't ask for anything better than that.

Recently I heard a sermon that really struck home with me. It was from a pastor named Dale Bronner and was titled "Deal with It." As I listened to Dr. Bronner speak about the teachings of the Bible in

2 Timothy, chapter two, I felt as if his words were aimed directly at me and the struggles that I still face with my feelings of responsibility toward my family.

He outlined the major points in the chapter, which was written to help Christians to deal with adversity. We were reminded that in all things, we are to praise and worship God, just as Paul did even while he was in prison. That was an immediate reminder to me that I have not always placed God at the forefront of my mind, but have let my personal worries consume my attentions. I know that when I first arrived at Florida State, I was bowled over by some of the amazing athletes around me who were still focused on their spiritual lives. This helped me to focus because it not only gave me a clear-cut goal—graduating from college—but also gave me an example of how a life in sports and a life of religious conviction could mix. It helped confirm that things do happen for a reason, and that I need to find the reason that God put me here, in the circumstances that He did, and make something of that.

"If your life is under attack, your gift will still be intact"—this was one of the taglines from the sermon, and it really made me think. When my mom first died, I'll admit, I was really mad with God. My greatest gift was my mom. That was everything. When He took the gift from me, that changed me so much. But my other gift was my talent, because that afforded me the opportunity to still be able to take care of my family. For me, I was so driven to keep developing my gift that I just continued to work hard.

Second Timothy charges its reader to not lose sight of his own place in the world. Pointing to this charge, Dr. Bronner urged us to remember our mission and our purpose. It is not selfish to be concerned with our own matters. We each have a charge and a responsibility for what we are to accomplish with the talents and opportunities we have been blessed with; to lose sight of those because of worry or hardship is as great a sin as selfishness.

In order to keep our focus and fulfill the calling of our lives, we need to lean on our family and our friends. This was an especially important reminder for me—our family should be a source of strength, encouragement, and renewal. For years, I have let my family be a source of stress and concern. I need to remember that my siblings have grown up and have established their own lives. I can finally relinquish my role as the father figure; I can let go and trust them to stand on their own. Finally (and this might be the most difficult thing for me), I can actually turn to them for guidance and accountability in the same way that they turned to me for so long. I also thought about my grandmother, who changed her entire life for us after our mom was killed, and I thought about the people in Baton Rouge who banded together and showed so much solidarity and support for us. This reflection helped to remind me that there are good people out there who want to help and who want to give of themselves. We just have to be willing to take them up on their offers and be grateful for their efforts.

The sermon went on to urge us to find a place of solitude so that we can have rest from the world and allow our mind and our body to rest and be restored. In other words, we don't need to be constantly moving; it is essential that we allow ourselves a break from the pain before we head back into the middle of things to carry on with life. Even though I didn't realize it at the time, I feel that Tallahassee was that time and place of solitude for me. I was alone so much because I chose to be. After Charlie graduated and I moved off campus, I lived by myself. I had so much time to really reflect and think, and that's what I did. It was crazy—I was an All-American running back who was getting all kinds of national attention, but there were times when I'd sit in the dorm room or my apartment just crying and thinking about my life. I needed that time of solitude in order to express the emotions that I wouldn't allow anyone else to see.

And, of course, we need to learn to let go—as Dr. Bronner phrased it, "Lighten your load, then tighten your life back up." I know that I need to finally release the worries and cares about my family that I've carried with me for so many years. The longer I continue to carry those burdens, the more they become fully engrained in my life. If I am willing to let go, I can focus on the things that God wants me to focus on—the things that He has put into my life that allow me to be a blessing to others.

I know that for a long time I let my life stagnate. I was miserable and the pain was just eating away at me, but I didn't want to deal with the emotion and let it run its course. Instead, I just coped with it by hiding my feelings. People couldn't really tell if I was experiencing any emotions. I didn't laugh, I didn't smile. I just had a still look on my face. All along, through my time in Tallahassee to Tampa to Atlanta, I found myself just living my life but never moving forward with it. I needed to reclaim my life—to take it back from the hurt and the memories and the responsibilities for other people. I had to claim it for myself. That is the "tightening it back up" that Dr. Bronner was discussing. Second Timothy reminds us that Jesus invites us to partake in his pain—that he suffered for us so that we don't need to be weighed down with worries and so that we can get on with the mission we are each given.

The final charge was to draw strength from God's word, and that has been something I have really been focused on. About two years ago I redevoted my life to Christ and started reading all that I could—not just my Bible but also personal devotion books, books about personal strength and conviction. One day I even met with the team chaplain at a little taco place and we just stayed there, eating tacos and praying. We started doing Bible studies and I could just feel the growth that was occurring in my spirit. I was finding strength and joy instead of depression and worry. It was a very liberating change.

The realization that came with Dr. Bronner's sermon might seem very unremarkable to most people, but it was very freeing for me. I had been hearing for years that it was okay for me to place my burden down, but I wasn't ready to hear that message yet. Suddenly, as I sat in church that August morning and listened to those words, I discovered that I was finally at a place in my life where I was ready to move on—and to allow my siblings to move on, too.

I was the first of us kids who had to grow up, and as I look back on my spiritual and emotional journey, I guess that in some ways, maybe I was the last, too.

CHAPTER 17

LEARNING TO LOVE

MY JOURNEY TO TRUE FAITH AND HEALING HAS BEEN long, but in the past few years I have felt myself finally start to emerge from the despair in which I felt trapped for so long. I feel ready to move forward with my life on a number of fronts that I had previously been afraid to face.

For years, I struggled with the subconscious connection between love and separation. I was too afraid to let anyone new into my life because I couldn't stand the thought of maybe losing that person. I had my family and my few select friends and mentors, but beyond that, I was not ready to open myself up to the possibility of allowing anyone else to get close to me.

I know that there are some people who might read about my journey and think to themselves, "Look, I know you lost your mother and I know that hurts, but you can't keep going back to that in every aspect of your life." My response to those people is that every person's emotional healing is different as they deal with significant loss and that my situation surrounding that process was hardly a typical one.

First, when my mother died, I didn't just lose my mom. I lost my best friend, I lost my mentor, I lost my hero, I lost my childhood, I lost my sense of innocence, and I lost my trust in the inherent goodness of people. That is a lot of loss to deal with all at once.

There have been people and gestures to counter that loss, of course. The people of Baton Rouge who stepped forward on behalf of my family after Mom's death were an amazing boost to my spirit. But there are also people who can't see beyond themselves and don't see where to draw the line, like the heckling rival fans during more than one college game who called, "Hey, Dunn—where's your mom?" They were trying to get to me and they succeeded, but not the way they intended. I knew that their jeers were just meant to throw me off my game, and while I refused to allow that to happen, the comments did really cut at my heart and made me question the decency of people.

And I don't just hurt for myself, but I hurt for my mother, too—that she didn't live to see any of her children graduate from high school or see us off to college; that she couldn't come to any more games or track meets. I know how much joy she drew from those events, and it pains me to think that she had that joy taken from her the night she was murdered. Of course I believe that she is in a better place, a place where there is no more pain or suffering. But I still can't help but feel angry at times not only for what we missed with her death but for what she missed, too.

Perhaps the most significant way I have finally been able to pull myself out of my emotional isolation is by watching the Christian examples around me and relying first on them to help get me through, and then getting to the point where I could begin seeking to rebuild a faith of my own.

I've joked sometimes that I consider myself a "Batholic." That is, I was raised Baptist, but my time and my siblings' time in Catholic school definitely influenced us as well. I find that I am really comfortable in just about any religious setting. Ultimately, though, I do not feel tied down to any one denomination. My mother was the same way. She fiercely believed in the concept of faith over religion, and taught us all to believe that we must ultimately answer to God and not to a denomination.

Coach Boudreaux has teased me about one instance when our high school track team was traveling and we attended mass in a mostly white retirement community near Orlando. There were several of us there who hadn't grown up Catholic and had never been to a mass outside the ones at school, and I guess we made it obvious when the time came when we were supposed to do the passing of the peace and shaking hands with one another. The older folks turned around to greet us, looking a little confused as to why there were a large number of high school athletes sitting behind them, and we just started hugging them enthusiastically, which is what we thought we were supposed to do. Thankfully, they just rolled with it and hugged right back, but Coach was just laughing hysterically in the pew.

Looking back on it now, I can see how that incident really exemplifies what I feel real faith should do—it should reach across the differences and embrace the similar purpose. My friendship with Charlie Ward was kind of the same way. He is very outspoken about his faith and is able to talk to people about prayer and love in a way that I just never could. I admire his humble spirit so much, but being a shy person already and then to be plagued with all the doubts and struggles that I was facing as a young man, I couldn't ever feel my faith manifest itself in that same way. And yet Charlie could reach past all of that and was able to help me start to recognize what it is that I needed to start focusing on.

I was able to let my guard down around Charlie because I felt he understood me on a different level. The same is true of Coach Bowden, who recognized what I needed and matched us up in the first place; and Clint Purvis, who was such a great source of strength for me as team chaplin for the Seminoles.

Chaplin Purvis encouraged me to recognize that God took my mother away from the struggles of her life and gave her peace. He prayed with me every time we met, and he would tell me, "God loves you enough to not only have taken care of your mom so that you don't have to worry about her, but He also loves you enough to give you a sense of understanding in all of this and to use this for His good."

More than once, he reminded me that God's intent is always for good to triumph over evil and that even though there will always be evil in the world—sin, crime, violence—this is not the way things are supposed to be. It is our responsibility to help set things right, to do our part to combat the negative things that surround us. I've thought about that fact a lot, and I think he's right.

My community work, in many ways, began out of a desire not only to give back but also to help ease my own pain. Now, from my experiences with the families I've met and the businesses and people who have been so generous with our foundation, I am finding a renewed sense of trust in people, in their kindness and their humanity. I don't see it as an anomaly anymore—I am starting to feel an awareness of goodness return in a way that I haven't felt in a very long time.

It's still hard for me sometimes, because I do feel so acutely aware of the evil in the world. I look at someone like Charlie Ward, who has such a beautiful, unshakable faith and who really sees the good in everything and everyone, and I have to admit that I am a little envious.

I know that the question of how a merciful God can allow bad things to happen to good people has been a source of theological debate since the beginning of time, so I do take a bit of comfort in the fact that I am not alone with my questions or my struggles. And I take a lot of comfort in seeing how far I've come.

I've also recently taken a step back and really started to evaluate my Homes for the Holidays program, because at first I didn't want any credit for it. I didn't really want my presence to be a big deal because for the longest time I never wanted to associate the project with my personal life because this program was about my mom. It wasn't that I was ashamed, but there was just so much anger, so many of the memories that I really wasn't ready to talk about. I wasn't able to really talk about a lot of things. I was happy about the program, but I really didn't reflect on the joy until I got home and I laid in bed at night—that's when I felt like I started to understand the magnitude of just what had happened, the events that had taken place that day.

I am a very nonchalant person. As long as I know that you are thankful and grateful, I am cool. I don't really need a lot. I know that I didn't really interact with the families very much at first. Now I tend to smile a lot more, interact a lot more. I engage with the families a lot more, crack jokes, and do a lot of crazy things. It used to be that it hurt too badly to be involved on a personal level any more than I already was. Now I say to them, "If you ever need to talk to me, if you need anything, if I can do anything at all, don't hesitate to call. I may just pop up at your house, you never know." I'll ask, "Can I have dinner sometime?" and they always invite me. I didn't used to be like that—I had to become happier with my life and happier in myself to make that change.

I've found myself relaxing a bit with the fact that people want my autograph, too. That was so hard for me for so long, but I can finally accept that it's okay for me to sign stuff for people who ask—after all, they tend to be the ones who are genuinely interested in my on-field stats rather than just my "nice guy" reputation.

I remember one of the first times I let myself loosen up on that issue was in Atlanta in 2000 during the Super Bowl, when I called up Randy Oravetz, the trainer at FSU. We were both there to watch the game and we met in the lobby of the Atlanta Marriott Marquis just to say hello and catch up. We were sitting and talking for maybe thirty minutes when a boy wearing my jersey came up and looked really scared. "Mr. Dunn," he said softly. "Can I have your autograph?" Even though he was being quiet and not drawing any attention, it was like every head in the place was on a swivel and they all spun around to look at us. You could hear a buzz immediately, as people were pointing me out to one another. For a moment I felt like saying, "Whoa—I'm just trying to talk with an old friend here. No need to get worked up about it. Go ask the famous players to sign something." But then I realized that people were excited because they respected me as an athlete, and I had to laugh and remind myself that I needed to be okay with that.

Other personal interactions have been even more of a challenge. I know I struggled for a long time over my relationship—or rather, my lack of a relationship—with my father. As already discussed, I always was a little bit hurt when I would see Derrick interact with his dad, knowing that he had an active part in Derrick's life. Derrick and I were close enough in age that I could recognize the importance that a male presence can have on a boy while he's growing up because Derrick's dad was there to help him through a lot of the same challenges I was facing. I think that it's important to point out that I don't have any resentment toward my father, either; I just don't really feel any emotion toward him, and in some ways that has been the hardest part.

I first met my father when I was thirteen or fourteen. Mom and I were at a track meet in Arlington, Texas, when my mom called me over to meet a man she was talking to. It turns out that it was my father; he was living in Dallas at the time and had driven over to watch the meet. He was a former track star himself, which was how he met my mother, and was now working as a coach.

It was shocking to meet him all at once, without any buildup or expectation. I also met his oldest son—my half-brother—who was about eight or ten years older than me. It was a polite meeting, but it did make my heart hurt a bit to know that my father was a part of his older son's life, but not mine. I was excited to meet him, though—to finally have a man to picture when I thought about my family.

As the years went on, I encountered my father a few more times. He came over to Baton Rouge a few times, and after Mom died, I called him to tell him and he drove over for the funeral and stayed for about a week to help out with things there.

I also saw him at a few games in college, and went up to visit him once at a small university in Kentucky where he was coaching at the time. But ultimately, he has never expressed an interest in being a part of my life, and it's never been something I've felt right about pursuing. He did come to the last Sugar Bowl in which I played, but beyond those few sporadic contacts, we just don't have a relationship. I don't even have his current contact information.

It's sad, but it's also made me evaluate the relationships that I do have in my life and what emotional investment really means. I think about Choo-Choo Brooks and how he is really the man I cling to. He is the one who really made the effort in my life. He taught me about football, about running track, about making good grades—he was always encouraging and always supportive. At all of my games and meets growing up, it would be Mom and Choo-Choo who were cheering me on and waiting to hug me afterward.

When I think about my life and where I want it to go next, I try to pattern myself to be what Choo-Choo has been for me: a communicator, a friend—someone who teaches. I would want to be the best husband and father I can be.

And that is a major step for me—to recognize that I do want to be a husband and a father. For a long time I felt that I couldn't tear myself away from my brothers and sisters and that my destiny was to try to keep the family together.

As I've gotten older and felt myself start to finally deal with a lot of the pain and fears, I have reached a point where I can not only start to let go of that burden but also where I want to start a family of my own. I want to be married and I want to have children. I've finally accepted that it's okay for me to focus on developing my own family life.

If there is one memory of my mother that comes back more than any other, it is the ending of my last high school football game. When it was all over, she came down from the stands and the two of us walked off the field together, holding hands. I loved it when she held my hand. Doesn't sound like a tough guy, huh? It is impossible for a lot of people to understand the love my mother and I had for each other.

Just a few weeks later, she was gone. The memory of that night of us walking off the football field has had an impact on a major part of my life since.

From January 1993 on, I have struggled with personal relationships. Nowhere is that more obvious to the people I've dated than the fact that I can't feel comfortable holding a woman's hand. That, as you might imagine, has been an issue for each person I've dated. I understand that women need that touch, that show of affection gained from holding hands. But when someone I'm dating reaches for my hand, my thoughts go to that night on the football field and I see my mom's hand in mine. For years, I would try as respectfully as possible to pull my hand away.

You see, that's the one memory of my mother that I want to hold onto, that I don't want to let go of. I've been holding onto it for so long and so tightly that I know I've deprived both myself and those I've dated. Part of me honestly feels that if I hold their hand I'm letting someone else into that special place I've reserved for my mom.

No one else compares to her, and sometimes when I'm getting close to someone I worry that I'm trying to replace her. I hope you can hear my conflict.

If there is one area where I've worked hardest in counseling, I promise you this is it. Since my mother's death, relationships have been a complete struggle.

First, there's the hand-holding and the mixed message I know that sends to my dates. Second, there's the responsibility I felt for so many years to be the man of the family to my younger brothers and sisters. Often I have heard from women I've dated that they've felt like they were always in second place because so much of my life revolved around getting my family what they needed, often before I got what I needed. There were periods when spending time with me as my date meant going to dinner with me and my siblings or going to one of their athletic events. That's tough on everyone. I tried not to let dates feel like they were second, but I can see how they did. I tried to multitask in the relationship area, but if something happened with my family, I felt like Daddy, and that's where my attention went. I felt that's what my mother would have had me do. I was responsible for their future, their success.

There's also the issue of answering to someone else. I know that once you're committed to someone and headed toward marriage, you have to be ready to share everything with that person, including decision-making. At this stage of my life, that's a real challenge. Since my mother's death I have been the decision-maker for me and my family. That's a big role to accept at eighteen, and I am sure I've made lots of bad decisions. But I made them and didn't have to answer to anyone else while doing so. If I needed to do something, I did it and asked no one's permission. That independent streak doesn't work well in relationships. To give that up is a huge struggle.

Finally, and this is a confession that's tough to make, I have long been scared of losing someone I love again, as I did that night in

1993. What if I gave myself to someone and she left me? What if she passed? Could I do that twice in one lifetime? Trust me, those questions have been a part of my daily life for years. Often, if I found myself getting too close to someone, I would take off, come up with a reason I had to go to another city for something. I didn't want to get too close because I didn't want them to leave me. I would get away just to avoid getting more attached.

Finding someone who understands this struggle—and is willing to let me grow through the doubts—is a real challenge. I have come to realize over the years that I hadn't progressed in relationships because I was holding onto these thoughts and memories of my mother, thoughts that kept me from saying to someone, "Will you marry me?"

I'm still not there. I've had special women in my life—each made important contributions to my growth—and I am in a relationship now with someone who has seen my struggles and who I really care about. And because this kind of relationship is hard for me, I don't think being out front and talking too much about it is a good idea. We need to be able to work with all the issues, and I think the public can be harsh on women who date professional athletes. I don't want that for her and I don't think it's the best way to handle this—especially since I am still working to figure it all out.

As if all that weren't complicated enough, I know the fact that I had no role models in marriage while growing up has made it even more difficult. My mother didn't marry. My grandmother was married, but her husband died years ago. My aunt, who I thought had a good marriage, ended up with a husband who killed himself. Many of my friends were from single-parent homes, and as I got older I saw a lot of teammates who had marriages that were challenging. My experience with the whole concept hasn't been the best.

Without question, I want to be a husband like my mother never had. I want to be a father like the father I never had. I want those things, and I truly believe they will happen. To get there, I have spent hours and hours in counseling. I've spent hours and hours in tough and painful conversations with the women I've dated. The idea of being completely committed to someone would at one stage make my palms get sweaty.

I want to get past that, to be committed. I want to hold hands. At least my palms don't sweat anymore when the word *commitment* comes up!

It is going to work out for me. I know it. When? I'm not sure. But it will happen.

When my mom passed away, that's when I really came to a footprint. I'd spent years believing in God, but at the same time I was angry with God. Like so many other people who face tragedies, I had all kinds of questions and confusion. There's a time when you're angry, but you come to the realization that you start to understand that things happen for a reason. It makes you become stronger because you know that things happen for a reason. God is only going to give you so much that you can handle, but when something first happens you have the natural reaction of anybody: I want to retaliate. I want to kill them. God, why do you do this? Why do you do that? You acknowledge that he's such a great God—but then you question everything. And when you get past that lashing out, you really start to understand. The more I prayed and the more I sat back, the more I started to really understand the rules. So I think for me that's when my faith really took off. And then I went to Florida State and I was rooming with Charlie and he was such a Christian. I had Coach Bowden and Clint Purvis and so many other people who were pulling me to make sure that I was on that path. It was as if God had brought all these people into my life to show me that even though this tragedy happened, everything could still be okay.

Charlie Ward has continued to be incredibly encouraging in my journey to peace. He's told me that he's grateful that I finally sought help in facing the pain and loss. He's let me know that he thought I was doing the right thing in the way I was handling my family back home while we were in college, even when I had doubts about it myself. And he's always reminded me that everything is a journey and it's about seeking peace and acceptance of God's will.

He even remarked recently that he doesn't think that it's just a coincidence that I'm not married yet. He said, "I think the Lord has to work on you first so you can be ready to take care of your responsibilities as a husband and a father." Charlie's words really struck home for me; I think maybe he's right. I needed to do more work on my own life before I could be trusted to share a life with someone else or give life to other human beings. It wasn't an option for me to focus on myself when I was younger, so God allowed me to wait until my siblings were grown up before we really started in on me.

And even though the change has been recent, it wasn't something that just occurred out of the blue. The groundwork was being laid for years. Dr. Kris Stowers, one of the FSU team physicians, is also a preacher, and he and I would meet and pray together sometimes when I was in Tallahassee. He used to remind me that very few people have dramatic, sudden changes that happen all at once. For most people, it takes time and a lot of false starts to heal and to really connect with God and their life's purpose. He urged me not to give up, but to keep trying and to keep searching and to file away everything I learned or saw or thought or felt, and that together those things would help to form the basis of the new life of peace that I would someday find.

That's hard to hear sometimes when you just want the hurt to leave. I didn't like to think of a long road ahead of me. But it turns out that Dr. Stowers was right. I wasn't healing because I wasn't ready to let go of everything I had carried with me. All of the people and experiences in my life since my mother's death helped to build me up, piece by tiny piece, until I was finally at a place where I could open myself up to love and joy and peace once again.

The biggest obstacle in my personal growth had to be the nagging question of "Why?" Until I felt I had really resolved the issue of why my mother had to die, I don't think I could really fully accept anything else.

The fact is that I know that more than likely, I would not be doing this foundation because my mom would be here. It wouldn't be something I truly understood. I think it's a blessing in disguise. Of course I didn't want the tragedy to happen, but I am able to live through other people, live a dream that my mom had. If she were still alive, I know my time and my energy would be devoted entirely to her. But now I have been able to give my time and energy to sixty-nine other families. I have been able to touch hundreds—and it's all because I lost the one who mattered the most to me.

God does things for a reason. He put Bobby Bowden in my life for a reason, Tony Dungy in my life for a reason, Arthur Blank in my life for a reason. There are reasons that different people come in and out of our lives, and I understand that. But you have some people who are so significant that they can help push you a little bit more. It's not necessarily them putting their hands on you, but you pay attention.

I am very observant, so I tend to pay attention to the little things. Certain things about Coach Dungy interested me so much that I just watched him and felt awed. He's a black head coach in the National Football League, and he took that role when there weren't that many black head coaches. I felt that here was a man who had worked unbelievably hard to become a head coach in this league, so I needed to pay attention to what he has to say. I took heed in what he said about the fact that if you are going to live somewhere, you need to get involved in the community. That statement stuck with me.

Things happen for a reason. My mom's life was taken for a reason. I always think about the fact—and I know this is crazy—that it seems like she was preparing me for the day when I'd have to take over for her. Maybe she knew her life was going to be taken at an early age, maybe she just wanted to raise me to be well-rounded, but she prepared me to be her little man. She taught me about decision-making; she gave me so much responsibility; she trusted me so much. It probably seemed weird for a child to be treated like an adult in so many ways, but I think about that now, and I know that she prepared me. I just had to accept the challenge. I didn't run away from it. I think she thought if the challenge cornered me, I would stand up to it and face it. I did it because I felt like I had no choice. In her eyes, I think she wanted me to do that. Or God was testing me to see if I could do it. Whatever the case, I feel like I have stood up to it and I have faced it.

And I have finally been able to defeat it.

CHAPTER 18

2007 SEASON

IT WAS A BASIC FOOTBALL PLAY, ONE THAT I'VE PROBA-
bly run a thousand times dating back to my youth days at
Philson Stadium; that's what we called the patch of dirt and grass on
the side of our neighbor's house on Bradley Street in East Baton
Rouge. That was a long time ago, but the games and years have certainly flown by—at times, seemingly in the blink of an eye.

As I stared at the line of scrimmage and set my feet on the spongy
FieldTurf in the Georgia Dome, my mind-set hadn't changed since
those early days. I wanted to gain as many yards as I could on this
carry and avoid the big hit.

The opponent was the Indianapolis Colts, the defending Super
Bowl champions. It's ironic how fate unravels at your feet. I started my
professional career eleven years earlier with the Tampa Bay Buccaneers, who were then coached by Tony Dungy. Coach Dungy was on
the sidelines this day, too, as the reigning head coach of the Colts.

It was Thanksgiving night, November 22, 2007, and I was poised
to reach a prestigious milestone in front of family, friends, and fans
in the Georgia Dome in downtown Atlanta. The achievement was

probably a bigger deal for others, but that's not to say I wasn't excited or grateful. Honestly, I think I've surprised people over the years with how hard I run and how tough I am. I haven't worn down despite my size. Just to be in my eleventh NFL season says a lot to all the people who doubted me.

With 14:34 left in the second quarter, I broke from our huddle and lined up in a single-back set behind quarterback Joey Harrington. Harrington barked a few quick signals and took the snap from center Todd McClure. I took the handoff from Harrington and plunged into the line behind McClure's right shoulder and hip. It wasn't fancy or sexy, but it was history.

A straight 2-yard run through the middle of the Indianapolis defense pushed me past the 10,000-yard career rushing mark, making me the twenty-second running back in NFL history to reach it.

The referee immediately flipped me the football as a keepsake, and I quickly tossed it underhanded to our equipment manager, Brian Boigner, on the sidelines for safekeeping. If I had the time, I would have pinned a note on the football that read: "Keep away from Grandma." I figured the ball would look nice on my living room mantle, unless, of course, my grandmother intercepted it first. She likes to tuck those types of mementos under her arm for her home in Baton Rouge.

McClure was one of the first players on the field to congratulate me. I was just trying to cherish the moment. As I stood there, I knew I was in the right place—on the field with my teammates. Not much was going right for us this season, but we were in this together, good times and bad. The team then set off some fireworks and flashed my name and picture on the scoreboards around the Georgia Dome. At the next stop in play, a highlight film of some of my runs from Tampa Bay and Atlanta was shown. The fans stood and applauded, and I really appreciated the gesture.

It was only two games earlier in a victory over Charlotte that Falcons owner Arthur Blank talked about me when he told the media that "As a person, he always amazes me, but at his age, to be performing the way he does on the field really [is amazing]. Whenever he has to step up, he always steps up. I'm sure Warrick has lost a step. It's just hard for me to see it."

I HAD ENTERED THE Colts game needing 26 yards to reach the milestone. On our opening drive, I had five carries for 23 yards and we ended the nineteen-play drive with a 34-yard field goal from Morten Anderson, whose NFL career, by the way, has spanned twenty-five years. I had one carry for 1 yard on our second possession. I finished the game with 70 yards on seventeen carries, but it wasn't nearly enough as we lost to the Colts 31–13.

The crazy part was that after the game when Coach Dungy congratulated me on reaching 10,000 yards, I told him he saw the first yard and he saw the 10,000th yard. It's truly remarkable. My teammate, tight end Alge Crumpler, explained to the *Atlanta Journal-Constitution* after the game that the only bright moment in the defeat was me eclipsing the 10,000-yard mark. "It takes a tremendous amount of work ethic, a tremendous amount of longevity and a tremendous amount of smarts to be able to do something like that. I'm glad to see him pass that mark today," Crumpler said.

The 10,000-yard club was actually quite popular in November 2007, as three runners reached that mark in a span of twenty days. I was one of two new members in week 12, when I was joined by La-Dainian Tomlinson of the San Diego Chargers. Tomlinson tied career rushing leader Emmitt Smith as the fourth-fastest in NFL history to reach the milestone, getting there in his 106th game.

(I reached the mark in my 151st game.) Earlier in November, Fred Taylor of the Jacksonville Jaguars surpassed the mark as well.

I realize that the 10,000-yard mark puts me in a category with some of the best runners to ever play the game, players such as Emmitt, Barry Sanders, Walter Payton, and Jim Brown. Ten of the twenty-three players who have eclipsed 10,000 yards are in the Hall of Fame. I probably won't understand the magnitude of it until I retire and get away from the game. As I said, what's made it even more special is the fact that I accomplished it in an era when many people didn't think I would do it, plus I wasn't a true featured back.

Eric Dickerson, for example, played eleven years in the NFL and finished with 13,259 yards on 2,996 carries—that's over 500 more carries than I've had in my career as the 2007 season wound down (I had 2,436 carries heading into the season's final month and had never run more than 286 times in a season). Emmitt, meanwhile, had 4,409 carries in his fifteen-year career.

The point is, I've always had to share snaps and stay constant and healthy, year in and year out. But I also respect the mark's significance because think about how many players have lined up at running back in NFL history. A friend mentioned that 251 running backs were listed on NFL's official website for the 2007 season alone. It's crazy.

Plus, there's another aspect that somebody brought to my attention: of the twenty-three players who have eclipsed 10,000 rushing yards, only five weighed 200 pounds or less—myself, Walter Payton, Thurman Thomas, Tony Dorsett, and Tiki Barber. Tony's listed playing weight was 192 pounds at five feet eleven. Until I had reached the mark at 187 pounds, Tony was the lightest running back to ever hit the 10,000-yard milestone. Then there's also that other number: age. When LaDainian eclipsed the 10,000-yard mark, he told the media, "It's been the benchmark for a lot of running backs in this

league. I take it you get 10,000 yards—but that means you are getting older."

Funny, I didn't feel old at thirty-two.

While the overall numbers may not have been there for me in
2007, I don't think I fell off in terms of ability and desire. Looking
back, though, it was a season that tested my teammates and I more
than any other, both as players and as people.

THE 2007 FOOTBALL SEASON for the Atlanta Falcons and myself could easily be described in one word: awful. In fact, it was
probably the worst football season of my professional career. No,
make it the worst I have experienced in all my years of playing this
great game.

The craziness surrounding our season came to a head during a
forty-eight-hour span in early December.

On Monday morning, December 10, quarterback Michael Vick,
the face of our franchise and one of the NFL's most exciting players,
was sentenced to twenty-three months in prison for his role in a federal dogfighting conspiracy that involved gambling and killing pit
bulls. Just hours after Vick's sentencing in Richmond, Virginia, we
suffered our fourth consecutive double-digit loss, 34–14, at home to
the New Orleans Saints on *Monday Night Football* before a national
television audience. Then, the following day, Tuesday, December 11,
our first-year head coach, Bobby Petrino, telephoned the Falcons
headquarters in Flowery Branch, just north of Atlanta, and resigned
after just thirteen games. Nearly six hours later, Petrino, in Fayette-
ville, Arkansas, was introduced as the new head coach at the University of Arkansas. And when we arrived at practice that Wednesday
afternoon to begin preparations for our road game at Tampa Bay,

assistant coach Emmitt Thomas was promoted to interim head coach for our final three games of the season.

I said it was craziness, with a capital C.

In all started in January 2007, when Mr. Blank fired Jim Mora after three seasons and hired Petrino away from the University of Louisville to his first NFL head coaching job. Mr. Blank hoped that Coach Petrino would inject offensive life into a team that failed to make the playoffs for two straight years. Well, make that three straight years now.

Petrino's hiring raised eyebrows from the start. He brought in new coaches and a new offense that was much different from the West Coast system we had used under Mora. Quite truthfully, and not to be disrespectful, Coach Petrino didn't know how to relate to professional players from the get-go. He alienated the veterans and was aloof with just about everyone in the organization. Petrino was openly criticized by two of our Pro Bowlers, Alge Crumpler and DeAngelo Hall, early in the season. When I reached the 10,000-yard career rushing mark against the Colts, Petrino didn't offer any words of congratulations until one of my offensive teammates encouraged him to do so.

Once news of Petrino's resignation surfaced, the media reported that, just like Steve Spurrier and Nick Saban before him, Petrino was simply the latest big-name ex-collegiate head coach to jump to the NFL for the big money and then quickly discover that the NFL is a far different game. Honestly, nobody was surprised when Petrino quit and rejoined the collegiate ranks. I think his exit was cowardly and classless—he left a note saying his decision was not easy but was made in the best interest of him and his family.

Even so, his resignation was another blow to an organization that had dealt with Vick's legal troubles since the first day of training camp, when a plane flew overhead pulling a sign that said: NEW TEAM NAME? DOG KILLERS?

It was just a bad year all around because of all the trials and tribulations that we had as a team. Honestly, it was a season you could never imagine having to go through as a player. We lost five of our first six games to open the year. Our lone victory was against Houston, 26–16, on September 30, in our fourth game. We won two straight games in November over San Francisco and Carolina, but that was followed by another three-game losing streak that only worsened. We could never dig out of the hole we put ourselves in.

Coach Petrino liked to run a power game, and our offensive line struggled with the transition from a zone-blocking scheme to man-to-man. Sometimes you have a system that helps a guy be very productive. Sometimes you have to make things work. I really don't know if Coach Petrino's system was the right fit for me, but I tried to make it work. I led the team in rushing in eight of our first twelve games, but I only had one 100-yard game—against San Francisco in week nine. Not helping matters was that we also had injury and personnel issues that slowed us.

Of course, we were in the center of a firestorm that rocked the NFL, and the Falcons franchise to its core, just prior to the season. That's when Vick was suspended by the NFL after he pled guilty on federal felony dogfighting charges.

After building a new offense around Vick's skills, Petrino had to adapt his scheme around quarterbacks Joey Harrington and Byron Leftwich. Harrington had signed with us in the spring of 2007, while Leftwich joined us two weeks into the regular season after being released by Jacksonville. Late in the season, a third quarterback, Chris Redman, who last saw extensive playing time in 2002 with Baltimore and sold insurance in 2006, started for us. All three are solid, talented quarterbacks, but they are not Michael Vick.

Only two months prior to the Vick bombshell, the Falcons traded backup quarterback Matt Schaub to Houston for two second-round draft picks. This move, on top of the loss of Vick, put us in a tough spot as a team. It's no secret that Vick's ability to run, evade the pass rush, and get the ball downfield would have helped Petrino run the offense more to his liking. Plus, Vick behind center would have made us a better team. But that all changed in an instant, and the initial shock of having to play without Vick hit everyone hard.

Life after Mike proved to be a long, hard work in progress.

It goes without saying that the team was hurt and confused by the news surrounding Vick. We struggled to comprehend how the guy we knew as a star on the field and a friend off it could have gotten himself into so much trouble. It made for a difficult work environment, especially when animal-rights protestors showed up at the Falcons' gates for our first training camp practice and we faced repeated questions from the media about Vick's absence. Vick's status received far more attention than anything else that happened during our preseason camp. It was obvious that the Falcons' ownership and management were forced to separate themselves from a player they had designated as the face of the franchise. The Falcons needed veterans like myself more than ever, on and off the field.

When I was repeatedly approached by the media for my opinion, finally I just said, "He's not on the team. That pretty much makes him an ex-teammate." I also told the *Atlanta Journal-Constitution*: "What it is right now, we have to move forward. I don't think anyone right now on this team is hoping that Mike comes back. If he comes back, that's great. Right now we're more to the point that the guys that are here, we're trying to get better with those guys and move on down the road."

I really like Mike. I do. While we didn't hang out after practice or games, we often talked about our families and what was going on in each other's lives. We also text-messaged each other to stay in touch. We had, and have, a good relationship. I was stunned by the news and I wasn't going to turn my back on Mike. But I also knew that as a team we needed to move on—we had no other choice—and focus on the players we had in camp.

In that split second, we went from a team that had positioned itself to be a contender to one that everyone picked to be one of the worst in the league. That was extremely difficult for veterans like me, but it was reality. Mr. Blank told the media late into our season that "our situation in Atlanta has probably been in some ways the most adverse for any club in the history of the NFL. Our head coach has stayed focused and we've done a good job of not feeling sorry for ourselves."

While we didn't feel sorry for ourselves, our thoughts and prayers were still with Mike. I am sure there are many Falcons fans who feel betrayed by Mike's actions. That's expected. But there are many others who continued to wear his number 7 jersey, and I know that people from his hometown of Newport News, Virginia, publicly talked about him as a generous benefactor who provided school supplies and athletic uniforms to the local youth.

Sure, we probably would have won a couple more games with Vick. He definitely would have made a difference, but we really don't know how the season would have turned out with him. Would Michael have adjusted to Petrino's offense? Would he have been able to pick up the offense and feel comfortable in it? It's pretty hard to say. I don't think anyone would have really felt great about the season we had.

I am hopeful that everything works out for Mike. One never knows what's in the future, but I know Mike was a guy who went through a lot in 2007. As players, we always reflect on woulda, coulda, and shoulda, but Mike lived a reality he had to face and one we had to accept. He stared at his future behind bars as our 2007 season wound down.

I last talked to Mike in late September 2007 when it was announced by the NFL that he had tested positive for marijuana. I picked up the telephone and called him. He didn't come out and apologize to me, but his tone to everyone was apologetic. Mike knows he messed up. He knows he put us as players, the organization, and himself in a situation that he's not proud of. I know he wished he could make it all go away and change things. But the reality is what it is.

The media reported Mike's situation as the lead story all over the country, laying it out in gory detail. Everything from the financing of the operation to the way the animals were killed became news.

When Mike was sentenced on December 10 to twenty-three months in prison for his role in a dogfighting conspiracy, everyone started to do the math. Mike will miss three consecutive NFL seasons—2007, 2008, and 2009—and will be twenty-nine years old when he gets out of prison. Will he return to the NFL? I don't know. He's an exceptional athlete, and if anyone could do it, Mike probably would be that person. But honestly, I am not sure what the future holds for Mike. Against the Saints later that night at the Georgia Dome, Mike was on the players' minds. DeAngelo Hall ran on the field during pregame introductions holding up a Vick poster and had "MV7" painted beneath his eyes. After Roddy White caught a 33-yard touchdown pass that briefly tied the game at seven, he pulled up his jersey and revealed a T-shirt with the handwritten message "Free Mike Vick."

Mike was gone, however, behind bars. And then Petrino was suddenly gone, too.

Our year went from bad to worse to crazy.

During the Coach Mora era, I registered three straight 1,000-yard seasons and our team led the league in rushing each time. The yards were more difficult to come by in 2007. For instance, I had just 292 yards through our first seven games.

You could see the frustration mount, especially in our veterans, some of whom publicly questioned Petrino's decisions. The fans also voiced their displeasure by staying away. Our poor start led to a home game TV blackout against San Francisco on November 4—the first non-sellout at the Georgia Dome in six years.

And as the regular season drew to a close, fans also wondered if Petrino might head back to the college ranks, pointing out the plights of Saban, Spurrier, Butch Davis, and other college coaches who struggled making the switch to the NFL. But Petrino, whose only other coaching job in the NFL was an assistant coach with the Jacksonville Jaguars from 1999 to 2001, indicated that he was committed to the Falcons.

After opening 1–6 and losing thirteen of our previous sixteen games dating back to 2006, it actually looked like we might be poised to turn the corner with November victories over San Francisco and Carolina. It was our first winning streak of the season, and we had climbed to the fringe of the playoff race. I told the media that "our leaders were helping us find our way out of this. Our guys haven't given up and we've stayed dedicated. I feel great right now. . . . I feel like it's my time to step up." But we couldn't find our footing against the Bucs and the Colts, and just like that, we were knocked backward again as the regular season wound down.

Bottom line, we had troubles scoring touchdowns. Our twenty-six points in a ten-point victory over Houston on September 30 was a season high after eleven games. To that point, we scored twenty points in three other games, twice in victories, and had not scored more than two touchdowns in a game. Our defense had played well to that point, and the unit topped the NFC with a plus-nine turnover differential. Opponents had converted only 33 percent on third down, number three in the league behind New England and Green Bay. We also started five rookies in our victory over the Carolina

Panthers in November, proof that the young guys were starting to learn how to be professionals.

Since our running game had fallen off so dramatically, I am sure there were some fans who questioned my ability. I knew I could still be effective if given the opportunities. I know the absence of Vick, who became the first quarterback in NFL history to run for more than 1,000 yards in 2006, played a role in our struggles.

But I also told the media that "I'm sure if he were back there he'd probably scramble or run around a bit and get some yards and we'd probably have rushed for over 100 yards in a game. I think we'd still be at the bottom echelon because of what we do offensively, not because Mike was making us look good in the running game. People keep saying I'm too old. It's been rough. If you watch the games and you really understand football it's not Warrick being unproductive. I've tried to maximize every carry that I've had . . . I guess sometimes when I'm watching film, I'm kind of surprised at some of the moves that I've made. I constantly challenge myself day in and day out to just go hard and leave it on the field. That's pretty much what I try to do, and whatever happens after that, to me, it just comes naturally. It's nothing that I'm planning to do. It just happens."

It also wasn't until early November that I finally began to physically feel like the player I used to be, as a result of my medical situation just before the start of training camp: I had back surgery on July 21 for a herniated disc. I felt some discomfort in my back and legs that just never subsided after my workouts. The Falcons medical staff told me that the discomfort would have lingered throughout the entire season had I not had the surgery. Earlier in the offseason, I also had shoulder surgery to repair damage to my rotator cuff. I rehabbed extensively following both surgeries, however, and I was actually back on the field within a month after back surgery.

Although I had just fourteen preseason plays underneath me, I started in our season opener against Minnesota. I know Petrino would have preferred a big, physical tailback to carry the load in his scheme, but it was up to me and Jerious Norwood to make it work. The early plan was for Jerious and me to rotate every other series unless one of us got hot. Once again, I knew I had to show that I could still make defenders miss me and that I could make plays. People see Jerious and get excited because he's so fast.

As the season progressed, however, we never seemed to get untracked offensively. I tried to make the most of my carries. Norwood stepped into the starter's role late in the season, though we continued to share carries. It's hard to convince people, because I am thirty-two years old, that I am not too old.

AND AS FATE WOULD have it, I had the chance to reach the 10,000-yard plateau prior to the Colts game against Tampa Bay four days earlier in the Georgia Dome. The Buccaneers drafted me out of Florida State, and it would have been neat to beat Tampa Bay and reach the mark in the same game. But it didn't happen. Actually, not much happened for our offense against the visiting Buccaneers.

I was coming off my best two rushing games of the season and only needed 58 yards to clear 10,000 career yards. But the Buccaneers, who have one of the league's quickest defenses, held us to a season-low 49 total yards rushing. I had 32 yards rushing on fifteen carries, leaving me 26 yards short.

I had my first 100-yard game of the season two weeks earlier against San Francisco—100 yards on twenty-seven carries. The following week against Carolina, I ran twenty-six times for 89 yards.

But we just never could get into a rhythm against the Buccaneers. While fans may argue otherwise, it really wasn't because we switched quarterbacks. Joey Harrington had won two straight games, but Coach Petrino elected to start Byron Leftwich, who had been sidelined by an ankle sprain.

Everyone knows that Byron has a great arm and he can make plays. However, he just didn't have a lot of time and he got hit a bunch of times in the pocket. We didn't handle their pressure well. The fans weren't thrilled, either, and they started chanting Harrington's name—"Joey, Joey"—during the first half. But Byron wasn't to blame. We committed silly penalties, dropped passes, made bad decisions. Honestly, we didn't come to play hard for four quarters, and that was frustrating. It was our fourth game of the season with one or no offensive touchdowns.

After building some momentum with wins over San Francisco and Carolina, we had visions of jumping back in the NFC South division race with a victory. But the Buccaneers extended their division lead to two games after Carolina and New Orleans also both lost, and we tumbled three games back with six games remaining in the regular season.

It would have been nice to reach 10,000 yards against the Buccaneers, since I have so many good friends on their sideline and fond memories of my five years in Tampa. I knew it would be crazy if it happened, and I am also sure those guys in Buccaneer uniforms— especially good friends Derrick Brooks and Ronde Barber—didn't want it to happen against them.

While individual milestones are not a big deal to me, I know my family wanted it to happen against the Buccaneers. And I had plenty of family and friends at the game, including my brother Derrick, who flew in from Baton Rouge for his first game of the year, and my agent, Jim Steiner, who came in from St. Louis.

As usual, my grandmother prepared enough food to feed a small army after the game. Trays of ribs, hamburgers, candied yams, rice, corn bread, and potato salad covered my kitchen counter. While it wasn't the celebration everyone had hoped for, it was still nice to see everyone. It was a great way to relax because up to that point, it had been a long, frustrating season for the Falcons and me.

SINCE WE PLAYED THE COLTS in an evening game on Thanksgiving Day, I caught a quick afternoon nap after our turkey-and-stuffing feast (Grandma outdid herself again). A small group of family and friends gathered at my townhouse for the holiday and the game. While we didn't talk about it, I knew what everyone had on their minds as I jumped into my car for the twenty-five-minute drive to the Georgia Dome:

Ten thousand yards.

Once everyone made it to our stadium suite, my sister Summer helped organize a little prediction contest: On what carry would I eclipse the 10,000-yard mark? First carry? Second? Tenth? I didn't know it at the time, but they held the same contest against the Buccaneers, and we all know how that went!

Summer is the first to tell you that she's pretty emotional when it comes to my football games. She will cheer for the Falcons and scream at the Falcons—more of the latter when she thinks I don't get the football enough. I know Summer was an emotional wreck for the game, and I can just imagine how she reacted as I inched closer to the mark.

I am not sure who won their contest, but I went over 10,000 yards on my seventh carry against the Colts. Derrick couldn't make the game, but he watched it at his home in Baton Rouge. Derrick knows that I am not a flamboyant person or one who wears his emotions on his sleeve, but he guessed that I was excited—and I was.

I REALIZE I AM RECOGNIZED more for my humanitarian efforts and housing program for single parents, but football has been extremely important to me. It's my career, my profession, my love. Heading into the 2007 season, I felt like I had at least two productive years left in my thirty-two-year-old body. But 2007 took its toll on me—not physically but mentally. I was mentally drained heading into the final month.

I knew that I needed to sit down in the offseason and make sure I was mentally refreshed for 2008. Other questions lingered. While changes were hinted at within the Falcons organization—would Atlanta and a new head coach jettison its veterans and rely more on youth?—I know I didn't want to leave the Falcons. But, again, I probably know better than anyone that no one knows what the future holds.

At that very moment against the Colts, as I picked myself off the turf and flipped the football to the sidelines as a keepsake, I was probably viewed as an ancient running back on his last legs. Physically, as I said, I felt fresh, I felt good, and I felt productive. The game was still fun. Come to think of it, my playing days at Philson Stadium don't seem that long ago.

Which only means that Mom must be somewhere close by, watching and smiling.

ACKNOWLEDGMENTS

Warrick Dunn's life has spanned only thirty-two years, but the number of lives he has improved spans the country. To tell his story, scores of others had to help—from family members to teammates, from mothers he has touched with the gift of a home to reporters who acknowledge never having covered anyone like him. ESPN's Andrea Kremer is a perfect example. Her feature on Warrick during the 2005 season became the first time Warrick opened up about his depression and counseling. The story remained on ESPN's website for months.

Each of Warrick's brothers and sisters—along with his wonderful grandmother—made themselves available for hours at a time, as did his youth coach, Maelen "Choo Choo" Brooks. Warrick's foundation, led today by Natalie Citarella Boe and in the past by Stephanie Waller, was always there to fill in the blanks and help arrange interviews with the families who now occupy homes provided by the foundation. WDF board members Christopher S. Knopik, Lee Hinkle, and Mike Hickey of Aaron's Rents helped explain Warrick's passion in ways even he couldn't. Warrick's longtime public-relations advisor, Lisa Brock, jumped in to make sure the right words were used during tough stretches. Ivan Blumberg and the great folks from Athletes for Hope, who included Warrick as a founding member, were invaluable.

The opening chapter of this book could not have happened without the extraordinary efforts of Angola State Prison warden Burl Cain, who agreed to arrange a meeting after former LSU basketball coach Dale Brown called in a favor. Nick Trenticosta, the attorney representing Kevan Brumfield, allowed his client to share that moment with Warrick, and I am sure he would agree that all of us in that tiny room—his client included—were changed forever.

Warrick's agent, Jim Steiner from CAA, and his literary representative, Janet Pawson, found the perfect publisher in HarperCollins, where editor Doug Grad is as good as they come. Doug's passion for this story is surpassed only by his deft editing skill. Research help came in big ways from the *Tallahassee Democrat*, the *Osceola Newspaper*, the *Seminole Boosters*, and WCTV in Tallahassee; the *Baton Rouge Advocate* in Louisiana; and the *Atlanta Journal-Constitution* in Georgia. Bill Vilona, sports editor of *Pensacola News-Journal* and Doug Carlson of the *Tampa Tribune* offered recollections of great career moments.

Gary Bogdon, the amazing photographer I was blessed to work with for ten years at *Sports Illustrated* captured Warrick for the cover of this book. As usual, his work tells the story in a way words cannot. It makes complete sense that Tony Dungy, who took time from his work as head coach of the Indianapolis Colts to write the very powerful foreword to this book, is Warrick's role model. The two are cut from the same bolt of cloth.

The others members of our writing and research team, led by the amazing Jim Henry, included Tiffany Brooks, Jenny Fernandez, and Chelsea Rodriguez. Without them, this book wouldn't happen. Thanks once again to all of you for both the help and for providing an inspiring place to work.